Praise for *Make Sure It's Deducti*

Evelyn Jacks is well-deserving of her reputation as Canada's m advisor. This book could save thousands of tax dollars for any employed, runs a small business, or is thinking of starting one.

GORDON PAPE, Bestselling Author

Ms Jacks draws on her expertise in a way that makes the argument for self-employment in this tax-oppressed country almost compelling.

JONATHAN CHEVREAU, *The National Post*

For guidelines on the home office and all self-employment issues, I would recommend you read Evelyn Jacks' book Make Sure It's Deductible *as a really good general and specific guide.*

DAVID CHRISTIANSON, *Winnipeg Free Press*

Evelyn Jacks knows tax and writes about it in a way the average person can understand. That's a very unusual combination. Reading her advice will make you richer, especially if you deduct business expenses the way she tells you to in this book.

ELLEN ROSEMAN, *The Toronto Star*

Jacks' style is direct and concise. For the answer to "What does this line on the tax return mean?" it is where I would turn first.

GEORGE HARTMAN, *Investment Executive*

MAKE
SURE IT'S
Fourth Edition

DEDUCTIBLE

Little-Known
TAX TIPS
for Your Canadian
Small Business

Evelyn Jacks

McGraw-Hill
Ryerson

Toronto   Montréal   Boston   Burr Ridge IL   Dubuque IA   Madison WI   New York
San Francisco   St. Louis   Bangkok   Bogotá   Caracas   Kuala Lumpur   Lisbon
London   Madrid   Mexico City   Milan   New Delhi   Santiago   Seoul
Singapore   Sydney   Taipei

ISBN: 978-0-07-171483-9
MHID: 0-07-171483-9

1 2 3 4 5 6 7 8 9 0   DOC/DOC 0 1 6 5 4 3 2 1 0 9

Library and Archives Canada Cataloguing in Publication

Jacks, Evelyn.
    Make sure it's deductible : little-known tax tips for your Canadian small business / Evelyn Jacks. — 4th ed.
Includes index.
ISBN: 978-0-07-171483-9

1. Income tax – Law and legislation – Canada – Popular works.
2. Small business – Taxation – Law and legislation – Canada – Popular works. I. Title.

HJ4662.A45J32   2009   343.7105'268   C2009-906151-1

Printed and bound in the United States of America.

For Cordell and Don, Cora and Enzo

You and the brilliance of your futures inspire me daily.

xoxo

About Evelyn Jacks

Evelyn Jacks is the founder and president of the *Knowledge Bureau*, Canada's leading national educational institute providing professional development in the tax and financial services industries.

Ms. Jacks has recently been appointed by Federal Finance Minister Jim Flaherty to the Task Force on Financial Literacy, which will deliver recommendations for a national strategy on financial literacy in 2010. She was previously appointed by the Premier of Manitoba to establish direction for a new provincial tax regime as a Commissioner for the Lower Tax Commission.

Ms. Jacks has written 45 bestselling consumer books on the subject of personal and business taxation, and personal wealth management. Most recently Knowledge Bureau has published the *Master Your . . . Personal Finances* series of books under her direction, providing financial education to decision-makers who want to have a better relationship with their advisors.

Ms. Jacks has received numerous distinguished awards in recognition of her contributions to excellence in financial education including the YM-YWCA's Business Woman of the Year and the prestigious National Canadian Woman Entrepreneur of the Year from the Rotman School of Business. She has also been recognized with an international Business Leadership Award by the Canadian Embassy in Washington, D.C.

For over 25 years, her companies have specialized in publishing and delivering certificate courses designed for the continuing education of tax and accounting practitioners as well as financial advisors focused on managing their clients' wealth.

Ms. Jacks has served as a Governor of the Manitoba Club and a Cabinet Member of the United Way. She has served on the Board of Associates at the University of Manitoba and as an Executive of the Winnipeg Chamber of Commerce, as well as on the boards of numerous other organizations.

Contents

Introduction   ix

Chapter 1:   Key Reasons Why Canadians Pay Too Much Tax   1
David, the typical one-source income earner. Taking a strategic view to saving taxes. Multiplying income sources. Using legitimate tax-savers. Understanding tax audit risk.

Chapter 2:   How to Tax Cost Average   19
Mary, the sales agent. Timing income. Deferring income. Making retroactive tax adjustments. Using carry-over provisions. Beware the CPP. Proprietorships vs. incorporation.

Chapter 3:   How to Start a Tax-Efficient Small Business   35
Marlen, the gourmet cook. When does a hobby become a business? Is there potential for profit? Meeting the onus of proof. Your Business Start Plan and Daily Business Journal. Classifying expenses. Claiming losses.

Chapter 4:   Write Off More Deductions Without Changing Your Life   61
Julie and Janet, artist and writer. What is a genuine tax-deductible expense? Statement of Business Activities. Current vs. capital expenses. Restricted and mixed-use expenses. Avoiding penalties.

Chapter 5:   Simple Rules for Writing Off Asset Purchases   91
Jared, the computer whiz. Capital Cost Allowance claims. Fast computer write-offs. Are expenses repairs or improvements? Buy or lease? Half-year rules. Adjusting returns on time.

Chapter 6:   Maximize Home Office and Auto Expense Benefits   107
Tom, the skilful woodworker. The second income. Keeping an auto log and worksheet. Calculating your home workspace. Calculating claims for the business portion of the expenses.

Chapter 7:   Profiles of the Self-Employed   121
Marcie, her babysitting business and other occupations. Sole proprietorship or partnership? Artists and writers. Child care providers. Farmers, expenses and special provisions.

Chapter 8:   How to Put Your Family to Work and Write It Off!   151

Raj and the family restaurant. Employing family members. Your obligations as an employer. Tax-free benefits for family members.

Chapter 9:   Often-Missed and Little-Known Family Tax Deductions   171

The Hampton family's enterprises. Income splitting and diversification. Various ways to increase your family's income— RRSPs, RRIFs, RESPs. Tax credits and write-offs.

Chapter 10:   How to Create Serious Wealth   209

Thomas and his software company. Planning to maximize benefits from the capital gains deduction. Qualified farm and fisher's property and shares in small business corporations.

Chapter 11:   How to Turn a Tax Audit Into a Profitable Experience   223

Rubin, the musician. The net worth assessment. Compliance, appeals and penalties. Some real life cases. Audit strategies.

Chapter 12:   Taxpayers and Their Advisors: The Top Check Lists   239

Marshall, who'd never filed a tax return. Choosing a tax advisor and the questions to ask. Ten skill-testing questions.

Conclusion   253

Index   256

Introduction

In a fast-paced world, where content snippets fly through virtual channels and one financial crisis after another assaults pocketbooks and savings, it would appear that the only certainties in life are death, taxes and change!

Especially when times are tough and people lose their livelihoods, being self-employed brings to the scene a sense of control over one's financial destiny. However, a big difference exists between starting your own small business to make a job for yourself and vision-based entrepreneurship, which requires passion, astute skills and detailed planning.

There are many obstacles along the way, not the least of which is the fact that in general the business owner must come up with the money to invest in the business first, before even one dime of the revenues earned rests securely in his or her pocket.

But perhaps the biggest paradigm shift for many new business owners is the realization that self-employment inherently involves a new, close relationship with the tax department. Known as CRA—the Canada Revenue Agency*—this partner can be generous and impatiently demanding at the same time. It is, in fact, against the law to be delinquent with your remittances of payroll and income taxes to the CRA.

On the plus side, however, the business owner has an advantage over the money that is earned from entrepreneurship, that others do not. When you own your own business, you see every dollar that's earned, *first*. That's powerful, because it gives you the opportunity for immediate financial clout, using larger dollars—*before-tax dollars*—to participate within the economy.

Yet sustainable access to those dollars can be complicated. Consider that an effective tax system is one that promotes the ideals of *fairness and equity, simplicity and compliance*. Unfortunately for taxpayers, some of these ideals are at odds with one another:

- Our tax system is based on *self-assessment*, an especially important concept for the self-employed. Taxpayers are expected to voluntarily

---

* Formerly known as Revenue Canada and Canada Customs and Revenue Agency.

comply with the requirement to file a tax return, correctly assess taxes owing and pay them on time, being aware that both audits and new tax law can be invoked retroactively.

- Taxpayers should expect equity from their tax system (i.e., that others in like circumstances pay at similar taxation levels). To be completely fair, however, the system must put into place special provisions for special groups of people—the sick and the disabled, the elderly, families, businesspeople, employees and investors—and take into account provincial taxation differences.
- The fairer the tax system, the more complex it will be. Complexity makes compliance with the law difficult for those making financial decisions throughout the year.
- Without compliance there is no equity.

You can see what we mean.

As a result, it is not necessarily true that two neighbours, each earning gross revenues of, let's say, $60,000, will pay the same level of tax. In fact, it's not always income level that determines the after-tax result—it's income *source* that will have the biggest bearing on your family's real wealth over the long run, a fact that few Canadians consider seriously.

What's more, the type of income earned, when it's earned and by whom, together with the application of generous rules for the deduction of expenses associated with earning certain income sources, will determine your family's after-tax status.

Only then can you really begin to consider the accumulation of family wealth on a sustainable basis and get ahead. It's what you are left with, after tax, that counts, *but it's how you plan to spend your before-tax dollar that makes all the difference to your lifestyle.*

Take Jean-Paul, for example, a 35-year-old self-employed electrical contractor, who suffered through a devastating divorce over a year ago. You could see the pain on his face as he spoke of missing his eight-year-old son, who moved with his mom to a small town more than four hours away. His commitment to the boy was unfaltering. Every weekend he drove the round trip to visit him.

"It's worth it to see my boy," Jean-Paul sighed, "but I am exhausted, and the travelling is costing me a fortune. Is there any way I could write some of this off?"

At first glance, his accountant explained the answer would be no. Driving to and from the small town to visit one's own child is considered to be a personal expense, not deductible.

But wait. Jean-Paul was self-employed. Did he ever bid on work in the area in which his child lived? No. Could he? Yes. In fact, a new school was expected to be built in the vicinity very soon. Was it too late to bid on the work? No.

Jean-Paul could legitimately write off the cost of driving to and from the town in which the work would be completed. Trips to place the bid, negotiate with the parties, supervise his work crew, etc., would all qualify for expense deductibility. So would the hotel bills he incurred while performing the work. His travel now had a dual purpose. Deductibility of at least a portion of the trip could be justified to the CRA, as there was a reasonable expectation of profit in the future. Jean-Paul took this into account when filing his tax return and accomplished his goals: the majority of his expenses were now tax deductible, leaving more in his pocket to spend on his beloved son.

He now makes a point of looking for work in the area over the weekends so that he can better balance business and personal resources *and arrange his affairs within the framework of the law to pay the least taxes legally possible.*

Often, taxpayers can increase their tax write-offs, and thereby improve their lifestyles, without dramatically changing the way they spend their money. It's all in the way you think about it. If you can make a business case to deduct an expenditure—even if you have to prorate out the cost for a personal component—the after-tax benefits will accumulate in double-digit yields.

That's the primary purpose behind this little book—to urge you to re-evaluate your existing income sources and annual expenditures. Is there a business purpose to any of them? Could there be? If so, what do you have to do to comply with CRA's audit requirements to ensure their acceptance? How can you plan to make decisions throughout the year to enhance your lifestyle with increased after-tax dollars? How can you be more astute and vigilant about claiming every tax deduction and credit you are entitled to?

If you have been in business for a while but are not sure if you have taken advantage of all your tax savings opportunities, be sure to check out the history of recent significant personal and small business tax changes in Chapter 12. This will help you to discuss key tax savings and tax planning opportunities with your professional advisors and tap into savings from your voluntary adjustments for errors or omissions.

With marginal tax costs in the range of 22% to 50% or more of every dollar you earn (depending upon your province of residence and your exposure to clawbacks of some of the tax provisions or social benefits you may be entitled to), it makes absolute "cents" to aggressively pursue your legal right to pay only the correct amount of tax and not one cent more.

You *can* take control of the taxes you pay! Make the decision today to take a fresh look at your next financial commitment and *make sure it's deductible!*

Evelyn Jacks

CHAPTER 1

Key Reasons Canadians Pay Too Much Tax

"The greatest discovery of my generation is that human beings can alter their lives by altering their attitudes of mind."
WILLIAM JAMES

KEY CONCEPTS

- There are 10 key reasons taxpayers overpay their taxes
- Tax can be reduced in multiple ways by operating a small business
- Small business owners face a higher audit risk than other taxpayers
- Documentation is necessary to beat a tax auditor
- Engagement in a "commercial activity" is required to legitimize tax write-offs
- The key to tax savings over time is tax-efficient decision-making all year long

REAL LIFE: David groaned as he completed this year's tax return. He thought he was doing well, supporting his family of four on his employment income of $65,000. He scrutinized his relatively simple tax return: one T4 slip and not much else. He paid close to $13,000 in taxes this year, and after his required source deductions of Canada Pension Plan (CPP), Employment Insurance (EI) and Income Tax (IT) were subtracted, David was left with less than $4,100 a month, barely enough to cover expenses of running a household with a stay-at-home mom and two small kids. How could this be? David, a typical Canadian dad, wondered if he needed a second job, or perhaps a self-employment opportunity.

THE PROBLEM

David, like so many other Canadians, pays too much tax, for very specific reasons. He:

1. Earns the majority of his income from one source (e.g., employment or pensions)
2. Allows too much to be taken from his paycheques for source deductions or remits too much in quarterly tax instalment payments
3. Has one person in the family who earns significantly more than the others
4. Focuses on earning income but fails to accumulate capital and build equity
5. Has no long-term savings goals
6. Does not have an order for investing his savings or plans for leaving an estate
7. Has trouble keeping records
8. Doesn't know himself, his investments or his business well enough to communicate effectively with his professional tax, legal or financial advisors
9. Fails to ask effective questions about important decisions he should be making regarding his current and future tax planning opportunities
10. Misses out on getting the right help to meet his financial needs and wants by looking at tax filing/tax planning options on an annual basis only

In short, paying attention to your after-tax results is important. Taxes are your largest lifetime expense and the largest eroder of your family's wealth, yet too often taxpayers delight in a large tax refund at the end of tax filing season, failing to understand that a tax refund is really an interest-free loan to the government.

That money, instead, could be supplementing your cash flow all year long, helping you to invest in yourself, build and grow.

THE SOLUTION: START A BUSINESS

There are millions of small businesses thriving in Canada today, owned and operated by entrepreneurs, professionals, commission salespersons, farmers, fishers, and revenue property owners. They are people who invest their time and money first in order to reap the rewards of both profit and equity in their enterprises later. In fact, they are tax advantaged! Owners of a small business can have both tax-efficient income today and the potential to substantially enhance their net worth by building equity for tomorrow. Our tax system makes it extremely lucrative to own and sell a properly structured small business venture.

Tax efficiency comes from the numerous opportunities small business owners have to do the following:

- Diversify income sources
- Control the tax timing of income and expenses
- Increase working capital by reducing or eliminating the withholding taxes
- Split income with family members, thereby reducing the household's marginal rate of tax
- Decrease personal living costs by writing off any business portion of such expenses
- Average tax costs over a period of years
- Build value within the goodwill and other assets of their business— and later realize gains on that equity tax free!
- Leverage their personal productivity by taking pro-active control of their retirement income and what they will leave to their heirs

As a new small business owner, you too can reap the benefits of these opportunities, and with a commitment to learning the rules of the tax-filing game, *you can position yourself to maximize the first dollar you earn as well as the last dollar you invest.*

All of this begins with an appreciation of the new relationship you will automatically start with your new partner—the tax department. Ensuring the quality of that relationship will be discussed throughout this book. To begin, consider some preliminary concepts you'll need to master as you prepare to make and save more after-tax dollars while you build your new business venture.

THE PARAMETERS

Four basic parameters must be observed in order to take advantage of the benefits provided to the self-employed under the law and to ensure you are "tax compliant" in your activities. For many novice business owners, this can represent a new approach to the annual tax-filing ritual.

1. **Family First—Reassess Your Tax and Financial Affairs**   Employees are used to receiving a regular paycheque, but this is not always the case when you run a small business. Conversely, sometimes the business simply makes too much money—a nice problem to have

but one that must be managed with tax efficiency to maximize the opportunity.

To smooth out income fluctuations on a tax-efficient basis, an important opportunity arises when the small business owner reviews not only the accuracy of his/her own individual tax return but also looks to the results on the returns of each family member to average out the income taxes the family pays as a unit. Doing so requires a close look at your family tax filing status both *in the current year and over a period of years.*

2. **Start a Commercial Activity and Write Off Your Losses** Earning business revenues is a process that involves risk—generally you must invest first to earn later. As mentioned, this is distinctly different from the earning of employment income, which occurs regularly and generally without risk to the employee.

The Income Tax Act (ITA) recognizes this natural evolution for commercial enterprises and will allow the deduction of legitimate business losses against other income of the year and in what are known as "carry over years"—3 years back and 20 years forward. This is true of both incorporated and unincorporated businesses; however, the power of earning start-up losses in your personal (unincorporated) hands is that business losses can be used to offset other personal income of the year.

However, if you are not careful, sometimes such losses can be disallowed by the tax department—retroactively—despite the fact that claims are fully supported by documentation. That happens *if you try to write off expenses that are really personal in nature, or if your activities are more of a hobby than commercial in nature.* This concept will be discussed in detail in subsequent chapters.

So here's what you need to know: *if a business clearly has a commercial basis to it, and if there is no personal element to the expenditures made on behalf of the business, the taxpayer is considered to be engaged in a commercial activity*, and therefore any losses are deductible. The Canada Revenue Agency (CRA) cannot deny those losses—even if there has never been and may never be a profit.

It's when there is a personal element to some of your business expenses that your losses may be disallowed, but you can still legitimize your tax write-offs. We'll show you how.

3. **Have a Source of Income From the Business** One of the ways to make sure your claims for expenditures made to start and grow your business are deductible is to make sure an income source,

or the potential for one, exists. That is, it's not enough to simply spend money to start a commercial activity, no matter how simple or small. Your activities should lead to an *income source* and the potential for *profit* from it, now *or in the future.* That's key. Your business *must be engaged in commercial activities, in the pursuit of profit.* Those who can show a reasonable expectation of profit from their activities will legitimize the deductions they are eligible for under the Income Tax Act.

4. **Make Sure You're Audit-Proof** A final and most important concept to remember is that if you are self-employed, the onus is on you to (1) "self-assess" income and deductions and (2) collect and re-mit source deductions and withholding taxes on your employees' paycheques and, in some cases, the sales taxes you collect on behalf of provincial and federal governments. All of this must be verifi-able, so it's true that your activities are subject to a *greater risk of scrutiny* by tax auditors. Your financial decision-making relating to the business involves a new level of responsibility throughout the year—there are tax audit requirements that require meticulous, retrievable documentation.

Not to worry—we'll suggest some coping strategies!

The important point, however, is this—small business owners have an even more purposeful and compelling reason to learn more about tax policy, tax law and tax news. And, despite the fact that some fear they can't understand it, you will quickly learn otherwise.

This is about money in your pocket; sharp attention to your right to your own tax savings opportunities is itself profitable. Here are some "starter tips."

Who Files a Return?

Canadian residents must report their taxable income to the government annually. Your obligation to file a Canadian tax return usually ends when you leave the country permanently, unless you continue to earn certain Canadian-source income after you leave, including Canadian business income.

However, make a note that you will want to file a tax return even if you are not required to pay additional taxes at tax time. That's because even those with no taxes payable can benefit from filing a tax return to take advantage of the redistribution of income in Canada through our "refundable" tax credit system and certain benefits like Old Age Security (OAS), Canada Pension Plan (CPP) and Employment Insurance (EI).

What's Taxable Income?

For Canadian residents, taxable income includes world-wide income, in Canadian funds, after allowable deductions and credits. You should also know that income sources are classified and subject to varying tax treatment. In other words, *not all income is taxed in the same manner,* creating potential advantages for the taxpayer who diversifies income sources.

How Is Employment Income Taxed?

Income and deductions from employment, including salary, wages, gratuities, bonuses and vacation pay, are specifically defined and outlined in the Income Tax Act, leaving little room for flexibility or interpretation in terms of how they are reported. Income must be reported on the return in the year received, and this includes not only cash but taxable benefits and employee stock options too.

Can Employees Claim Tax Deductions?

Sometimes, yes. Employees, however, may not take tax deductions for any expenditures except those listed by the Income Tax Act—even if the taxpayer legitimately makes the expenditure in pursuit of his/her duties from an office or employment.

A good example of these restrictions concerns the acquisition of certain equipment, computers or cell phones. An employee may not claim a deduction—known as a Capital Cost Allowance (CCA)—for the cost of depreciating assets *other than motor vehicles, aircraft or musical instruments* used in pursuit of income from his/her office or employment. Certain special provisions exist for tradespeople's tools, however, and power saws used by forestry workers.

Another example concerns the deductibility of meals consumed by the employee while away on company business. The employee must be absent from the employer's place of business for a period of not less than 12 hours in order to claim his/her meal expenses. Further, to claim any deductible expenses, a certificate signed by the employer (Form T2200, *Declaration of Conditions of Employment*) must be available for CRA to verify that the employee was required, under the employment contract, to pay the tax-deductible expenses being claimed and was not reimbursed for the costs.

How Is the Income of the Self-Employed Taxed?

The Income Tax Act states that a taxpayer's income for the year from a business or property is the taxpayer's "profit." This word is not specifically defined in the Act but does infer that the activity conducted has a business or commercial purpose, as previously discussed. It encompasses the concept that those expenditures that cause the taxpayer's gross income to be reduced to its taxable net income are legitimate, provided they have an income-earning purpose and are not personal in nature. Professionals will look to Generally Accepted Accounting Principles (GAAP), as defined in the Canadian Institute of Chartered Accountants' *CICA Handbook,* in computing profits.

However, sometimes the Act itself sets out exceptions to those rules. For example, the deduction for meals and entertainment expenses is usually limited to 50% of their cost. There are other provisions—for the claiming of your home office workspace, for example, or the advertisements you might make in foreign magazines, or the fines or penalties you incur as you conduct your day-to-day affairs—that are subject to restrictions as well.

It is also important to understand that the Income Tax Act separates the sources of income from a business—which is actively pursued—from sources of income from "property," which accrues with only a passive effort by the taxpayer. Income from property generally includes dividends, employee profit-sharing plans, retirement compensation arrangements, income from royalties and interest from investment contracts. Capital gains are classified on a completely separate basis, as discussed later.

What Deductions Can Be Claimed by the Self-Employed?

In order to claim deductions for a small business, you must be able to show that:

- Your expenditures were made or incurred to produce a profit, now or in the foreseeable future
- The amount of the expenditure was reasonable
- The expenditure did not include any personal and living expenses

However, this is also where the "onus of proof" arises—remember that it is your responsibility to show both potential for profit now or in the future and reasonableness in all documentation. You must also make allowances for any personal components of the cost. *Do this by prorating your total costs according to their relevant business/personal use components.*

This includes the deduction for interest expenses. In the case of those who borrow funds to invest in their enterprises or property, it is important to note that there must be potential for income from the property—profits, rents, dividends or interest—for the interest amounts to be deductible at all.

You should also know that "capital appreciation" is not considered to be business income. That's important.

How Is Capital Appreciation Taxed?

Currently, the Income Tax Act requires only 50% of capital gains received in the year to be included as income, and that these gains can be offset by capital losses of the current year, or any prior year since 1972, adjusted for changes that have been made in the past to the "income inclusion rates" for capital gains.

There are certain exceptions to this rule that in fact allows for tax-free gains—for gains on the sale of the principal residence, gains made on the disposition of certain properties when replacement properties are acquired, and tax-free rollovers of assets to children and/or spouses in certain cases.

Striving to earn profits and then to benefit from the appreciation in value of an asset throughout the ownership period and then at the time of disposition is tax wise. So how do you do this? Here's what you need to know:

- Asset appreciation is never taxed until disposition, which can include "actual disposition" sale, gift or "deemed disposition." An asset is *deemed* to be disposed by way of transfer, conversion to personal use, emigration, expropriation or death.
- Capital gains on assets usually qualify for a tax exemption of 50%.
- In certain cases, a capital gains deduction is possible when assets are disposed of. This is currently known as the $750,000 Capital Gains Exemption (CGE), and each taxpayer in the family who disposes of an eligible asset is entitled to one. On the tax return, 50% of the CGE will be claimed, and this is known as the capital gains deduction.
- Except in the case of death or other deemed dispositions, you do have some control over when you sell or otherwise dispose of an asset. Therefore, you have the potential to reduce the marginal tax rate on your investments through purposeful timing. For example, you could reduce your tax burden by disposing of the asset over two tax years (half in December, half in January) or by offsetting capital gains in the year with allowable capital losses, and so on.

TAX ADVISOR

Before any taxpayer begins a new small business, it is important to go through a personal and family income assessment procedure. Start this procedure as follows:

Complete a Current Year Tax Review

Prepare a tax summary to confirm how your current year income sources are earned and how they are taxed. Figure 1.1 shows a sample plan for Linda Baker. Linda started an *unincorporated small business* during the tax year.*

Note the following on her personal tax return:

- She has a tax refund originating from the withholding taxes deducted from her employment income. This refund has been largely generated by the loss she has reported from her business start-up activities.
- Her total amount payable for the year represents approximately 9% of her total income.
- Her Registered Retirement Savings Plan (RRSP) contribution limit for next year is calculated as 18% of her earned income of the current year. This represents some potential for real tax savings in her future, as discussed below.

Analyze Current RRSP Contribution Room

Small business owners often have all their eggs in one basket, investing everything in their enterprises. In fact this is often at the expense of their security in retirement. While the returns on your investment in the business can be very good for the family, in the absence of any other assets working for you and your future, your financial future in fact is at risk.

For this particular reason—and all the other good ones that strike a chord with average taxpayers—the RRSP is a "must-have" investment for business owners. It provides a way for you to invest in a tax-deferred savings vehicle that can enable a legitimate way to split income with your spouse† (through a spousal RRSP) while reducing the taxes you pay today and deferring the tax on your investment earnings to the future. Those are two powerful advantages—more cash today through tax

---

* For the purposes of this book, estimated figures for tax year 2009 are used.
† Or common-law partner.

Figure 1.1	Tax Summary for Linda Baker

Tax Summary
for
Linda Baker

Calculation of Taxable income

Income

Employment Income	$ 25,000.00
Business Income	$ (4,320.60)
Total Income	$ 20,679.40

Deductions from Total Income

None

Net Income	$ 20,679.40

Deductions from Net Income

None

Taxable Income	$ 20,679.40

Calculation of Federal Tax

Federal Tax on Taxable Income $ 3,101.91

Federal Non-Refundable Credits

Basic Personal Amount	$ 10,320.00	
CPP through employment	$ 1,064.25	
EI premiums	$ 432.50	
Canada Employment Credit	$ 1,044.00	
Total non-refundable credits	$ 12,860.75	
Total non-refundable credits 15%	$ 1,929.11	
Federal Tax	$ 1,172.80	$ 1,172.80

Calculation of Ontario Tax

Ontario Tax on Taxable Income $ 1,251.10

Ontario Non-Refundable Credits

Basic Personal Amount	$ 8,881.00	
CPP through employment	$ 1,064.25	
EI premiums	$ 432.50	
Total non-refundable credits	$ 10,377.75	
Total non-refundable credits × 6.05%	$ 627.85	
Ontario Health Tax	$ 40.76	
Ontario Tax	$ 664.01	$ 664.01
Total payable		$ 1,836.81

Calculation of Refund or Balance Due

Refundable Credits

Income tax deducted	$ 3,575.00	
Total Credits	$ 3,575.00	$ 3,575.00
Refund		$ 1,738.19

2010 RRSP contribution Limit	$ 3,722

savings and more cash tomorrow through enhanced investment compounding power with 100% (pre-tax) dollars.

To illustrate, the table below shows Linda's approximate tax savings at different levels of RRSP contributions.

RRSP Contribution	Tax Savings
$ 500	$135
$1,000	$251
$1,500	$357
$2,000	$462
$2,500	$567
$3,000	$672
$3,500	$778

Had Linda planned to save some money through an RRSP, she would have gained a double-digit return on her investment this year—just through her tax savings.

Remember, to contribute to an RRSP, you must have:

- Filed a return to report the qualifying "earned income" from active sources like employment or business income, and
- Made a contribution to an RRSP within the calendar year or 60 days after the calendar year

Tap Into the Tax-Free Savings Account

The very best type of investment, after one that saves you tax dollars on a double-digit basis, is one in which the earnings from the investment are completely tax free. The Tax-Free Savings Account (TFSA) is such an investment, available to any adult in Canada since 2009. It is important that any "redundant income" you have, after meeting your living costs and making your RRSP contributions, should really be invested here next.

Speak to your tax advisor about making your TFSA contribution an annual event. You must file a tax return to qualify to build "TFSA contribution room," which can be carried forward from year to year. This means that even if you don't have the money to invest in one today, your contribution room follows you until you can afford to do it. However, it would be a shame to miss out on the tax-free earnings—interest, dividends or capital gains—this savings vehicle will build for you over time. The younger you are, the more powerful the opportunity.

Know Your Current Average and Marginal Tax Rates on Income Sources You Earn

Linda's employment income, as well as her net business income (in this case a loss) will be taxed at her **marginal tax rate**—the rate of tax she pays on the next dollar of income earned in her tax bracket. Her **average tax rate** on total income for the year, however, will be less. This is the total amount of tax she actually pays on her total income.

These are important concepts. You need to know them to answer questions such as:

- How much will I keep of the next dollar I earn?
- How much should be properly withheld from my gross earnings for my tax remittances throughout the year?

The difference between marginal and average tax rates illustrates the "progressivity" in our tax system:

- The more you make, the more you pay.
- Non-refundable tax credits and tax deductions can be used to reduce the tax you pay.

Linda is very interested, for example, in her eligibility for non-refundable tax credits, such as the basic personal amount, or "tax free zone," and how her required contributions to the Canada Pension Plan (CPP) and Employment Insurance (EI) contributed through her former employer impact her tax results. These "personal amounts"—and others like her medical expenses and charitable donations—reduce her taxes payable.

Remember that income from different sources attracts different rates of tax. It is interesting to note that in her current tax bracket, dividends Linda might earn from her investment in a privately held small business corporation would be taxed at a much lower rate than interest earnings. Further, beginning in 2006, a second layer of even more advantageous tax treatment was extended to taxpayers who earned dividends from share ownership in corporations that paid tax at what's known as "general rates." Those corporations earn income over a "small business deduction" limit. It makes Linda wonder about incorporating her proprietorship and whether investments outside the business should be focused on publicly traded companies. More about that later.

Linda is also interested to learn that capital gains on any asset dispositions would be taxed at one-half her marginal tax rate on ordinary income. She has been talking to her financial advisors about how to incorporate this type of income source into her financial plans. It's important to have a well diversified investment portfolio so that taxes payable on total income earned during the year can be "averaged downward" over a lifetime of investing and saving.

What's challenging to taxpayers like Linda is that marginal and average tax rates change continuously both on the federal and provincial level. So do types and levels of various personal tax credits.

For an updated look at the current rules, visit www.knowledge bureau.com, look for "Breaking News" and subscribe to the online newsletter where indicated—*to keep you up to date.*

Prepare a Tax Review for Each Family Member

Whenever you file a tax return, one of your objectives should be to attempt to reduce taxes not just for each individual but for the family unit as a whole. You should look into the legitimate ways to split income with family members, take advantage of transferable deductions and credits, and tax deferral opportunities for your family's investments.

Every family member should make an RRSP contribution whenever possible. The criteria for making the investment have nothing to do with age—you need to have qualifying "earned income" to invest. That means your 16-year-old can have one.

And every adult in the family should make an annual TFSA investment too. These are very basic "must-dos" that every family should discuss with their advisors, especially if you are in business for yourself.

Assess Previous Errors and Omissions

Because a small business owner is subject to greater scrutiny by tax auditors, it is important for you to clean up any past filing problems with CRA before you start your business.

For example, if you have failed to file tax returns in the past, you may wish to consider filing them now. CRA may owe you money with regard to overpaid taxes at source or refundable tax credits you may be eligible for. If you had eligible earned income in those years, you will also create increased RRSP contribution room, which CRA will not yet have calculated. In addition, the creation of TFSA contribution room is very important, as you have just learned.

Also, if you voluntarily comply with the law to correct understated income or overstated deductions or credits, you will avoid gross negligence and tax evasion penalties. It is always important to clear up your tax-filing status, and it could pay off for you in the future. For example, you may someday have to rely on CRA's taxpayer relief provisions to grant you a waiver of interest and penalties should a severe hardship occur in your circumstances. More on that later.

And, if you find you have missed an important provision in your prior filed returns—like GST rebates on employment expenses, medical expenses, charitable donations, disability tax credits, safety deposit box charges or moving expenses—file Form T1 ADJ to request an adjustment. You can do so over a prior 10-year period for most federal provisions.

Find Out More: Incorporated Business or Proprietorship?

If you are serious about running a for-profit business, be aware that a business can be formed in a variety of organizational structures. For most people who begin an owner-operated business, an unincorporated structure, also known as a *proprietorship*, is best at the start. For a proprietorship, the income, expenses and capital transactions are reported on the T1 General personal tax return and added to other income of the year, in the case of net profits. Losses from the business offset other income of the current year, or if excess losses exist after this, these non-capital losses can offset other income of the previous 3 years or income in the next 20 years. They can, therefore, be lucrative.

The incorporated company, on the other hand, is a separate legal entity. Under this scenario, legal liability is limited, and earnings may be retained in the company or distributed on an after-tax basis to shareholders; losses, however, stay within the corporate structure. The shareholder, who is generally also the owner-manager, can earn salary, dividends or other income from the business. This provides for a great opportunity to diversify income sources, average down marginal tax rates and split income within the family.

A third form of business organization is the partnership, which may be incorporated or not.

We'll discuss the tax implications of different business structures in more depth later; however, unless otherwise stated, in the chapters that follow, we will assume our reader is operating an unincorporated small business.

Plan to Tax Cost Average

Once you have all the basic steps above in place, you are well positioned to begin to integrate tax efficiency into your normal business activities and the financial decisions you need to make all year long. In fact, you can plan to average your tax costs for the current year, the prior years and future years by applying the provisions available to you within the Income Tax Act.

We'll show you how in Chapter 2, "How to Tax Cost Average."

RECAP. YOU NEED TO KNOW:

1. How diversifying your income can decrease taxes payable
2. What your "onus of proof" is
3. How to prorate costs incurred for both business/personal use
4. The difference between business income and capital appreciation
5. How gains on a principal residence are taxed
6. The difference between marginal and average or effective tax rates
7. How to account for previous errors and omissions on tax returns
8. The difference between incorporated and unincorporated enterprises
9. The importance of RRSP contributions for small business owners
10. The importance of making TFSA contributions

YOU NEED TO ASK: Your tax advisor to help you

1. **Assess your current tax-filing profile:** What you want to know is how your current income sources are being taxed. Make sure you know what your marginal tax rates are on all new dollars earned. Finally, find out what deductions and credits apply to you.

2. **Find new money:** Many people overpay their taxes every year and then fail to go back and ask for a refund due to errors and omissions on their returns. This is possible by requesting a formal adjustment to returns, which can be filed over a prior 10-year period. Ask your tax advisor to prepare a thorough prior-filing review for each family member. This is particularly important if you have been changing advisors from year to year or have missed filing tax returns in any prior years. Make sure you ask for your overpaid dollars back, if applicable.

3. **Launch your future with RRSP tax savings:** Make sure you isolate the ways to reduce future taxes now. One way to do this is to have your tax advisor prepare an RRSP contribution room analysis for each family member. You'll want to receive a tax refund for ev-

ery dollar contributed, as this new money can be used to finance your business or personal expenses or split retirement income with your spouse. It also diversifies your investments, prepares you to tap into tax-advantaged investments like the TFSA and maximizes your personal productivity by providing a "Plan B" on your retirement savings strategies if you cannot accumulate enough through the lifecycle of your business. Carry forward undeducted contributions in cases where income is too low to derive a benefit from the RRSP contribution. Where income levels are high, make sure RRSP deductions are taken.

4. **Prepare to "tax cost average":** Some carry-over provisions are available to taxpayers to average tax costs over time. Those are the ones to isolate and record now. Examples are prior capital and non-capital loss balances, unclaimed moving expenses or unused medical expenses and charitable donations.

5. **Do some "tax planning R & D":** Find out how your self-employment can help you diversify income—first, from the operations of the enterprise, and second, by building a potentially saleable concern. Talk to your tax advisor about your proposed business plans, your business structure at start-up and in the future. Receive information about obligations to CRA for income taxes, source deductions and GST/HST remittances, as well as business name licensing, trademark applications and the like. It is important to protect all of your equity in your income-producing assets.

6. **Plan to split business income with family members:** By starting a proprietorship—perhaps a simple home-based business—you have increased the potential to reap double-digit returns from your tax filing opportunities, simply by giving family members an opportunity to work for you. Try not to earn all the profits yourself, so that you can equalize income levels and maximize the "tax-free zones" available through the basic personal amount every tax filer is entitled to. Find tasks within your business that can be delegated to others, and then consider employing family members who are willing to take on the job a stranger would normally be hired for. Pay them at fair market value to do so. More on this later.

7. **Be vigilant about keeping track of all expenditures:** Start a document filing system and open a separate bank account. Small business owners can reap double-digit tax savings on each dollar they *spend* in their small business ventures, depending on their income levels and marginal tax rates in their province of residence. But to deduct

costs you must keep track of all money spent in the establishment of your business enterprise, even if you are not yet earning revenues. Store your receipts. Hire a bookkeeper if you're not good at this.

8. **Get ready to give birth to your business:** Remember that the birth of a small business requires careful nurturing to grow into a profitable entity that has enduring value—potentially to a future buyer. Both money and time must be expended in advance for revenues to begin to flow. This involves the formalization of the financial path your business will take to its maturity as well as an injection of capital. CRA will want to know the details of that birth and its growth patterns when assessing your tax return. Keep track of all initiatives that precede the revenue flow in your business.

. . . .

CHAPTER 2

How to Tax Cost Average

"We make our habits, and then our habits make us."
JOHN DRYDEN

KEY CONCEPTS

- Control the tax you pay with a detailed tax and business plan that anticipates your income, deductions and credits
- Consider that your tax filing results may be influenced by carry-over provisions which may span 10 to 20 years
- Save "permissive deductions"—like Capital Cost Allowance—for the future if they are worth more to you then
- Claim every deduction you are entitled to, keeping in mind that those with mixed business/personal components may need to be prorated
- Split income with family members, but watch the costs of Canada Pension Plan contributions, which affect each lower-income earner over 18 and your cash flow
- Defer taxable income to the future whenever possible

REAL LIFE: How would you like to save tens of thousands of dollars in taxes over the next several years? What would you do with the extra money? How would it change your life? The good news is that it's possible, you can do it and it's also easy. In fact, this recently happened to Mary, a single entrepreneur living in Ontario.

Unable to afford a dream camping trip to beautiful BC with her boyfriend, Mary decided to have her tax advisor prepare a current year tax review. Perhaps there was something she was missing out on by filing her own return. Mary makes $50,000 a year from her efforts as a manufacturer's agent, which is shown on the T4A slip sent to her at the end of the year. She reports the amounts as self-employment income on her tax return, and that's it, she's done. "A simple return," she'd say every year, "no hassles."

Turns out, Mary's erroneous self-assessment has been costly. She is significantly overpaying her taxes. In preparing her return as she described it— which is perfectly legal and correct, by the way—she owes close to $10,000 at year end. Let's project that liability forward for a moment. Should her income stay constant over the next 10 years, she'll have paid over $100,000 in taxes—more than what's left to pay on her home mortgage.

In addition, because the annual amount she owes the government at year end is over $3,000, she is required to make quarterly tax instalment payments throughout the year. This will take approximately $2,500 out of her pocket *every calendar quarter.* What does this mean to Mary's lifestyle? No holidays this summer, fall, winter or spring.

THE PROBLEM

Most people overpay their taxes year in and year out because they think about their tax obligations only once a year, at tax-filing time. Unfortunately, at this point you are usually only reconciling history. Aside from maximizing every tax deduction and credit you and your family are entitled to, there are few pro-active measures available to reduce the tax burden of the tax year in question.

In fact, the difference between a "taxpayer" and a "tax saver" lies in the desire to gain control of one's future tax bill by planning all year long. A "tax saver" also controls the amount of taxes being paid to the government over a period of years—looking back and forward—to get a new result: *a tax cost that on average is significantly lower than the current liability.*

It is the self-employed who are in the best position to minimize tax in this way. As discussed in Chapter 1, business income, which is generally taxed within the calendar year in the case of proprietors, can be reduced by all reasonable expenses incurred to earn income as long as the commercial venture has a reasonable expectation of profit. Proprietors can also utilize business loss application rules to their advantage—that is, to reduce other income of the year.

Employees, on the other hand, are limited to writing off only a very specific group of itemized expenses, and then only with the certification of their employers.

So the tax saver's goal is to reduce the taxes paid over a period of years to avoid one of the taxpayer's greatest risks—the real-dollar cost of under-utilizing available and legitimate tax provisions during one's lifetime.

THE SOLUTION

The key to reducing the taxes you pay is to put yourself and your family in the position of controlling:

- The type of income earned
- When it's earned
- Who reports it
- How much of it is subject to tax

Your goal is to create an effective plan not only to earn an income but to increase after-tax wealth, implemented over a period of years, all within the framework of the law, of course. It is your legitimate right—and duty—to arrange your affairs within the framework of the law to pay the correct amount of taxes, but no more.

One way to do this is to *tax cost average*.

Your *tax cost* is the real dollars you send to CRA every year. If you net $50,000 a year from your proprietorship, for example, your tax cost for the year may be about $10,000 (the exact amount depends on your province of residence and the various individual credits and deductions you may be entitled to).

Tax cost averaging is the deliberate use of existing tax provisions available to reduce the taxes you pay *over a period of years*. This involves the diversification of income sources, the application of all existing tax provisions to reduce your current tax bill and the maximization of carry-over provisions available to average out the good years and the bad.

Tax cost averaging involves the projection of taxes payable through a multi-year overview, generally encompassing the tax results from:

1. The current year
2. The prior three years against which to apply capital losses of the current year
3. The next 20 years—the time frame in which unused losses from your business can be carried forward

Maximizing loss carry-over periods can be a very worthwhile endeavor. But in addition several other tax provisions can affect your income—and therefore your taxes payable—year over year. This can include Capital Cost Allowance (CCA) deductions available to reduce net business income, carry-forwards of unclaimed home office expenses, RRSP contribution room available or unclaimed RRSP contributions. A more complete list follows later in the chapter.

Ask your tax advisor about some of these provisions and how they affect you. He or she will help you develop a "Tax Savings Blueprint" over a period of years. This is just like a business plan but focused on tax-efficiency projections. Many tax software programs provide just those types of reports to help you understand not only what has happened on your tax return this year but what your tax filing trendlines and future tax savings opportunities are. It's important to look over these and discuss them. Many tax advisors consider these "what if" solutions to be a part of a professional solution to your annual tax preparation exercise.

In short, it is important that your annual visit with your tax advisor be purposeful, not only to meet your obligations to file your annual tax return but also to define and bring structure to your *projected after-tax results* so that you can make good decisions to achieve them throughout the year. Anticipating and understanding the effects of those decisions on your cash flow, this year and within your 24-year "carry-forward" window, can help you maximize all provisions that apply to your changing personal and business lifecycles. Over time, this focus on *your future tax position* can return five- and six-figure tax savings—sometimes more—depending on the size of your business enterprise.

You'll need the help of an astute tax advisor with whom you are in sync on both tax law and the evolution of your business. The opportunity for tax savings often arises out of change—changes in tax law, changes in the structure of your business affairs, as well as changes in your personal life. Don't deal with someone who is focused only on the past year's results.

Remember that tax law changes continuously. You need your advisor to stay on top of them for you and to explain the implications as they relate to your plans for the future. Look for someone who can do that for you in language you understand.

You, on the other hand, are the expert at your business and the plans for its future and are therefore in control of the execution of those plans. When you combine (1) a clear understanding of tax options available to maximize your precious resources of time and money with (2) the vision you have for your business, you will get tax-efficient results—in short, more money in your pockets. But you need to share all of this with your advisors too. They can then do a better job for you.

This is especially important when it comes time to face a tax audit, which can be very time-consuming and expensive and can distract you from what you do best—running your business—if you are unprepared. More about managing that later.

THE TAX ADVISOR

Mary was delighted to find out about the tax cost averaging process when she visited her tax advisor. He showed her how to reclaim some control over her tax costs. She hadn't known, for example, about the allowable claims for:

- Automobile expenses ($2,500, after taking into account any personal driving)
- Workplace in the home expenses ($1,200, after making allowance for personal use)
- Operating expenses, like promotions and travelling expenses (which amounted to another $3,500)
- How to use and maximize her RRSP contribution room

By drawing up a Tax Savings Blueprint—some "what if" scenarios about what could be achieved with her money—Mary's advisor illustrated the financial results available to a better-informed taxpayer with four simple reports:

1. A thorough investigation of her current year's tax filing status
2. An adjustment for prior year errors and omissions
3. Corrections to her current year's return to set up her future tax efficiencies
4. Projections of quarterly tax remittances required

The Current Year Investigation   Mary's loosely kept books and records revealed the following:

- The additional deductions of $7,200 identified above would save Mary close to $2,500 in taxes.
- Mary had never claimed any of these expenses before—a potential for recovery of overpaid taxes of the past.
- Mary has accumulated $19,500 in unused RRSP accumulation room—a potential for future tax savings.

Adjustments for the Past   Mary's advisor can now take further action and request adjustments to prior filed returns where errors or omissions occurred. In looking over last year's return, he finds $2,500 more in tax savings. Now it looks like Mary and her boyfriend can afford that holiday after all!

Adjustments for the Current and Future Years   There is more good news. Thanks to lower tax obligations on her current year return, Mary can reduce her quarterly tax instalment payment obligations throughout the rest of this calendar year and the first half of the next, increasing her cash flow by just over $600 each quarter or $200 a month. This gives Mary more cash to invest or grow her business. Two calendar years are now affected positively with increased after-tax cash flow.

Mary's advisor wisely counsels her to consider all tax savings as a windfall to be used to leverage and accumulate wealth. Her next logical step should be to invest part of this tax windfall into her RRSP to save even more tax dollars.

Given her plentiful RRSP room, Mary decides to contribute $3,000 to her RRSP this year and vows to do so every year. She is thereby successful in reducing her taxes for the past tax year, but, more importantly, she also further decreases her quarterly instalment owings throughout this calendar year and the first part of the next. Again Mary has increased her cash flow and significantly increased her opportunities to grow her wealth.

When her increased tax refund is received, Mary decides to invest it in a Tax-Free Savings Account. Then, together with the tax-free earnings within that account, she makes a down payment on the new car she's wanted for years. That acquisition is also tax efficient. Fixed costs (like Capital Cost Allowance and interest charges) and operating costs (like gas, repairs, car washes and parking) are deductible against business income earned, after taking into account any personal portion of the expenses. This is music to Mary's ears.

By year three of her "tax enlightenment," Mary decides to use the tax savings from the increased Capital Cost Allowance write-off she earned by acquiring the car to buy another asset—a new laptop computer. The CCA write-off from this asset finances the cost of her office supplies. It just keeps getting better—tax savings from one business expenditure finance another! This is fun!

By the time Mary and her tax advisor were through analyzing "what if" scenarios on her Tax Savings Blueprint and putting them into action, Mary was paying approximately $4,000 per year less in taxes. Mary could hardly believe it as her accountant projected the power of those savings forward—without a tax focus, she could have been overpaying her taxes by $40,000 in 10 years, $80,000 in 20 and so on. There is a trick to tax planning all right—you can't afford not to do it!

Minimize Quarterly Tax Instalments

It is important to see the big picture when it comes to your potential tax savings. Five-figure tax saving returns over a 10-year period are possible for some and can translate into numerous new investments both inside and outside registered accounts, sending the taxpayer along the road to maximum wealth creation.

However, your cash flow and investment opportunities can be significantly impacted when you overpay quarterly tax instalments. These payments are required when your taxes payable exceed $3,000 when you file your tax return. Make sure that when income fluctuates, your quarterly instalments are adjusted. Also, use RRSP contributions, charitable contributions and other tax provisions purposefully when you are near that quarterly instalment tax threshold.

THE TAX PARAMETERS

If Mary's story whetted your appetite for tax savings, please take a moment now to learn more about the tax theory surrounding the *tax cost averaging* process. Following are a series of parameters to help you understand the benefits of tax cost averaging:

1. Know your personal tax brackets and rates.
2. Build tax-exempt income sources.
3. Know and use your carry-forward provisions.
4. Defer taxation of income into the future.
5. Watch the CPP tax.
6. Diversify your taxable income sources.
7. Build equity that will be tax free.
8. Be audit-proof.
9. Make it your business to know tax changes.
10. Understand that retroactive tax adjustments may have their limits.

Know Your Personal Tax Brackets and Rates

Personal incomes are categorized into various tax brackets, and then tax rates are applied to them. This happens on both the federal and provincial tax forms. Ask your tax advisor to show you what tax bracket your income falls into, or look at Schedule 1 of your federal tax return to get a basic idea. At the time of writing, the approximate tax brackets and tax rates on the federal tax return were as follows (know that these amounts are subject to indexing by increases in the consumer price index every year):

The Basic Personal Amount (BPA)	$10,320
$10,321 to $40,726	15%
$40,727 to $81,452	22%
$81,453 to $126,264	26%
Over $126,264	29%

As you can see, those with income levels over $126,264 generally pay the highest federal marginal tax rates on personal taxable income levels. However, these results will differ from province to province and over time with federal law changes. The tax brackets are also indexed annually.

Maximize Opportunities to Build Tax-Exempt Income

Many people don't realize that there are certain income sources that are, in fact, completely exempt from tax. They include the following:

- Income from a Tax-Free Savings Account (TFSA)
- Amounts received from refundable tax credits like the Child Tax Benefit or Goods and Services Tax Credit (teenagers should be reminded to file a return for the year they reach age 18 in order to claim this credit for themselves the quarter after they turn 19)
- Gifts or inheritances (non-cash gifts from employers are generally tax free under $500)
- Life insurance policy proceeds on death of the insured
- Profit from the sale of a person's principal residence

Further reinvestment of these sources generates taxable investment earnings in the hands of the recipient unless invested in another tax-exempt source.

Know and Use Your Carry-Over Provisions

Each taxpayer should make it her business (1) to keep track of all carry-over provisions available over the course of her tax-filing lifetime and (2) to ask her tax advisor for an updated record of them every year. Here are some common examples:

- Undepreciated capital cost (UCC) balances as well as costs of asset acquisition and disposition
- Undeducted moving expenses

- Undeducted home office expenses
- RRSP carry-forward room or undeducted contributions
- TFSA carry-forward room
- Undeducted past-service contributions to Registered Pension Plans (RPPs)
- Capital gains deduction availability
- Prior years' capital and non-capital losses
- Prior years' business investment losses
- Undeducted medical expenses
- Undeducted charitable donations
- Undeducted tuition, education and text book amounts
- Undeducted student loan interest
- Minimum tax carry-overs
- Undeducted labour-sponsored funds tax credits
- Refunds of investment tax credits

Defer Taxation of Income into the Future

Try to invest the first dollar you earn, rather than the last one left over after taxation, by using your opportunities for tax deferral. Moving tax into the future increases your earning power today. There are several ways to accomplish this:

- Assess which of your potential income sources are taxed on a cash basis and which are taxed on an accrual basis. Capital transactions, for example, are taxed on the cash basis in the year the transaction actually occurs. Business transactions are generally subject to accrual accounting rules, which require reporting of income as it is earned, rather than when it is received, and expenses when they are incurred, rather than when they are actually paid.
- Time dispositions of assets advantageously, given the cash reporting rules. For example, you might choose to sell your revenue properties strategically if you expect a large taxable gain: one-half in the current year; one-half in the new year. The same logic could be applied to any capital or depreciable asset. The right price and willing buyer are, of course, prerequisites.
- In the case of depreciable business assets, try to push the disposition into the next taxation year if the transaction will be happening late in the year and if the buyer is willing to wait. This could be especially wise if a recapture of previous CCA deductions will occur. More details appear in later chapters.

- When signing contracts for new work in your business, record start dates in the new fiscal year if work on the project will not begin until then.
- Buy mutual funds in the new year to push any potential distributions into the next taxation year.
- If incorporated, pay dividends in January rather than December.
- Time severance package receipts over two tax years or move them into the next year if that otherwise makes sense.
- Take bonuses and raises in January rather than December.

Watch the CPP "Tax"

When you own a business, you are responsible for making contributions to the Canada Pension Plan for your employees. If you are the proprietor of an unincorporated business, you must make them for yourself too. In fact, you must contribute both "employer" and "employee" portions to the plan. This actually happens when you file your annual tax return.

This obligation can cause hardship for new sole proprietors, who may not expect to pay their own CPP contributions all at once at tax time. It's an expensive hit, amounting to over $4,200 a year when contributory earning levels exceed $46,000. (These rates change annually so be sure to subscribe to updates under "Breaking News" at www.knowledge bureau.com.)

The employer's portion of the CPP has implications in family income splitting as well. While every tax dollar that you can split with family members may put the family unit in a lower average tax position, when you take the employer's portion of CPP into account in the calculations, the marginal tax rates on business income spike considerably.

Therefore, when calculating the benefits of employing family members, you must take into account the cash flow you need to fund their CPP premiums. While the first $3,500 of earnings is exempt from the CPP and only those over 18 must contribute to the plan, everyone must pay until income exceeds the $46,000 threshold.

That means that there is a diminishing marginal cost for those whose incomes exceed the maximum contributory amount and an additional marginal cost for those whose incomes exceed $3,500.

The tax calculations on the personal tax return are tricky too. In the case of a proprietor, 50% of his or her premium is deductible as a non-refundable tax credit, the other half as a deduction that reduces net income. This tax treatment is on par with that afforded to other employees/employers who work in a corporate environment.

Careful tax planning, however, can help you reduce the tax burden of your CPP obligations, particularly if you own assets in your business. You might consider planning to reduce net income subject to CPP contributions with your deductions for Capital Cost Allowances, for example.

CCA is taken *at the taxpayer's option* to account for the diminishing value of income-producing assets and is used to reduce the net income of the business, upon which CPP premiums are based. So when your business income is low you may wish to elect to save your CCA deductions for the future, especially if you have lots of non-refundable tax credits to take advantage of. You can then reduce net business income later as CPP obligations rise with increased undepreciated capital cost balances.

As always, you'll want to maximize use of tax expenditures like RRSP contributions, medical expenses, charitable donations and so on to reduce this year's taxes further, all of which can often be claimed in different tax years to maximize your tax benefits. Ask your accountant about these provisions.

But don't fall into this trap: if you choose to reduce your income subject to CPP too often or choose to take only dividends from an incorporated business, for example, then you'll miss out on receiving a periodic pension from the CPP later in life.

Diversify Your Income Sources

Here's a quick look at different tax results stemming from your decision to earn a variety of different income types for a taxpayer in the province of Ontario. (Ask your tax professional to prepare an exact computation for you as part of your annual Tax Savings Blueprint, or use your favourite tax software program to do so.):

Prov. Taxable Income Range	Ordinary Income	Capital Gains	Small Corp. Div.	Eligible Div.
Up to $10,320	0%	0%	0%	0%
$10,321 to $12,053	15.00%	7.50%	2.08%	−5.75%
$12,054 to $36,848	21.05%	10.52%	3.23%	−7.71%
$36,849 to $40,726	24.15%	12.07%	7.11%	−3.21%
$40,727 to $64,882	31.15%	15.58%	15.57%	6.94%
$64,883 to $73,698	32.98%	16.49%	16.86%	7.45%
$73,699 to $76,440	35.39%	17.70%	19.88%	10.94%
$76,441 to $81,452	39.41%	19.70%	22.59%	12.91%
$81,453 to $126,264	43.41%	21.70%	27.59%	18.71%
Over $126,264	46.41%	23.20%	31.34%	23.05%

It is interesting to note that income from dividends and capital gains earned produce the most advantageous tax results; in the case of dividends, that's due to the effects of the dividend tax credit. This credit offsets the gross-up of dividends required under the personal tax system.

You'll note that there are two types of dividends in Canada today—those that are eligible for an enhanced "gross-up" and dividend tax credit, and those that are not. Privately held small business corporations whose income is subject to the small business deduction will produce "ineligible" dividends for its shareholders; publicly traded companies and those small businesses whose income is subject to general rates of tax will produce eligible dividends.

When dividends produce a "negative tax" effect, it means that they offset other income of the year—a very good thing, especially when other income sources—such as pension income—have few deductions to offset them. Astute business planning can have favorable effects on retirement income planning too.

Build Equity That Will Be Tax Free

Most business owners are so concerned about surviving the day-to-day challenges of making enough money to cover all expenses that they often forget about the possible rewards, down the road, for the hours of unpaid labour they invest in their businesses in the start-up years. That is, if they build an entity someone else wants to buy in the future, they'll earn a capital gain that could be tax free in some cases. Below is a true-to-life example.

REAL LIFE: Maggie, a 40-year-old mother, started a cleaning business last year. She cleaned one house every Friday. She soon developed a reputation for her integrity and work ethic, and within six months, Maggie and her staff of three were cleaning two houses a day, six days a week. After the first year, Maggie was grossing $60,000 a year and taking on even more staff to increase her revenues. Halfway through the second year, Maggie was offered $80,000 by a franchise company for her list of clients. She decided to sell her business. Not a bad return for a 24-month effort.

Had Maggie been operating a proprietorship* she would have reported a taxable gain on goodwill. However, had this business been incorporated, Maggie may have qualified for the capital gains deduction, and her gain on the sale of her shares would have been tax free.

---

* Other than a qualified farming or fishing operation.

This scenario begs the question: *When should I incorporate?* This is an important question to discuss with your tax advisor, as additional opportunities to diversify income sources and average out taxes payable can arise. Some of the factors to consider include:

- The importance of limited liability to the business owner
- The difference in tax rates payable on business income
- The importance of income diversification: employment income, dividends from after-tax profits, bonuses paid out of the corporation
- Whether there are current year losses (losses held in a proprietorship offset all other income in the year, the prior 3 years and for up to 20 years in the future)
- The likelihood of a future sale of the business
- The value of the business at the time of change in structure
- The opportunity of income splitting within the family unit
- The eligibility of shareholders for the capital gains deduction

These issues should be revisited with your tax advisor whenever you anticipate significant new opportunities, or at least annually. Also see Chapter 10.

Be Audit-Proof!

File every tax return in anticipation of a tax audit. It's a fact that small business owners have a greater potential of audit because the government must rely on those taxpayers to "self-assess" business income and deductions. The penalties for tax evasion are stiff, as you'll find out in Chapter 11. Of particular interest to a tax auditor are any expenses that may contain a personal component, such as entertainment, home office or auto expenses.

If you can't do documentation well, hire a bookkeeper immediately. Tax cost averaging is easier when your books and records are in order. So is decision-making for the future of your business.

Make It Your Business to Know Tax Changes

Another great way to tax cost average is to keep on top of all the most recent tax changes, announced with every federal and provincial budget. The documents often review prior provisions, and you may find you've missed a few recoverable ones. If so, always go back and review prior-filed returns for any potential errors or omissions. In addition, you may find some new tax write-offs and deferral opportunities. For the latest federal budget summary, visit www.knowledgebureau.com to tap into a number of resources to keep you up to date.

Retroactive Tax Adjustments May Have Limits

CRA may allow an adjustment for some of the unclaimed operating expenses of prior years, but know that special rules may apply. For example, the Capital Cost Allowance deduction will not be allowed if the adjustment request comes more than 90 days after receiving a Notice of Assessment or Reassessment. (Note that if CRA audits your files, however, retroactive claims for CCA are generally allowed as you wish to apply them, as if the return were being filed for the first time.)

Requests to adjust home office and operating expenses will likely be allowed retroactively as well if receipts are provided. However, with every adjustment request, there is always the potential for a more thorough audit. Therefore adjustment requests should never be made frivolously.

Know that requests to voluntarily adjust returns that contain an overstatement of deductions or understatement of income are always a good idea. By doing so you can avoid penalties that could be extremely expensive, or in seriously abusive cases, land you in jail.

TAX ADVISOR

To average out the money you will pay CRA over the long term, you'll need to be aware of the tax-planning choices available from the past, today and, as time goes by, in the future. It is therefore important to have a good working relationship with a tax professional who clearly understands those tax parameters and how they affect your current and future financial planning goals and who can discuss them in a way that makes sense to you. Look for a team of professional advisors—accountant, lawyer, financial planner, banker, life insurance advisor—who will inform you of all your options so that you can make the most tax-efficient decisions about your time and money.

Communication with your professionals begins with you, though. Be sure to provide the background information your advisors need to make the best recommendations for you. Here's how you can facilitate the process:

- Together with your advisors, chart your tax cost over your carry-forward time frames using historical data, current year data and projections for the future.

- Develop your own standard Tax Savings Blueprint outlining the "what if" scenarios that are most meaningful for you throughout the year.
- Update the blueprint annually as your business and personal life-cycles change, and integrate these templates with your investment strategies too.

At the end of this process, you should have a basic understanding of the following:

- Estimated tax calculations for the entire review period, using current tax law, and/or known proposals for change
- An analysis of the marginal tax rates paid or payable in the period for each family member
- A plan to average out income, apply deductions and credits, as well as carry-backs and carry-forwards, so as to pay the least amount of tax, at the lowest average rate possible in the period, for the household as a unit
- The minimization of tax prepayment, through quarterly tax instalments or required statutory deductions

RECAP. YOU NEED TO KNOW:

1. The difference between tax preparation and your effective use of tax planning options
2. How unused provisions can be carried forward or back to reduce taxes in carry-over years
3. Why loss carry-overs and discretionary deductions like capital cost allowances are particularly lucrative to planning your cash flow
4. How changing tax law—particularly tax brackets and marginal tax rates—affects your after-tax return on investment
5. How reinvestment of tax savings into tax deferral structures—like the RRSP—can produce even bigger tax rewards
6. Which income sources are tax-exempt and which are tax "preferred," generating lower marginal tax rates, or in some cases, a negative tax
7. That quarterly tax instalments should never be overpaid
8. What to do when errors or omissions are made on your tax return
9. That tax efficiencies should be calculated forward over one's working lifetime to bring purpose to investigative tax queries between taxpayers and their advisors

YOU NEED TO ASK: Your tax advisor for help to ace tax cost averaging and cut your lifetime tax bill

1. **"What if" scenarios:** Ask your tax advisor to help you develop a Tax Savings Blueprint to make tax-efficient decisions all year long. This blueprint is a standard format for "what if" scenarios that will help you understand your financial decisions in the context of your personal marginal tax rates, family income splitting and opportunities to reduce your taxes over a defined window of past, present and future tax years in which you can use "carry-over" provisions to reduce your taxes payable.

2. **How to diversify the types of income you earn** today and in the future, and when you realize it for tax purposes. In this way you can average the taxes charged on your overall investment portfolio.

3. **What is the cost of CPP premiums?** Take special note of the effect of Canada Pension Plan premium obligations over the next several years and plan your business deductions and income-splitting affairs with this liability in mind.

4. **How to split income with family members** using all provisions available under the law.

5. **How to defer taxation of income** into the future.

6. **How to earn profits and build equity** in all future business planning decisions. Sometimes timing is everything.

7. **How to leverage the cost of time and money with proper documentation:** Miss no tax deductions due to poor bookkeeping skills.

8. **How to make on-going retroactive tax adjustments** and then use them whenever the opportunity arises to reduce previously overpaid taxes or to bring forward provisions that will reduce future tax liabilities.

9. **How to use your up-to-date record of all carry-over provisions** available for your reference at all times. Make sure that if you change accountants the new professional knows about these too.

10. **How to build tax-exempt income or capital sources:** Maximize opportunities to receive tax-exempt income now, in the future and within your estate. This includes investments in tax-exempt principal residences and life insurance policies, qualified small business corporations and the new Tax-Free Savings Account.

CHAPTER 3

How to Start a Tax-Efficient Small Business

"Ultimately we know deeply that the other side of every fear is freedom."
MARILYN FERGUSON

KEY CONCEPTS

- Recognize a start-up: Is it a personal hobby or is it a commercial venture with a reasonable expectation of profit?
- Be ready to meet subjective as well as hard-copy tests in an audit
- Formal business plans and cash flow projections can help
- Meet hard-copy tests with documentation for amounts claimed
- Open a separate business bank account; use a separate business credit card
- Classify business expenses into operating costs and capital costs
- Strip out personal use components
- Claim your tax losses

REAL LIFE: Marlen Macleod loved to cook. Over the years she had invented a number of taste-bud-tempting new creations, but a few stood out as memorable to her family and friends. There was the tomato aspic that was special at Thanksgiving, the miniature chocolate sculptures on her cream puffs at Christmas time and her crown roast of pork barbequed exquisitely for her mother's birthday bash every August. In fact, after one particularly sumptuous girth-enhancing session, Marlen's friends remarked, "You know, you should really go into business!"

This common scene, played out daily in countless homes and workplaces throughout Canada, often initiates entrepreneurship in those with both a wonderful product (or service) and a vision for taking it to market. Yet the flame of a small business owner's inspiration can quickly be doused if steps are not taken to shelter a fledgling enterprise from the gusts of CRA's audit department.

Happily, in this case, Marlen went on to become the town caterer and is today making plans to franchise her business methods nation-wide. However, she almost lost it all when a tax auditor refused to see the potential in her and her start-up venture.

THE PROBLEM

Just when does a passion or hobby become a viable commercial enterprise with a reasonable expectation of profit? The Income Tax Act provides limited guidance, defining a business as follows:

> A business includes a profession, calling, trade, manufacture or undertaking *of any kind whatever*. . . [including] an adventure or concern in the nature of trade, but does not include an office or employment.

This means that if you can make a profit from activities as diverse as gardening, walking your neighbours' dogs while they are on holidays, drawing ads or finding mates for the lovelorn, CRA will be obliged to agree that you are in fact in business. Unfortunately, the nature of business start-ups is usually such that you must spend both time and money before you reap the rewards. Those rewards, which are often several years away, hopefully will justify the risks.

In the meantime, CRA's auditors have a window of time in which to probe your affairs and make a judgement call on the deductibility of your expenditures. Unless fraud is suspected, the time frame over which your tax affairs can be audited is generally three years—usually the current tax year and up to two years back. The bad news? If you have been writing off business losses against other income, and particularly if there is any personal aspect to your affairs, CRA can take a narrow view of your business results to date and judge whether the activities are more personal than commercial in nature.

In those cases, there is potential trouble. Even if you are writing off business losses resulting from legitimate deductions that are fully documented, an auditor can take a hard-nosed approach and deem those expenses in support of a hobby instead of in support of a viable business, particularly if there is no apparent source of income from the activities during the audit period.

Over the last several years, the courts have consistently ruled in favor of the taxpayer when "reasonable expectation of profit" (REOP) tests have been invoked by the CRA as a reason to disallow business losses, ruling that it should not be the intent of the law to second-guess the business judgment of the taxpayer. Rather, it is the nature of the taxpayer's activity that must be evaluated, and, more importantly, if there are no personal aspects to the activities, they necessarily involve the pursuit of profit and therefore should be viewed as commercial in nature by tax auditors. (Ask your advisors about the details of the Stewart and Walls cases, in which the Supreme Court of Canada restricted the tax department's power in determining whether a taxpayer has a source of income for tax purposes.)

However, there are still important steps to take to ensure you can show the evolution of your "hobby" or "start-up" into a viable commercial business, in order to ensure that your business losses are deductible against other income sources of the year.

THE SOLUTION

Start-up ventures can be a challenge for a CRA auditor and taxpayer alike. It's difficult, for example, not to get a little emotional when you've struggled to keep your part-time business afloat for a couple of years, only to find yourself nose to nose with an auditor who is inferring you are cunningly trying, by writing off your business losses, to avoid paying tax on your income from the day job that's keeping you all fed in the meantime. This can be particularly distressing if you've run into some unanticipated roadblocks along the way and have had to find a job to avoid more dire financial consequences.

As you begin your new relationship with CRA as a part-time entrepreneur, you need to understand two things up front:

Don't Take It Personally   Unfortunately there are those taxpayers who do try to bend the rules or cheat the tax system, and they are the very ones who validate the tax compliance activities at CRA. Tax auditing has its place in ensuring that small businesses in Canada compete on a level playing field, where honest taxpayers can rest assured that tax cheats aren't undercutting pricing because they aren't paying their taxes.

Your role in a tax audit is to provide the information required for the auditor to understand and agree that you have a viable business enterprise with a reasonable expectation of profit *in the future*. See it as an exercise in both communication and education, and approach this part of any audit with confidence. Remember, *it is usually the person with the most knowledge who is the most successful*. At this point, that's you, because no one knows your business and its future better than you do.

Know the Rules and How to Play the Game   The day you decided to open your business is the day you stepped up to the plate to play ball with CRA. You're in the game, and it's more than just a pastime; you're in the big leagues now. Imagine for a moment a baseball player capable of hitting a home run. By not studying in advance the tendencies of the pitcher, he could nevertheless easily strike out. Likewise, you could be heading directly toward a lucrative long-term contract for your business, but if you don't bother to know the tax rules, CRA could strike you out despite your skills, ability and work ethic. To that end, in the pursuit of all of your business activities, you should be prepared to demonstrate that you are in fact, a pro, and know the tax auditor's arsenal! Doing so begins with detailed documentation of your affairs.

THE PARAMETERS

Professionals—those who get paid to do what they love best—conduct themselves in a *consistent*, professional manner. When business is your calling, your professional conduct is under scrutiny by your clients, your employees, your suppliers, your competitors, and yes, even CRA. For this reason, a specific code of conduct is required, particularly when it comes to your tax-filing obligations. *Make it your business to get this right.*

Open a Separate Business Bank Account

Never co-mingle personal and business funds. Further, obtain a separate credit card for the business. Never put business charges on your personal charge cards. In this way you can avoid "mixed business-personal use" and keep your commercial activities clearly separated from your personal activities.

Remember, when the nature of your activities has no personal components, there is no reason for the tax auditor to search further to determine whether you have a potential source of business income to report or not. When you separate your personal and business affairs, the activities in question by the audit will be clearly commercial in nature, and the deduction of your expenditures must be allowed if there is a link to potential profits in the future, regardless of whether or not they actually materialize.

Sometimes, however, personal components are present by necessity; for example, a family car is sometimes used for business purposes too. We'll address how to handle these situations a bit later.

Business Start Criteria

So when are you considered to be in business for the purposes of deducting your start-up expenses? Did the expenses you incurred precede the start of the business, or did they take place after the business had commenced? When did the business actually start?

To assist taxpayers, CRA issues a number of "Interpretation Bulletins" on such grey areas to explain assessing policies relating to CRA's interpretation of the law. While these interpretation bulletins do not have the force of the law, they can be used as guidelines. CRA's IT 364, "Commencement of Business Operations," outlines business start criteria:

- A business starts whenever some significant activity that forms a regular part of the income-earning process takes place.
- There must be a specific concept of the type of business activity that will be carried on.
- An organizational structure must be in place to undertake the essential preliminaries, to show whether this is a one-time transaction, or an on-going enterprise.

The full utilization of start-up costs over the lifetime of your business is most important, as they can help you reduce profits in the future or reach back and gain access to past taxes paid. You learned about that in the last chapter, which discussed carry-over provisions relating to business losses.

Figure 3.1 provides examples of activities that indicate whether or not business is considered by CRA to have started.

Hobby vs. Business

After determining a business start date, you'll have to convince CRA that you have a commercial business that has a source of income in the future and a reasonable expectation of profit. This can be difficult, especially if you are transitioning from a hobby to a commercial enterprise. The taxman might take a hard line if:

- The business is not making enough money to cover expenditures, and it looks doubtful it ever will.
- The income from the business is not the chief source of income.
- You are not separating personal from business expenses.

Figure 3.1	CRA's Considerations on Business Start-ups

Type of Activity	A Business Start?
Purchase of materials for resale	Yes
Review of various business opportunities	No
Market surveys to establish place or method of carrying on a business	Yes
Construction of a hotel has started, together with staff recruitment, training, advertising, and purchasing of supplies	Yes
Overviewing preliminary plans to determine if the hotel business is the right business opportunity	No
Steps are taken to obtain a required regulatory licence before business activities begin	Yes
Assurances are negotiated from suppliers that they will perform, in advance of business commencement	Yes
Steps are taken to obtain a patent	No
Manufacture of the patented goods begins	Yes

To be fair, many successful businesses start out as a hobby. You enjoy an activity, perfect your skills and come to see a business possibility. There are many such examples:

- The professor of music who writes in her spare time, touring with a local band of musicians to summer folk festivals to build up her name and image
- The photographer who is employed by a newspaper during the day and takes breath-taking wedding photographs on the weekend
- The mechanic who has invested thousands of dollars in his video and computer equipment in order to document the history of his passion—vintage vehicles—in what he hopes will be a bestselling coffee table book next Christmas
- The farmer who works in the city as a teacher by day and raises his prize exotic poultry—geese, ducks and ostrich—when he comes home
- The housewife and mother of four who has turned her recipe for after-school nutritional "candy" into a Christmas fair bestseller

The best way to prove that a hobby-turned-business has a reasonable expectation of profit in the future is to keep a detailed record of activities demonstrating that you've crossed the line from the pursuit of pleasure to the pursuit of profit. You can do this best by keeping a *Daily Business Journal* (see Figure 3.3). It also helps to show how close you are to landing the deals you need to make yours a profitable venture.

Establish Your Business Start and Your Fiscal Year End

Unincorporated small businesses must end their fiscal period for reporting business income and deductions at December 31. An election may be made to select an off-calendar year end in specific cases when there is a bona fide business reason to postpone the business year end. This could happen in the case of a retail outlet, for instance, which experiences its largest sales in the month of December.

A corporation, on the other hand, may choose any 12-month period in which to end its fiscal reporting period—June 1 to May 31, February 1 to January 31 and so on. Discuss the right fiscal year end for your enterprise with your tax advisor.

Set Up Your Tax-Filing Framework

For most businesses, there is a specific fiscal "framework" for approaching various tax-filing obligations. This framework boils down to seven easy parameters:

1. **Methods of Reporting Income.** There are two methods of reporting income:
   - **The cash method:** Income is reported for tax purposes when it is actually received, and expenses are deducted when they are actually paid. This method is usually available only to farmers and very small businesses.
   - **The accrual method:** Most businesses must use the accrual method of accounting. Income is reported when "earned" (rather than received), and expenses are deducted as they are "incurred" (rather than actually paid). Professionals, like doctors and dentists, may report on a modified accrual basis to take into account "work-in-progress," while other businesses may take special reserves to adjust income reporting in certain instances.
2. **The Requirement to Collect and Pay the GST.** As a small business owner in Canada, you may be required to collect the Goods and Services Tax (GST) if you make "taxable" goods and services in your business, also known as "supplies" for the purposes of this tax. Taxable supplies are taxed at a rate of 0% (if the supply is zero-

rated), 5% or 13%, depending on whether the supply is made or in a participating province that charges the Harmonized Sales Tax (HST). The participating provinces are Nova Scotia, New Brunswick, Newfoundland and Labrador and include the Nova Scotia and Newfoundland offshore areas. Ontario and BC will become participating provinces for HST purposes on July 1, 2010.

GST/HST is imposed on every taxable supply made in Canada. In addition, supplies that are made outside Canada but enjoyed in Canada will also be subject to tax when they are imported into Canada.

The GST/HST is a tax paid by the "end user." In other words, it is the "recipient" of the supply who must pay the GST/HST. It is important to identify the recipient of the supply because in some cases the recipient can recover the GST/HST paid as an "input tax credit." This is generally allowed if you are a GST/HST registrant making zero-rated or taxable supplies for an end user. Registrants engaged exclusively in commercial activities can recover GST/HST paid on purchases and expenses by claiming a full (meaning 100%) input tax credit on their GST/HST returns.

- **Who can avoid the GST/HST?** Although almost everyone pays GST/HST on taxable supplies, there are some exceptions. Certain organizations and groups, including some governments and First Nations, may not have to pay this tax. The First Nations Goods and Services Tax (FNGST) is a tax of 5% applied to taxable supplies of certain types of goods, called listed goods, on specified First Nations land. Listed goods are generally alcohol, tobacco and fuel, although each First Nation chooses independently which listed goods will be subject to FNGST on its lands.

    FNGST is very similar to GST/HST and is collected in exactly the same manner as GST/HST. However, where FNGST applies to the supply of a listed good, the GST/HST does not apply, so that all supplies are subject to tax only once.

    Small suppliers, those with gross revenues under $30,000, need not collect the tax (but may elect to). Specifically, a small supplier is defined as a person whose world-wide taxable supplies are equal to or less than $30,000 in either a calendar quarter or over the last four consecutive calendar quarters. This definition is used for sole proprietorships, partnerships, trusts and corporations. In applying this definition, you are required to add together taxes collected on taxable supplies made by all persons with whom you are associated.

If the $30,000 threshold is exceeded in a calendar quarter, you are required to be registered to collect the GST/HST, starting with the supply that takes total revenue over $30,000. That is, there is no grace period allowed—you must register at that time, although 30 days are allowed for the registration form (RC1) to be submitted.

If the $30,000 threshold is exceeded over four calendar quarters, you cease to be a small supplier and are required to be registered on the first day of the second month following the end of the last calendar quarter (i.e., a one-month grace period is allowed).

There are many rules involving GST/HST compliance obligations. Be sure to cover these with your tax advisor carefully.

3. **Deduction of Operating Expenses.** Operating expenses are also known as "business inputs" in GST jargon, or those expenditures that are necessary for you to produce the goods and services that bring in revenue. These expenses comprise items that are "used up,"—such as supplies, advertising and promotions, rent, salary, communications costs, licences, etc.— and are usually 100% deductible in the fiscal year in which they occur, unless there are specific restrictions in place. When gross revenues earned are reduced by operating expenses, the result may be either net operating loss or an operating profit.

4. **Computation of Capital Cost Allowances.** When you acquire an asset with a useful life of more than one year, you must classify that asset into prescribed classes set out in the Income Tax Act in order to get tax relief from the cost of its acquisition and then the cost of its diminishing value due to on-going use in the business. Prescribed rates of depreciation are claimed for those assets, and the result is a deduction claimed for Capital Cost Allowance (CCA) on the tax return. This subject is discussed in more detail in Chapter 5.

Why is CCA important to you? The CCA claim provides a series of tax-planning opportunities that can put more money in your pocket at tax time. First, know that you can make the claim for this deduction *at your option*. That means you can "save" it for use in a future year when it's worth more to you.

For example, if your operating expenses have already exceeded your gross revenues—that is, you have a loss—it may be wise not to take the CCA deduction in the current year. Or, you may have enough personal amounts available on the tax return to reduce any taxes payable without needing to take any CCA deduction. The personal amounts generally cannot be carried forward (exceptions include medical expenses, charitable donations and the tuition, education and textbook credits), while the undepreciated balance of your capital assets can be carried forward. So, in the event of a loss on the year, it's best to use the CCA deduction in the future.

By choosing to "save" a higher undepreciated balance of value in your assets for use in a more tax-advantaged way in the future, when income may be higher and therefore taxable, you'll save more money then.

On the other hand, if the CCA deduction helps to increase or create a business loss that can be carried back to recover taxes paid in the prior three years, you may wish to maximize the available claim. This is not important if you were not taxable in those years. Again, ask your tax advisor to look over your prior filed returns to help you with this.

In addition, you have learned that by reducing net business income with a CCA deduction, you may be able to save money on your CPP liability. This is significant for businesses in which net profit exceeds the $46,000 range.

Finally, know a key concept about CCA that is often problematic for the uninformed during a tax audit—you don't want to make the mistake of taking a 100% deduction for an "operating" expenditure only to find later that CRA is going to reclassify the expense as a "capital" one. For instance, say a taxpayer writes off the replacement of a roof on his rental building as a fully deductible expense, only to find that CRA reclassifies the outlay as a capital one upon which CCA should be claimed. This is a common mistake and can make a big difference in the taxes payable for the year.

Other provisions apply to your capital asset purchases. It is important to keep track of asset values on acquisition and disposition— they may be transferred from personal use to business use and vice versa—and to ask your tax advisor if a GST/HST rebate or input tax credit was received, or if you qualify for an investment tax credit, or if a special accelerated rate applies to your purchases, such as the 100% write-off on computer equipment, a provision available at the time of writing.

Ask your advisor about all these provisions and terms and how they relate to your particular business every year.

5. **Personal Use Allocation.** Most home-based business owners spend long hours trying to get their businesses off the ground and use all

available resources to do so, including their family members, homes, cars, and other supplies. Many business owners make the mistake of underclaiming expenses that have a legitimate business component. Chapter 9 takes a closer look at how to legitimize business-use components of specific expenses.

To be sure, the Income Tax Act is very specific about personal or living expenses of the taxpayer—*they may not be deducted*, other than travel expenses incurred by the taxpayer while away from home in the course of carrying on a business.

Personal and living expenses are specifically defined in the Act in Section 248. They include the expenses of the personal property, costs of a life insurance policy or expenses of properties that are maintained by a trust.

However, what you need to know is that, as long as you make proper allowances for any personal component of an expense, *the business portion of the expense* should be tax deductible, provided that the expense is connected to the earning of income from a commercial business that has a reasonable expectation of profit.

If you're in the business of selling cosmetics, for example, you might write off all the expenses of make-up and skin care products that are used for resale. But if you fail to add back into income a reasonable amount for personal consumption, you can expect trouble from tax auditors unless you can prove you never use any of the products yourself.

In another example, a masonry contractor who ships a portion of interlocking bricks to his new home and a portion to his client's worksite would need to allocate the personal use portion of the expenses or write off only the portion of the expense that pertained to his client.

Similar adjustments must be made by those who run clothing stores, grocery stores, farms, fishing enterprises and the like. In addition, costs of using capital assets that have both a personal and business usage—such as a car or your home office—must reflect reductions for personal use. Expect to be asked for the personal use allocation during an audit.

6. **Computation of Auto Expenses.** One of the most common deductions of the small or home-based business owner, auto expenses are usually discussed at tax time when the computation of a separate worksheet is required to account for fixed and operating expenses and your personal and business use of the vehicle.

   Operating expenses include goods that are "used up," such as gas and oil, and fixed expenses include items such as interest on your car loan or capital cost allowance. These expenses must be prorated or divided according to the business driving you did during the year, over the total distance driven. It's necessary to have an auto log that reports both business and personal driving in order for you to come up with the deductibility ratio. Details are discussed in Chapter 6. Note that certain expenses can be claimed on an unreceipted basis—coin parking, car washes, etc., where it is not possible to receive a receipt. Keep a log of such expenditures.

7. **Computation of Home Workspace Costs.** Most home-based or small business owners will also be writing off home workspace costs, which is legitimate only if you have a separate area exclusively set aside for the business and if you regularly see clients or conduct your business from there. This is also computed on a separate worksheet in order to properly accomplish the proration of all total expenses of the home including utilities, interest, insurance, property taxes, etc. Additionally, there is a special restriction to be aware of: *home workspace expenses may not be used to create or increase an operating loss.* When an operating loss occurs, the balance of the home workspace expenses must be carried forward for use in future years when there is an operating profit. See Chapter 6 for more details.

Record Keeping: Meeting the Onus of Proof

For any expense to be deductible, two requirements must be met:

- You have to meet an onus of proof, showing that the expenses were actually incurred, are reasonable and are supported with proper documentation.
- You have to incur the expense in order to produce a potential source of income from your commercial activities.

Usually, in a court of law, you are considered innocent until proven guilty. However, compliance under the Income Tax Act has a slightly different twist—CRA doesn't have to accept your return as filed. Rather, you have an obligation to prove that every figure on that return is correct, reasonable and legitimate. There are two sections of the Income Tax Act that offer guidance on this subject:

- Section 67, which introduces the requirement for "reasonableness": "In computing income, no deduction shall be made in respect of an outlay or expense . . . except to the extent that (it) was reasonable in the circumstances."

- Section 18, which zeros in on the concept of "intent": "In computing the income of a taxpayer from a business or property, no deduction shall be made in respect of an outlay or expense except to the extent that it was made or incurred by the taxpayer for the purpose of gaining or producing income from the business or property."

To support your case for "reasonableness," you have to do two things:

- Keep meticulous records of all income and expenditures, including auto and home office usage logs.
- Keep your personal and business affairs completely separate, as discussed above.

In addition, the auditor must consider the following: gross income, net income, cost of goods sold, capital investment, cash flow, personal involvement, experience and training, plans for future development and all other relevant factors that will be used to determine whether business income is from a commercial activity and consequently whether any losses will be deductible in full or in part.

Record Retention

When it comes to record keeping, it matters not how sophisticated your computer system and software are. The finest reports will not by-pass CRA's requirement for hard copy or microfilming. Guidelines for proper electronic imaging must be met and can be obtained by calling the Canadian General Standards Board (1-800-665-2472).

You will be required to produce records in an organized, retrievable and readable manner, including:

- Accounts
- Agreements
- Books
- Charts
- Diagrams
- Forms
- Images
- Invoices

- Letters
- Maps
- Memoranda
- Optical disks
- Plans
- Returns
- Source documents*
- Statements
- Tables
- Telegrams
- Vouchers
- Any other record that contains information, whether in writing or any other form

It is also necessary to keep an automobile distance log. Note that electronic documents must be in a format readable by CRA auditors on CRA equipment. Contact CRA for more information.

Your records must be kept at your place of business or your residence and must be available to tax auditors at all reasonable times. CRA does in fact show up at doorsteps and may reassess your tax returns at any time up to three years after the date on the original Notice of Assessment or Reassessment.

If at any time fraud is suspected, however, the agency can go as far back in your records as it wants, subject only to the record retention period. *That is, you are required to keep books and records for only six years from the end of the last taxation year in which the records and books relate.* You can request permission to destroy your records earlier than that, using Form T137; however, this may be an invitation for a tax audit first.

Know the Value of Your Tax Losses

When your total business expenditures exceed your income for the year, the resulting non-capital loss can be used to offset all other income of the year. If there is an excess loss, the remaining balance can be carried back for up to 3 years or carried forward for up to 20 years.

So let's say that last year your total taxable income was $115,000. This year, after losing your job, you start a business and incur a $10,000 non-capital loss. What's the value of that loss if you carry it back and offset

---

* Source documents include sales invoices, purchase invoices, cash register receipts, formal written contracts, credit card receipts, delivery slips, deposit slips, work orders, dockets, cheques, bank statements, tax returns, accountant's working papers and general correspondence, according to Information Circular 78-10.

last year's income? Well, at a 45% tax bracket, that's $4,500—which can go a long way to financing continual growth in your business. So you want to get this right!

But this is exactly the type of situation that can raise the flags in CRA's audit department, especially if you've been claiming these losses over a number of years. You'll need to be prepared to prove that the expenses were both reasonable and were incurred to earn income from a commercial business with a reasonable expectation of profit.

THE TAX ADVISOR

The following actions will be necessary to start your business venture. Do them on your own or together with your tax advisors.

Register Your Business

When you have determined your business start date, open a separate bank account for your business, then see your tax accountant and/or lawyer, who will help you with the following compliance discussion points. Take Figure 3.2 along as a guide.

Tax Compliance Discussion Points

- Whether to obtain a Business Number, which is required to remit income taxes, collect and remit GST/HST and/or to make payroll remittances on behalf of employees
- When to make payroll, GST/HST and PST remittances to avoid late-filing penalties
- When periodic tax instalment payments are necessary
- Whether to register business names, trademarks and copyrights
- Whether provincial sales tax collections and remittances will be necessary
- Whether family assets need further protection through life insurance
- Whether additional life insurance, disability and medical insurance should be obtained
- How your estate planning will be affected by the start-up venture
- Parameters in writing contracts with others
- How to protect yourself and your family from lawsuits by others
- Whether or not to incorporate your business and when

Figure 3.2	**Tax Compliance Discussion Points**

Directions for Use: Discussion topics with taxpayers and their advisors.

A. Form of Business Organization: Incorporated or Unincorporated

Issues: Questions   Potential Solutions:

_____

_____

_____

_____

_____

B. CRA COMPLIANCE REQUIREMENTS

1. Business Number:
2. GST/HST Issues:
3. Provincial Sales Tax Issues:
4. Payroll Remittance Issues:
5. Taxable and Tax Free Benefits:
6. Requirements to Remit Instalment Payments:
7. Errors Omissions, Penalties:
8. Filing Requirements: T1, T2, T3, T4, T5, TD1, T1213

C. BUSINESS START PLAN

1. Fiscal Year End & Reporting Methods
2. Legal: Business Name, Trademarks, Copyrights, Asset Protection, Will Planning
3. Contracts Required, Formats
4. Business Plan, Budget, Cash Flow Plan
5. Capital Asset Acquisition Plan
6. Sales and Marketing Plan
7. Separate Banking, Borrowing Schedules
8. Negotiate Terms of Payment: Creditors & Suppliers
9. Daily Business Journal & Auto Log
10. Home Workspace Sketch & Area
11. Owner-Manager Compensation Plan
12. Employee, Supplier, Client Contracts
13. Employee Role Descriptions & Contracts
14. Training Programs
15. Risk Management: Personal Insurance, Disaster Recovery

Write Your Business Start Plan

The checklist in Figure 3.3 should be consulted throughout the year to help you make major business start-up decisions.

By covering the items in this business start plan with your advisors, you will have most of the information a tax auditor will need to recognize that you have taken steps not only to start a business formally or to turn a hobby into a business, but also that there is a reasonable expectation of profit from your venture sometime in the future.

Start a Daily Business Journal

As you can tell from our previous discussions, even the commencement date of a business can be a debated matter when it comes to a tax audit. The best defense for the business owner is to begin journalizing any and all activities that relate to the business as soon as possible. This documentation can take any format you are comfortable with, but the key is to make notes of the following:

- Every phone call made to do research, enquire about finding a supplier, get a business licence, lease a location, buy a computer, etc. (electronic calendars provide a great perpetual record)
- Every networking appointment (keep all business cards from potential customers, suppliers or others who will be associated with you in your business, or keep an electronic contact record)
- Every lead, meeting, conference, etc., that brings you to the next step in your business development
- Every hour worked on the project
- All distances driven in pursuit of your business activities

A sample format follows in Figure 3.4. This Daily Business Journal can be your key to tax audit survival. It shows commercial intent and reasonableness at the same time. It helps you meet your subjective audit test.

Keep your journal faithfully. It is the story of your business's past, present and future—a crucial element in *making sure it's deductible*!

Formalize Your Books and Keep All Receipts

If you're a hopeless bookkeeper, do yourself and CRA a favour by hiring someone to do this job for you, at least monthly. You simply can't afford not to. You'll be busy starting up the business, recruiting staff, finding capital to cover the costs and managing the distribution of your goods

Figure 3.3	Your Business Start Plan

Circumstance	Decision	Action Plan
Business Starts	Formalize Tax Position	- Prepare Business Plan: 1,3, 5 Years - Consult Professional Team - Prepare annual budget - Prepare cash flow journal - Start Daily Business Journal - Register business name/trademarks - Obtain Business Number - Start recordkeeping system, auto log, home office log
Obtain Assets Used in Business	Buy, Lease or Convert Existing Assets to Business Use	- Obtain fair market value of car, home computer, other assets to be used in business - Establish business location - Separate home workspace area - Obtain estimates on buying new or used - Obtain estimates on leasing options, tax advantages
Operating Expenses Commence	How Will Expenses Be Paid?	- Obtain line of credit or make equity contribution - Arrange terms from suppliers - Get business cards, design logos, letterhead printed - Establish separate business phone lines, cell, fax/e-mail communications - Prepare marketing materials
Plan Owner-Manager Compensation	How Will I Be Paid?	- Proprietorship: remuneration, draw - Corporation: salary, bonus, dividends or shareholders loan?
Plan Income Splitting with Family Members	How Will I Pay Income to my Spouse or Children?	- Establish job descriptions, pay at FMV - Write employment contracts - Begin source remittances
Enhance Family Lifestyle	How Can I Utilize Company-Paid Benefits?	- Company Pension Plans - Company Group Health Plans - RRSP Contributions, RPP, IPP Contributions* - Taxable/tax-free perks
Establish Operating Procedures	How Can I Expand?	- Document Policies and Procedures - Establish Organizational Structure - Prepare Marketing Plans - Prepare Development Plans - Prepare Product Distribution Plans - Prepare Quality Control Procedures - Prepare Follow-up Procedures - Prepare Client Relationship Procedures
Plan Equity Accumulation	How Will I Be Paid Out?	- Prepare Personal Net Worth Statement - Establish family succession plans - Establish current valuation of business - Set a price . . . you never know when an offer may come along - Plan for tax-free capital gains
Plan for Your Demise	What Taxes Will Be Payable?	- Anticipate deemed disposition rules - Ensure life insurance will cover taxes - Family trust/testamentary trust planning

* Registered Retirement Savings Plan, Registered Pension Plan, Individual Pension Plan.

| Figure 3.4 | Sample of a Daily Business Journal | | | |

Date:

Time	To Do	Incoming Items	Follow-up	Expense Details
6:00 a.m.	Breakfast			km: 36,544
7:00	e-mail		Meet L. Jones	
8:00	Meeting T. Cook		Prepare Quote	Coffee $5.00
9:00	Prepare Market Plan			
10:00	"			
11:00	Mail/Telephone Calls	See log attached		
12:00 p.m.	Meet Banker @ Tini's			Lunch $35.00 km 36,660 B
1:00				
2:00	L. Jones @ Earl's		Prepare Quote	Coffee $5.00 km 36,670 B
3:00	Market Plan			
4:00	Meet Printer @ shop		Proof designs	km 36,750 B
5:00	Exercise			km 36,780 P
6:00	Supper			km 36,800 P
7:00	Finish Market plan			
8:00	e-mail			
9:00	Family time			

Total Expenses: $45.00   **Total Travel: 256 km**   **Business Travel: 206 km**

and services. As you've learned, you'll also be responsible for keeping your Daily Business Journal (Figure 3.4), a critical tool in ensuring that your expenditures are deductible during a tax audit. Poor record keeping can stall your business, so put this critical component into place.

Figure 3.5 outlines the minimum reporting structure you'll need in order to keep on top of your business activities on a daily, weekly, monthly and quarterly basis. It's important to keep these records right from the start. Aside from the tax compliance requirements, they will provide you with the ability to compare next year's results with your start-up year and to budget for and chart the growth of your business.

Figure 3.5	Required Reports		

Daily	Weekly Totals	Monthly	Quarterly
Bank Deposits	Bank Deposits	Income Statement	Income Statement
Dollar Volume	Dollar Volume	Balance Sheet	Balance Sheet
Units Sold	Units Sold	Sales Statistics	Sales Statistics
Staff Hours	Staff Hours	Marketing Statistics*	Marketing Statistics*
Prospects Contacted	NSF Cheque Records	Payroll Remittances	GST/HST Reporting
	Accounts Payable	Cash Flow Requirements	
	Prospects Contacted		

* Cumulative Results: Prospects Contacted, Units Sold, Dollar Volume, Comparison to Prior Year

Tax Filing Deadlines

Most people know that April 30 is the personal tax filing deadline. Unincorporated proprietors can avoid penalties by filing by midnight on June 15. But interest is payable on balances due starting May 1, so make a habit of filing by April 30.

In the case of corporations, corporate returns must be filed within six months of the end of the corporation's fiscal year, even if there is no tax payable. This requirement applies to tax-exempt corporations, inactive corporations and non-profit organizations. The only exception is a registered charity; however, this type of corporation must file an information return within six months of the end of its fiscal year.

Write It Off, Write It All Off

So now that you know basic parameters of tax compliance, go ahead, look upon every expenditure you make in terms of its potential for reducing your taxes (see Chapter 9). Always ask yourself: "Is this deductible?" If you are not sure, keep the receipt and ask your tax pro. Receipts and invoices are valuable and necessary—don't lose track of them. (Remember, when it comes to your taxes, it's all about retrieval!) You'll learn in the next chapter that your expenditures can fall into certain classifications for tax purposes, but for now, what's important is that when it comes to your receipts, you *save everything*.

Log Your Automobile Costs and Business Driving

Start an auto log immediately. Record all expenses of operating the vehicle, the fair market value of the vehicle at the time you started using it for business activities and the distance you drive. Both personal and

Figure 3.6	Auto Log Template

Date	Km Start	Km Finish	Destination	Reason for Trip	Gas/Oil	M & R	Wash	Park	Other

business kilometres must be faithfully kept—at least for a reasonable, representative time period—to help you claim your auto expenses on your return. A sample format is shown in Figure 3.6.

Plan How to Take Your Tax-Efficient Profits

Leaving CRA to concentrate on catching the tax cheats, you should now have your tax compliance house in order with your set-up of procedures. With those basics out of the way, you can concentrate on organizing your affairs to make and report your profits in the most tax-efficient manner. That's where you should be spending the time and money with your advisors in the first place. Remember the reason you are in business—to make profits and build equity over the long run to your best advantage.

Figure 3.7 details differences in owner-manager compensation among three types of business structures: a proprietorship, a corporation and a partnership. There are lots of details, so don't wait until tax filing time to have a chat with your advisors about which structure is best for you. By giving yourself lead time, you'll be able to plan for tax efficiency for your compensation and tax-deductible income splitting for family members too. By choosing a tax-efficient organizational structure at the right time, you'll maximize start-up losses, which will allow you to reach back and recover previously paid personal taxes and then set up your operating structure to take full advantage of lower tax rates to be applied to your business profits in the future.

Figure 3.7	Compensation Planning Under Various Business Structures

Unincorporated Proprietor	Incorporated Business	Partnership
Taxed on net profits of the business, not salary or draws	- Taxed as employee - Taxed on certain benefits - Taxed on dividends received as a shareholder - Taxed on sale of equity	Whether incorporated or not, the profits are split and allocated to partners based on details of the partnership agreement.

A Proprietor Can Reduce Taxable Income By:

- Filing a tax return on time to minimize interest and penalties
- Reducing net business income (or taxable profits) with CCA deductions, paying operational expenses before year end, buying capital assets before year end, keeping auto log books to maximize car expenses and paying family members to split income and create RRSP room for them
- Making maximum RRSP contributions for each family member
- Minimizing quarterly instalment payments
- Deferring income into the future with the timing of contracts, if doing so makes good business sense

An Incorporated Business Owner May Reduce Taxable Income Personally By:

- **Planning personal compensation structures:** Mind the top of personal tax brackets in drawing employment income and dividends from the business. Set the level of employment income from the corporation to pay yourself a salary that maximizes your retirement income plans—CPP, RRSP and TFSA contributions, for example—but minimizes source deductions, which affect the cash flow needed by the business. No source deductions, for example, are required on dividend payments (the after-tax distribution of profits); however, quarterly tax instalment requirements may arise personally when taxes payable at tax filing time exceed $3,000 for the year. This integration of the personal and corporate taxation structure is an important lesson the owner-manager will want to learn well to maximize cash flow and wealth planning. You will want to bring in the expertise of financial and insurance advisors to ensure investment and insurance strategies match up with cash flow and tax planning in the family business.
- **Planning bonuses:** Discuss the wisdom of declaring year-end bonus payments when the corporation makes a profit, especially when this exceeds the current small business deduction level. These payments might be taken over two calendar years to minimize personal tax. Withholding taxes on bonuses can also be annualized to avoid a sudden spike in taxes in a particular pay period. Or, you can decide to pay the bonuses to your family members who work with you, if by doing so you minimize the family tax liability as a whole and if this is otherwise in line with employee compensation programs.

- **Declaring dividend payments:** Make these throughout the year if you need the money, but consider making at least one in January of the next tax year. You won't have to pay source deductions in advance through the company, and you'll have use of the money for a full 16 months more: January 1, Year 1, to April 30 of the following year for example.
- **Paying perks:** Consider paying taxable and tax-free benefits to yourself and family members instead of cash, thereby allowing larger after-tax corporate dollars to help pay for lifestyle. (The benefits of employing family members will be discussed in more detail in Chapter 8.) For example, you may be able to have the company fund education of family members when that education benefits the business.
- **Accounting for interest on shareholders loans**: If you own a corporation, it is possible for you to take a shareholder's loan. Under general rules, if this amount is not repaid within one year of the end of the tax year in which it was made, the amounts are added to your income. Also know that an "imputed interest" charge must be assessed to the owner when money is taken from the company in this way.

However, loans made to shareholders who are also employees are considered exempt from income inclusion if the loans were made because of the employment conditions (i.e., a loan to acquire a company car) and bona fide repayments were arranged.

Make sure to speak with your tax advisor about structuring compensation packages to take advantage of as many of these tax efficiencies as possible.

RECAP. YOU NEED TO KNOW:

1. The difference between a hobby and a business
2. What constitutes a reasonable expectation of profit from a commercial venture
3. How to determine when a business has started up with the result that income is taxable and expenses are deductible
4. How to establish a fiscal year end for your business
5. What reporting method—cash or accrual—your business should use
6. The difference between operating expenses and capital expenses on a tax return

7. Basic GST/HST collection, reporting and filing requirements

8. How to set up claims for auto and home office expenses when there is mixed (personal-business) use

9. How long to retain records and in what format

10. How to think about your options in organizing your business and personal compensation structure—to incorporate or not?

YOU NEED TO ASK: Your tax advisor for help in setting up your tax-efficient small business

1. **Understand your new relationship with CRA:** Make a point of understanding your obligations to report income under the law; keep records; and make remittances such as instalments, source deductions and GST/HST. Be prepared to open your books to CRA's audit scrutiny and to meet hard and soft copy requirements.

2. **Know when your business is considered to have started:** When did it go from being a sideline or hobby to a viable going concern? The key: when was there a reasonable expectation of profit or earning income from the business? Your activities must lead to a potential income source.

3. **Establish your fiscal year end:** This is normally December 31 for most unincorporated small business organizations; however, speak to your tax advisor if you feel there is a bona fide business reason to choose a non-calendar year end.

4. **Know how to document and separate personal use components of any expenditures** and when to open separate bank and charge card accounts for your business. Your tax advisor will guide you on record-keeping requirements that will not only save time on a tax audit in the future but will also save you money on professional charges along the way.

5. **Write a formal business start plan** including a marketing and cash flow analysis plan. Create a formal budget and establish the ability to make comparative reports in the future. These documents will all go a long way to winning a tax audit focused on your commercial viability.

6. **Start keeping a Daily Business Journal** to document your networking and contacts with suppliers and others who will help you build and grow your business. Keep your auto distance travel logs in the journal as well.

7. **Know that deductible expenditures must be classified properly** to facilitate proper tax application and long-term tax planning. Be sure to separate the cost of capital acquisitions from day-to-day operating expenses. In fact, speak to your tax advisor before you make large capital purchases. More about this in the chapters that follow.

8. **Know the value of your tax losses** and how to apply them to other income in the current year and in the carry-over periods in order to tax cost average.

9. **Meet the onus of proof** annually. The ability to defend the "grey areas" is a position of power you do not want to relinquish to a tax auditor, who doesn't know your business or your business plans as well as you do. You can show the potential from profit from your commercial venture better than the auditor can. Don't give up your edge by keeping poor records during the year.

10. **Review your business organization structure often,** at least every six months. Is the proprietorship the best format, or should you be considering a partnership or incorporation? Is there a better way to split income with family members or a better compensation structure for the owner-manager? Discuss these items with your advisors.

· ·

CHAPTER 4

Write Off More Deductions Without Changing Your Life

"You must first clearly see a thing in your mind before you can do it."
ALEX MORRISON

KEY CONCEPTS

- It's important to prepare your tax return to your family's best benefit
- For the "grey" areas, look to precedent-setting court appeals
- You've got to know your "deductibles"
- There is a difference in writing off current vs. capital expenses
- Prepaid expenses are treated differently again
- Restricted expense rules are often audited first
- Proration of mixed-use expenditures is mandatory—and easy
- Loss deductibility can be lucrative

REAL LIFE: Julie was blessed with a special gift—the ability to express herself in painting beautiful Canadian landscapes for reprint on greeting cards. Her studio was in her home, where she produced, marketed and distributed the cards nation-wide. Her twin sister, Janet, was a writer employed by the local paper. Her quick wit and quirky sense of humour landed her the role of feature freelance columnist, a job she enjoyed. She also wrote thoughtful messages for her sister's works on a contract basis. To escape the pressure of writing a daily column, she often joined Julie in the beautiful mountains of British Columbia, where the sisters gained inspiration and insight for their respective art forms.

The sisters, both earning income in the $75,000 range, found they were paying remarkably dissimilar amounts of tax. This prompted a visit to their tax advisor, who confirmed that both their returns had been prepared mathematically correctly—but not to their best overall benefit.

Janet, it appeared, was passive about claiming all the deductions she was entitled to. Julie, who knew more about her rights and obligations, fared better. Their advisor, however, found that they could both decrease the amount of taxes they were paying without dramatically changing their lives. They needed to take a fresh look at their respective costs and to stay on top of changes in tax law and in their businesses.

However, like many Canadian taxpayers, the twins were afraid of appearing too aggressive because the last thing they needed was trouble with CRA! They wanted to stay under the radar.

THE PROBLEM

Every day, Canadian businesspeople contemplate a variety of business transactions, wondering, "Will it be deductible?" How does one make the call? Identifying deductibles is a real concern for many taxpayers, and legitimately so.

We will show you how to make your expenditures tax deductible in this chapter, but before we drill down into the specific rules you need to follow (with the help of your tax advisor), you need to understand that even if you play by all the rules, your claims are not guaranteed.

The problem is that our Income Tax Act alone does not provide sufficient guidance to assess deductible business expenses. There are, in addition, a number of administrative policies CRA follows, and these policies, together with the law itself, are prone to a variety of subjective interpretations by both sides.

What's more, the Income Tax Act grants to CRA a number of arbitrary powers. The Minister does not have to accept your return as filed. In fact, under Section 152(7), CRA has the right to change your tax return if they don't agree with the way you've filed it. They can change your income figures, your deductions or your credits prior to the expiration of a normal "reassessment period," which is three years. Your tax-filing fate, therefore, can rest with an auditor who perceives your *tax and personal affairs* quite differently than you do. Given this reality, it's often difficult to say in advance whether your business expense will ultimately be deductible or not.

For some, this is scary stuff. These grey areas of interpretation by two opposing parties is somewhat weighted in favour of the taxman, according to the historical win/lose status. It's enough to make some taxpayers feel like they are playing ball against a team that knows more of the rules and also has all the referees on its side. Does the audit process itself lead to inequality of two taxpayers with like enterprises and income levels? Do those who get audited pay more tax than those who don't?

Not necessarily. You have learned previously that the courts have made a clear distinction between a "commercial activity" and a "personal activity" in addressing CRA's assessing policies on the matter. You can now rest more assured that if the business clearly has a commercial basis, and there is no personal element to the business, reasonable business expenditures that result in losses are deductible. CRA no longer can use the argument that a loss can be disallowed if the auditor cannot see a reasonable expectation of profit from an enterprise that is clearly commercial in nature. As long as the business does not have a "hobby" or personal element, CRA cannot deny the loss, even if there has never been a profit or never may be.

And so, the assessment policies of CRA are often challenged by taxpayers in cases before the courts, and often the law is changed as a result. It's interesting to follow these, *as it is the combination of tax law, assessment policy and jurisprudence that makes up the "heart and soul" of our tax collection system.* If you don't agree with how your tax return has been assessed, you have the right to appeal the results. It's important that you know this and also that it is your right to arrange your affairs within the framework of the law so as to pay the least taxes allowed by the law.

Following are some interesting results of court challenges, initiated by those who prepared to fight for tax deductibility under a variety of circumstances, ranging from the thorny reasonable expectation of profit issue to business start criteria, reasonableness of "mixed use" expenditures, income classification and the important role of compliance regarding your documentation in fighting for your rights.

It's Not Personal

In a landmark case that went to the Supreme Court of Canada (*Stewart v. Queen* [2002]), the taxpayer claimed losses pursuant to Section 20 of the Income Tax Act for the costs of interest paid on loans made to purchase four condominium units for rental purposes. In this case, the taxpayer borrowed heavily to purchase the condos and paid interest on the mortgages, resulting in significant losses.

CRA denied these losses on the grounds that there was no "reasonable expectation of profit." They argued that the taxpayer had not shown a profit in several years and wasn't projected to show one in the next 10 years. They also argued that the deductions should not be allowed because the taxpayer was investing in the properties in the hope that their value at some point would yield a high capital gain.

In rendering its decision, the Supreme Court of Canada essentially changed the existing law and its interpretation regarding the onerous and often contested "reasonable expectation of profit test." The decision stated that this test had become a tool used by the CRA and the courts to "second-guess" the legitimate business purposes of taxpayers. The decision went on to state that the test was vague and arbitrary and sometimes resulted in unfair treatment of taxpayers. A new test was adopted to determine if a person's activities were a source of income: whether or not the activity is commercial or personal. Where it clearly is a commercial activity, the deduction or loss should be allowed.

In short, in the view of the court, the taxpayer's condo ownership was clearly a "commercial activity" as opposed to a "personal activity."

This case, and a companion case, *Walls v. Canada*, established a much more secure playing field for business owners, who must invest first and see the results of their efforts later. Judging the wisdom of those investments is something that is much easier to do in retrospect, of course. Unlike tax auditors, *most businesspeople do not have the benefit of hindsight when making business decisions.*

Fuel for the Body

In an interesting case at the Tax Court level (*Scott*, 98), a self-employed foot and public transit courier tried to claim the daily cost of food and water needed to sustain him during his fast-paced work days. The Tax Court dismissed his case, stating they found those expenses to be personal in nature. The Federal Court of Appeal disagreed. While food and beverages consumed during a workday are normally considered to be a personal expense, the court found that, in this case, the courier had to eat and drink more than normal; in fact, if fuel for an auto was deductible, so should fuel for the body be. The result? A reasonable amount of the expenses should be allowed as a tax deduction.

Sufficient Start-up Time

In a case involving a rental property (*Gideon*, 98), a doctor and her husband acquired a rental property that suffered losses resulting from adverse economic factors. Despite the fact that they charged rent proven to be reasonable, that they reduced the mortgage quickly to minimize interest payments and that the rental losses were steadily decreasing over time, CRA took a hard-line position and reassessed the couple's tax returns to disallow the rental losses claimed over a period of three years. The Federal Court of Appeal overturned the decision, scolding CRA for failing to allow the taxpayers sufficient start-up time in which to make a profit. Given the way in which the taxpayers conducted their business, it appeared to the judge that there was a reasonable expectation of profit in the future.

Home Sales Produced Profits, Not Capital Gains

Recent housing booms have been the source of many significant profits—and potentially some losses. What will be the status of those profits and losses? History can be a guide here. During a prior real estate boom, a taxpayer built a series of houses and resold each of them in a short period of time (*Mullin, 98*). A number of these homes were built in a subdivision owned by the taxpayer's father. In this case, one house was allowed as a tax-exempt principal residence, as the taxpayer and his wife lived in the home. However, the taxpayer had not been able to convince the judge that the other homes were built for investment purposes (hence qualifying for capital gains treatment) because of the "quick flip" in sales. As a result, 100% of the profits from those sales were included in income.

The Dentist and His Sheep

Part-time farmers have also been known to have a tough time with CRA assessments. That's because they are often subject to what's known as restricted farm loss rules. (Chapter 7 discusses these rules in more depth.) In one case, CRA restricted the farming losses of a dentist who raised cattle for five years and then decided to raise sheep. The good doctor was able to beat the taxman, who wanted to restrict his loss write-offs. By proving he had spent 60 hours or more each week in pursuit of his farming activities while he practised dentistry fewer than 24 hours per week, and by showing that his investment in the farm was substantial, the dentist was able to convince the judge that over the past several years, his chief source of income had actually changed—now it was the farming operation (*Langtot, 98*).

Credibility Wins Over the Judge

The commission sales agent faced the wrath of the taxman when his records and log books were, well, skimpy. The Judge at the Tax Court of Canada, however, found him to be totally credible and allowed him to claim expenses as a deduction. The "Model Citizen Factor" pays off again (*Rusnak, 98*).

These cases reinforce what you've already learned about setting consistent foundations for business start-ups. Because you have the ability to tell the story of your business circumstances, your intent now and in the future, and your activities in pursuit of future profits, you likely have the components for a successful case. In fact, for some, a tax audit can actually be a profitable experience (see Chapter 10).

So now you may be asking yourself how you can make sure it's all deductible and avoid a time-consuming and often expensive tax court challenge. In truth, there is never a guarantee your return won't be chosen for audit. However, there is much you can do to avoid a devastating financial impact.

THE SOLUTION

If you want to make sure your expenditures are tax deductible, the Income Tax Act can provide much guidance for your pro-activity in disagreeing with a tax auditor:

> ". . . no deduction shall be made in respect of an outlay or expense except to the extent that it was made or incurred by the taxpayer *for the purpose of gaining or producing income from the business . . .*"
> ITA Section 18(1) (a)

> "It is not necessary to show that income actually resulted from the particular outlay or expenditure itself. It is sufficient that the outlay or expense was a *part of the income-earning process.*"
> CRA's Interpretation Bulletin IT-487

> "An expense would not be disallowed simply because the income-earning process produced a loss as long as *the intention* in making the expenditure was to produce income. Outlays or expenses made or incurred *to maintain income* or *to reduce other expenses* are also deductible as their purpose would be to increase income, whether or not such an increase resulted."
> CRA's Interpretation Bulletin IT-487

Remember, there must be an *intent* to produce a viable source of income or a potential for that source sometime in the *foreseeable future.* Many taxpayers and their advisors under-develop this argument during an appeals process and lose their case.

This shouldn't happen, as no one knows *the potential for future profits* of your business better than you do. The auditor can only make a judgment call on what *is* and what *was* in the reassessment period. You, however, can paint the vision of the potential for income, which is your right and privilege under the Income Tax Act. In addition, you must follow the rules that are clearly defined for tax deductibility of your expenditures under a variety of classifications.

Let's focus on those rules to "make sure it's deductible" now.

THE PARAMETERS

Essentially, your business expenditures fall into five types:

1. Current
2. Capital
3. Prepaid
4. Restricted
5. Not allowable

Current Expenses   These are used up in the course of earning income from the business. Examples are office supplies, wages, rent and other overhead costs. These costs are usually fully deductible against revenues.

Capital Expenses   These expenditures are for the acquisition of income-producing assets with a useful life of more than one year. This includes cars, buildings, equipment and machinery. These expenses are subject to Capital Cost Allowance (CCA) rates and classes, which allow for a declining balance method of accounting for the cost of wear and tear, resulting in a deduction from business income. You've previously learned that this optional CCA deduction can be used in tax planning activities. You'll learn more about the specifics of making the claim in the next chapter.

Prepaid Costs   Most businesses must report income and expenses on the accrual method of accounting. In that case, the prepaid expense is prorated and deductible in the year the benefit is received. Only those on the cash method of accounting (generally only farmers, fishers and very small businesses) may claim the full costs in the year paid.

Restricted Expenses   These include the costs of meals and entertainment (50% deductible) and the costs of attending conventions (only two per year). Home workspace expenses are another example, restricted to net income from the business.

Non-allowable Expenses   Fines or penalties imposed after March 22, 2004, by any level of government (including foreign governments) will not be tax deductible. Also not allowable is the cost of a golf membership or certain advertising in foreign media. Personal expenses of any kind are not allowable business expenses.

Be sure to cover each category with your tax advisor to prepare properly for tax filing time. In the case of a proprietorship, your deductible expenses are assembled on a Statement of Business or Professional Activities (see Figure 4.1), also known as Form T2125. You'll want to make sure that every number provided on this statement is supported by your retrieval boxes of hard copy.

The Statement of Business or Professional Activities

CRA provides an excellent form to follow in developing a compliance strategy for your tax reporting of deductible items when you run an unincorporated business. Form T2125, *Statement of Business or Professional Activities,* requires first that you report your "adjusted gross sales" from your business or professional income. (Note that different forms are available for farmers or fishers.)

Adjusted gross sales are the total of sales, commissions or other fees earned in your business or, in the case of professionals, fees that include work-in-progress, which we will define later.

From those total sales, the following are deducted: net amount of federal or provincial sales taxes; any returns, allowances or discounts; work-in-progress at the end of the year; or certain elections to exclude work-in-progress that were included in the gross sales figure.

These categories should be discussed with your bookkeeper, who should set up the following accounts:

- Gross sales (which you can break out into types of sales), before taxes
- GST/HST collected
- Provincial sales taxes collected
- Returns of sold items
- Allowances on sold items
- Discounts included in gross sales
- Work-in-progress

Also set up an account for any reserves on income, which were deducted last year, and any other income sources that are outside the normal

Figure 4.1	Form T2125, Statement of Business or Professional Activities

Canada Revenue Agency   Agence du revenu du Canada

Statement of
Business or Professional Activities

- For each business or profession, complete a **separate** Form T2125.
- File each completed Form T2125 with your *Income Tax and Benefit Return*.
- For more information on how to complete this form, see Guide T4002, *Business and Professional Income*.

Identification

Your name

Your social insurance number

Business name

Business Number

Business address

City, province, or territory   Postal code

Fiscal period   Year   Month   Day   Year   Month   Day   Was 2008 your last year of business?   Yes ☐   No ☐
From: To:

Main product or service

Industry code (see the appendix in the *Business and Professional Income* guide)

Tax shelter identification number   Partnership filer identification number   Your percentage of the partnership   %

Name and address of person or firm preparing this form

Part 1 – Business income

2. ☐ If you have business income, tick this box and complete this part. **Do not complete parts 1 and 2 on the same form.**

Sales, commissions, or fees .... A

Minus

Goods and services tax/harmonized sales tax (GST/HST) and provincial sales tax (PST)
(if included in sales above) ....

Returns, allowances, and discounts (if included in sales above) ....

Total of the above two lines   ▶   B

Adjusted gross sales (line A **minus** line B)   C
Enter this amount on line 8000 in Part 3, below

Part 2 – Professional income

3. ☐ If you have professional income, tick this box and complete this part. **Do not complete parts 1 and 2 on the same form.**

Professional fees (includes work-in-progress) .... D

Minus

Goods and services tax/harmonized sales tax (GST/HST) and provincial sales tax (PST)
(if included in fees above) ....

Work-in-progress (WIP), end of the year, per election to exclude WIP (see Chapter 2 of the guide)

Total of the above two lines   ▶   E

Subtotal (line D **minus** line E)

Plus

Work-in-progress (WIP), start of the year, per election to exclude WIP (see Chapter 2 of the guide) ....

Adjusted professional fees (total of the above two lines)   F
Enter this amount on line 8000 in Part 3, below

Part 3 – Gross business or professional income

Adjusted gross sales (from line C in Part 1) or adjusted professional fees (from line F in Part 2) .... 8000 G

Plus

Reserves deducted last year 8290

Other income 8230

Total of the above two lines   ▶   H

Gross business or professional income (line G **plus** line H) 8299

Enter this amount on the appropriate line of your income tax and benefit return: business on line 162, professional on line 164, or commission on line 166

T2125 E   (Vous pouvez obtenir ce formulaire en français à **www.arc.gc.ca** ou au **1-800-959-3376**.)   Page 1 of 5   Canada

Figure 4.1	Form T2125, Statement of Business or Professional Activities (continued)

Part 4 – Cost of goods sold and gross profit

If you have business income, complete this part. Enter only the business part of the costs.

Gross business income from line 8299 in Part 3 on page 1 I

Opening inventory (include raw materials, goods in process, and finished goods) **8300**

Purchases during the year (net of returns, allowances, and discounts) **8320**

Subcontracts **8360**

Direct wage costs **8340**

Other costs **8450**

Total of the above five lines

Minus
Closing inventory (include raw materials, goods in process, and finished goods) **8500**

Cost of goods sold **8518** ▶ J

Gross profit (line I **minus** line J) **8519**

Part 5 – Net income (loss) before adjustments

Gross profit from line 8519 in Part 4 above, or gross income from line 8299 in Part 3 on page 1 . . . . K

Expenses (enter only the business part)

Advertising **8521**

Meals and entertainment (allowable part only) **8523**

Bad debts **8590**

Insurance **8690**

Interest **8710**

Business tax, fees, licences, dues, memberships, and subscriptions **8760**

Office expenses **8810**

Supplies **8811**

Legal, accounting, and other professional fees **8860**

Management and administration fees **8871**

Rent **8910**

Maintenance and repairs **8960**

Salaries, wages, and benefits (including employer's contributions) **9060**

Property taxes **9180**

Travel (including transportation fees, accommodations, and allowable part of meals) **9200**

Telephone and utilities **9220**

Fuel costs (except for motor vehicles) **9224**

Delivery, freight, and express **9275**

Motor vehicle expenses (not including CCA) (see Chart A on page 5) **9281**

Allowance on eligible capital property **9935**

Capital cost allowance (CCA) (from Area A on page 4) **9936**

Other expenses

9270

Total business expenses **9368** ▶ L

Net income (loss) before adjustments (line K **minus** line L) **9369**

Part 6 – Your net income (loss)

Your share of the amount on line 9369 in Part 5 above . . . . M

Minus – Other amounts deductible from your share of net partnership income (loss)
(from the chart on page 3) . . . . **9943** N

Net income (loss) after adjustments (line M **minus** line N) . . . . O

Minus – Business-use-of-home expenses (from the chart on page 3) . . . . **9945** P

Your net income (loss) (line O **minus** line P) **9946**

Enter this amount on the appropriate line of your income tax and benefit return: business on line 135, professional on line 137, or commission on line 139

Page 2 of 5

Figure 4.1	Form T2125, Statement of Business or Professional Activities (continued)

Other amounts deductible from your share of net partnership income (loss)

Claim expenses you incurred that were not included in the partnership statement of income and expenses, and for which the partnership did not reimburse you.

Total (enter this amount on line 9943 in Part 6 on page 2)

Calculation of business-use-of-home expenses

Heat

Electricity

Insurance

Maintenance

Mortgage interest

Property taxes

Other expenses

Subtotal

Minus – Personal use part

Subtotal

Plus – Capital cost allowance (business part only)

– Amount carried forward from previous year

Subtotal   1

Minus – Net income (loss) after adjustments (from line O in Part 6 on page 2) – If negative, enter "0."   2

Business-use-of-home expenses available to carry forward (line **1** minus line 2) – If negative, enter "0."

Allowable claim (the lesser of amounts 1 or 2 above) – Enter this amount on line 9945 in Part 6.

Details of other partners

Name and address	Share of net income or (loss) $	Percentage of partnership %
Name and address	Share of net income or (loss) $	Percentage of partnership %
Name and address	Share of net income or (loss) $	Percentage of partnership %
Name and address	Share of net income or (loss) $	Percentage of partnership %

Details of equity

Total business liabilities	9931	
Drawings in 2008	9932	
Capital contributions in 2008	9933	

Page 3 of 5

sales lines. Those amounts are added to calculate your total gross business or professional income.

Cost of Goods Sold

Those who stock inventory have to keep meticulous track of opening inventory, purchases, the cost of sub-contracting, direct wage costs and other costs in producing the inventory. From all of these items, the closing inventory value is subtracted to arrive at cost of goods sold. This figure reduces gross business and professional income to become gross profit.

You'll notice that only the business portion of costs is to be included here. This is particularly important for direct sellers in the cleaning, jewelry and other home sales enterprises. Those who use any part of their purchases for personal consumption—grocery items, cleaning supplies, jewelry worn personally, clothing worn personally, etc.—must account for this. You may not write off the costs of any inventory items that are used personally. Make sure you keep a separate log to identify such items and their value and be prepared to show this in a tax audit. In that way the auditor can see you have accounted for personal use.

Gross Profit

This is a very important point of analysis for CRA. For example, let's say your net sales were $25,000 during the year, but after computing your cost of goods sold, your gross profit is a negative $5,000. From this figure, all other expenses of running the operation—from advertising to interest costs to salaries and travel costs—must be paid. This is a red flag for auditors, who will wonder why your profit margins are so low.

Margin Analysis

A close look at your gross profit tells the auditor the story of your enterprise's viability. If your retail pricing to the customer is not high enough to cover your operating expenses, there is no reasonable expectation of profit. Fact is, you'll always be in a loss position, even if all your other operating expenses are legitimate and well-documented.

It is doubtful that anyone goes into business to lose money. Most serious business owners would want to reassess time and efforts closely to decide whether or not to continue in the same vein, given the poor showing at their gross profit line. Change is necessary to stay afloat. *So, to make sure your expenditures are deductible and that resulting operational losses can be used to offset other income of the year, plan for reasonable profit margins now or in the future.*

Business Expenses Only

You'll notice the Statement of Business or Professional Activities calls for the *business portion of expenses only*. As mentioned above, all expenditures of the business must be prorated if there is any personal use component. Always document the nature of your expenditures. If you can, get into the habit of writing a note on the back of the receipt or invoice:

- Lunch, James Cook, re quote on supplies
- Gift, L. Smith, re thanks for contract
- Dinner, T. Tromblin, re rental property
- Flyers re Maryville campaign

Calculate Adjustments to Net Income

Deductions of operating expenses help unincorporated business owners arrive at their net income for tax purposes. However, several adjustments may be required before the figures are transferred to the personal tax return. The adjustments can include:

- Amounts deductible from your share of partnership income or losses
- Business use of home workspace expenses

The form goes on to provide charts to calculate the above, as well as deductions for capital cost allowances and motor vehicle expenses. We will discuss those costs in Chapters 5 and 6. For now, we'll focus on operating expenses used up in the pursuit of profit in your enterprise. This is what's important to you as you gather documentation for your bookkeeper and accountant throughout the year.

Avoid Pitfalls Claiming Common Business Expenses

Accounting and Legal Fees   The key pitfall taxpayers run into here is that they write off accounting and legal fees in full in cases where they really relate to capital transactions. CRA has issued IT-99 to address certain specific cases when legal or accounting fees will be deductible.

They will be 100% deductible when paid in the course of normal business activities such as preparing contracts, collecting trade debts, preparing minutes of directors' meetings, conducting appeals for sales or property tax assessments and so on. The fees may even be deductible in defense of a charge of performance of illegal activities, depending on the relationship of the conduct to the income-earning activities. (Also see comments regarding Damages.) Fees for preparing income tax returns and assistance in preparing an appeal on assessment of income taxes, interest or penalties, CPP or EI premiums will be deductible, as will the costs of preparing advance tax rulings.

However, when legal and accounting fees are incurred on the acquisition of capital property, they are *normally included in the cost of the property* or as an outlay or expense in the case of dispositions of capital property.

Legal fees surrounding successful corporate acquisitions will be treated as *capital expenses added to the cost base of the shares acquired*.

Legal and accounting fees incurred in an abortive attempt to acquire shares would normally *not be deductible at all* unless the taxpayer can demonstrate that he/she intended to make the business a part of a similar business already operated by the taxpayer. (See IT-143 and IT-259.)

Convention Expenses   This is a real problem area for taxpayers at audit time. First, self-employed taxpayers may claim the costs of *only two conventions* a year provided that they are held by a business or professional organization. While you need not be a member of the organization, you must have an income-earning purpose related to your business in attending the convention. In addition, IT-131 explains another little-known requirement—that the convention be "held at a location that may reasonably be regarded as consistent with the territorial scope of the organization." An ocean cruise held by a Canadian organization, for instance, probably wouldn't qualify. Taxpayers must be cautious in choosing their convention locations—as only two per year are deductible in the first place—and ensure they can prove that attending a convention in another country is *directly related to their business or profession*. Further information can be found in IT-357 and should be discussed with your tax advisor.

Damages and Settlements Paid   If you incur damages resulting from a normal risk of your business operations, a deduction for the costs, including interest payments or wrongful dismissal payments, will normally be allowed as fully deductible, unless the damages are on account of capital, in which case they would be classified as "eligible capital property." In such cases, three-quarters of the value of the damages are scheduled in the Cumulative Eligible Capital account and may be deducted at a rate of 7% of that value per year.

Non-competition Agreements or Restrictive Covenants   Here's a consideration for any business owner who sells his or her company and agrees to work under an employment contract that includes a non-competition clause. Generally, where it is reasonable to conclude that part of the amount paid on the acquisition of property relates to a restrictive covenant, that amount must be valued separately and treated as a payment for the restrictive covenant. Further, any amount paid by a purchaser for a restrictive covenant is deductible to the purchaser and taxable to the vendor as "other income" that is not earned income for RRSP purposes. Where the payments form a part of the proceeds of sale of the goodwill of the business or the cost of shares, amounts received in exchange for the agreement not to compete can be classified as an "eligible capital expenditure" or in some cases, a capital gain. Discuss these options carefully with your advisors well in advance of the sale of your business.

Health Care Premiums

For tax years after 1997, CRA will allow you to deduct from your business income any premiums paid to a private health plan on behalf of yourself, your employees and your spouse or children. For these premiums to be deductible on your personal tax return, you must meet certain criteria:

- Your income from the business in the current or preceding year must exceed 50% of your income for the year, and your other income must not exceed $10,000
- Premiums are paid to a government-authorized Private Health Services Plan (PHSP)
- The premiums are not claimed as a medical expense by anyone else
- The deduction depends on several criteria, including how many qualifying (non-family) employees are insured and for what part of the year

The deduction is either the lowest amount that is or would be paid for non-family members or:

- An annual dollar maximum of $1,500 for yourself and each adult family member covered by the plan plus
- $750 for each family member who is under 18 years of age at the beginning of the fiscal year

Note: If you do not pay the premiums for any employee covered by the plan, the limit for yourself is zero.

If the period of coverage is less than one year, the amounts are pro-rated. Where you have no non-arm's-length employees, you are limited to the dollar maximums described above.

Hospitality, Meals and Entertainment

CRA issued IT-518 to overview their position with regard to the deductibility of food, beverages and entertainment. Reasonable amounts may of course be deducted if the costs were incurred in the course of earning income from a business or property. The total costs must, however, be restricted to 50% of the amounts actually paid or payable. Note this 50% limitation *will not apply* to the computation of the personal tax liability on the T1 General in the following cases:

- The claiming of moving expenses using Form T1M
- The claiming of child care expenses using Form T778
- The claiming of medical expenses

However, it is important to know that the 50% limitation does apply to taxes, gratuities and restaurant gift certificates purchased for your clients. The small business owner must be aware of several exceptions to the 50% restriction that will result in 100% claims on his/her Statement of Business or Professional Activities, as discussed below:

- **Hospitality business:** Costs of food, beverages or entertainment provided in the ordinary course of business, which is the business of providing food, beverages or entertainment to others in return for compensation. Restaurants, hotels and airlines, therefore, are all exempt from the 50% restriction on food, beverages or entertainment provided to their customers.
- **Food and beverage business:** If the business you conduct is the business of making food, beverages or entertainment, the cost of promotional samples is 100% deductible. However, any time you take someone out for a business meal, the costs will be subject to the 50% rule.
- **Registered charities:** The 50% restriction will not apply if the food, beverages or entertainment are for a fund-raising event to primarily benefit a charity. The 50% rule will apply to the price of admission to an event that is part of the regular activities of the charity. For in-

stance, Morena invites her client, Gustav, to the annual fund-raising dinner of the Manitoba Theatre for Young People. The expenses in that case are not subject to the 50% rule. Next week, she will be giving Gustav tickets to the group's five new plays to be held over the next seven months. The cost of those tickets is subject to the 50% rule.

- **Consultant's billings:** If you do work for a company that entails travel or work "on location," and if the costs of meals are billed to the client and reimbursed to you, you are able to fully deduct those meal expenses, as the reimbursement would be included in your income.
- **Meals at conferences:** Where an all-inclusive fee is paid, entitling the participant to food, beverages and/or entertainment, the 50% restriction applies to an allocation of $50 per day. All other costs will be fully deductible.
- **Beverages en route:** You can fully deduct the cost of any meals and beverages served or entertainment provided on planes, trains or buses (but not ships, boats or ferries), so keep a log of those expenditures, as receipts are normally not available, and CRA will allow a reasonable amount as your claim.
- **Employer-sponsored events:** When you entertain your staff, you'll be able to avoid the 50% limitation on food, beverages and entertainment, provided that these are generally available to and enjoyed by all employees at a particular place, such as a Christmas party. *Such events are limited to six per year*. In general, you can spend $100 per person (including transportation) before having to add a taxable benefit to the employee's pay (see IT-470).
- **Employer-operated restaurants or cafeterias:** Costs of food and beverages here are not subject to the 50% rule, but subsidized meals do present a taxable benefit to the employees. Restricted facilities like an executive lounge or dining room are always subject to the 50% limitation.

Note that the following activities *will qualify as entertainment subject to the 50% rule*:

- Tickets to theatre, concerts, athletic events
- Private boxes at sporting events
- Cost of a cruise
- Admission to a fashion show
- Hospitality suites

- Entertaining at athletic or sporting clubs
- Entertaining while on vacation
- Cost of taxes, gratuities and cover charges
- Cost of security escorts
- Cost of escorts or tour guides*

Interest Costs

Interest costs on money borrowed at a reasonable interest rate to earn income from a business or property will generally be deductible. Interest expenses will not be deductible in the following cases:

- The loan is interest free, or the interest costs payable are not reasonable
- The money is not used directly in the pursuit of income from a business with a reasonable expectation of profit

Note: Income from property does not include capital gains accruals. Therefore income in the form of dividends, rents or interest must be present for interest deductibility on loans used to acquire capital properties to be allowed.

CRA has set out its current interpretations on interest deductibility in IT-533, which business owners should know:

- **Tracing/linking:** The onus is on the taxpayer to trace funds to a current and eligible usage. Taxpayers must demonstrate that aggregate eligible expenditures from co-mingled accounts, for example, exceed the amount borrowed and deposited to that account.
- **Income-producing accounts:** CRA accepts that the use of borrowed money can be for an ancillary, rather than primary, income-producing purpose. This will be determined as a question of fact.
- **Borrowing to pay dividends:** The interest expense amounts will be deductible.
- **Borrowing to make loans to employees and shareholders:** Interest will be deductible if there is a reasonable expectation of income. This comes from the effort of the employee, and such loans would be therefore viewed as a form of remuneration.
- **Borrowing to contribute capital:** Interest may be deductible if the borrowed funds can be linked to an income-producing purpose (i.e., the issuing of dividends).

---

* Costs of "escort services" are not deductible at all. So now you know.

- **Borrowing to honour a guarantee:** Interest costs are generally not deductible unless it can be shown that the transaction will increase the potential for dividends to be received. If the taxpayer receives consideration of some kind for fair market value, such amounts are a source of income, and therefore any interest expense incurred to earn it will be deductible.
- **Leveraged buy-outs:** Interest on money borrowed to acquire common shares will be deductible. CRA comments further by saying there is no arm's-length requirement in this case.
- **Limitation on interest deduction on purchase of undeveloped land:** The deduction for interest and property taxes on land is limited to the net income from the land. These limitations do not apply to land used in the course of business other than land development. Interest and property taxes not deductible may be added to the cost base of the land.
- **Interest paid on capital property that is no longer owned:** When a taxpayer borrows money to acquire a capital property for the purposes of earning income from that property and subsequently disposes of the property for an amount less than the amount borrowed to acquire the property, it is deemed that the taxpayer continues to use the property for the purpose of earning income from property. In other words, if the proceeds of the sale are used to pay back the money borrowed, then the interest payable on any outstanding balance will continue to be deductible.
- **Capitalizing interest:** Many business owners are unaware of the election to *capitalize* the cost of borrowed money used to acquire depreciable property. This election can be made for the current year and the three previous years, and for one, some or all of the properties acquired. It can also be made for all the money borrowed or some of it. An election under Section 21(1) or (3) of the Income Tax Act must be made and submitted with the tax return each year to opt for the treatment. Then the amount of the interest is simply added to the capital cost of the property and written off as part of the CCA claim each year. Using this method, you can effectively move your interest deduction to future years when you have a higher income level. Look to IT-121 for more details.

Training Expenses

How much of your training costs—including travel, food, beverages and lodging paid to attend a training course—can you actually claim as a business deduction? There are several important rules outlined in IT-357R2:

New Skill or Upgrading?   Training costs will not be deductible if they are considered to be "capital" in nature—that is, if they result in a lasting benefit to the taxpayer. This could include the acquisition of a new skill or qualification. However, if training is taken to maintain, update or upgrade an existing skill, the costs are 100% deductible—that is, unless they are also being claimed as a non-refundable tax credit under the tuition fee amount.

Examples of expenses that are 100% deductible:

- A professional development course taken to maintain professional standards
- A tax course taken by a lawyer or accountant, whether or not he/she has previously done such work
- A course on modern building materials taken by an architect

Therefore, training costs to attend a course that results in a degree, diploma, professional qualification or similar certificate are considered to be "capital" in nature. The costs would be scheduled in the Cumulative Eligible Capital account. Examples include:

- Training by a medical practitioner to qualify as a specialist
- A lawyer taking an engineering course unrelated to his/her legal practice
- A professor taking a sideline course to acquire skills in a sideline business

Personal Portion   Any portion of the costs that are personal in nature cannot be deducted. Personal costs are assessed on a case-by-case basis using factors such as the duration and location of the course, as well as the number of days in which no training occurred. It is also important that the costs not be misclassified. If they are really convention expenses, you could be restricted to the two-per-year and territorial-scope rules identified earlier.

Location and Duration   Deductibility of expenses will be questioned if courses are taken abroad or in a resort, particularly if you follow up the course with a personal holiday. If equivalent training was available locally, your expenses for the trip to study at the exotic location will likely be considered personal. Costs for expenses of food and lodging will not be allowed for any days in which no training occurred. CRA will make an exception and allow costs for arrival and departure dates as well as weekends. Remember that the costs of claiming food and auto are subject to the normal limitations.

Deductibility of Seminars   Are seminars classified as conventions or training courses? This is a question of fact. Conventions generally include a formal meeting of members of an organization or association. Training courses generally have a classroom format and a formal course of study that results in testing and the possibility of certification. Training courses are treated more favourably in that you can attend more than two in a year; however, Interpretation Bulletin 357 makes a noteworthy comment: "The total time taken in attending courses in any one year must not be so great as to interfere with the carrying on of the taxpayer's business. If that happens, expenses will not be deductible."

Stay Informed: Resources Are Many, Varied and Often Free

In conclusion, if you are wondering about the deductibility of a specific classification of expenses, don't hesitate to seek guidance from an interpretation bulletin or other source of tax information from CRA. This will give you guidance on the position the agency will likely take on the issue and provide you with peace of mind.

Also consider subscribing to *EverGreen Explanatory Notes*, an on-line resource from www.knowledgebureau.com that serves as a one-stop gateway to all of the information bulletins, circulars, guides and forms, along with instructional notes and examples.

Remember, if you decide to take an aggressive stance and claim deductions for items that could be called into question, you want to make sure you have a bona fide business purpose documented for each expenditure and that your business has a reasonable expectation of profiting from your activities and expenditures.

TAX ADVISOR

To audit-proof your expenditures and *Make Sure It's Deductible,* take advantage of the check lists in Figures 4.2 and 4.3. They'll help you make sound judgement calls that ensure your books are prepared in your favour. Consider two compliance standards:

Hard Copy Classification

When considering an outlay, classify it as an operating or capital expense and prepare your records as detailed in Figure 4.2.

Business/Personal Use Classification

Make a list of all expenditures that have both a personal and business component to determine if any of those items are tax deductible, as shown in Figure 4.3. Chart common family expenses and determine whether any of them should be claimed as business expenses, bearing in mind that they must have a direct bearing on the income-earning activities of the business and be reasonable under the circumstances.

Penalties for Tax Evasion, Other Missteps

It can be expensive to break tax law. Income tax evasion—the willful understatement of income or overstatement of expenditures—can result in large fines and even imprisonment. Talk to your tax advisor about staying onside and avoiding the following penalties:

1. **Failure to file a return of income:** This results in a penalty equal to 5% of the person's unpaid tax payable plus 1% for each complete month past the filing due date up to a maximum of 12 months.

2. **Repeated failure to file:** Repeat offenders within a three-year period will be fined an amount equal to 10% of their unpaid tax payable plus 2% for each complete month past the filing due date up to a maximum of 20 months.

3. **False statements or omissions:** For persons who knowingly (or, under circumstances amounting to gross negligence) make, participate

Figure 4.2	Classification of Expenses

Expense: _____ Total $_____ HST/GST $_____ PST$_____

Authorized by: _____ Date Paid: _____

1. What is the classification of the expense?   ☐ Operating   ☐ Capital

2. Will the expense impact future revenues?   _____

3. Is the expense reasonable under the circumstances? Why? _____

4. Will the expense reduce costs to improve bottom lines? _____

5. Is there a personal use component? If so what %? _____

Figure 4.3	Business Component of Mixed-Use Expenses				
Expense	**Do You Have Receipts?**		**Can You Claim the Expense? Talk to your tax advisor about these grey areas**	**Can You Use It?**	
	Yes	No		Yes	No
A. Personal Groceries			Usually no, but entertaining for business purposes is tax deductible (50% usually), as is the expense of feeding children in a babysitting business (100%). Personal use must always be isolated, however.		
Clothing			Usually no, however certain clothing is deductible, provided it is unsuitable for street wear; example, judges' robes, entertainers' costumes. These must be depreciated, rather than written off in full.		
Footwear			Usually no, however, employed dancers and certain self-employed taxpayers may make a claim in certain cases if their special footwear is "used up" in the pursuit of business income. For example, those who run a winter resort might write off the cost of snowshoes worn by instructors, or ballerinas may write off the cost of their shoes.		
Entertainment			Yes, but generally restricted to 50% of costs; except for events that are staff gatherings — but no more than 6 times a year. If you entertain in your home, keep receipts of food, liquor, etc., specific to the event. Keep entertainment log to record name and address of person being entertained.		
Utilities			Yes, a portion of these expenses are deductible if workspace in home claim is otherwise allowed. Keep total bills, but prorate expenses according to square footage of office space.		
Repairs/ Maintenance			Yes, certain employed musicians, other employees, and the self-employed may make this claim for repairs to home office, revenue properties, certain equipment. Personal use must be isolated.		
Mortgage (Home) Payments			Yes. But only interest costs (not principal) are deductible by the self-employed, according to the space used for business purposes.		
Insurance Payments			Yes, if home office claims, musicians' instrument costs, auto expense claims and insurance for other equipment costs are otherwise allowable.		
Car Payments			Never for personal driving; however, costs of running an auto are deductible, if used for business or employment purposes and written off according to information on distance travelled in auto log.		

Figure 4.3			Business Component of Mixed-Use Expenses (continued)		

Expense	Do You Have Receipts?		Can You Claim the Expense? Talk to your tax advisor about these grey areas	Can You Use It?	
	Yes	No		Yes	No
Tuition Fees			Claim as a tax credit rather than a deduction if over $100 and paid to a designated educational institute. Sometimes can be claimed as an expense of business as a training cost, in which case either the credit or the deduction must be chosen. For higher-income earners, the deduction may result in a higher claim.		
Gifts			Personal, no. If made to a client of a self-employed taxpayer or, in some cases, an employed commissioned salesperson, yes. Note gift certificates to restaurants are subject to the 50% restriction on meals.		
Medical/Pharmacy			Claim as a medical expense credit on the return. Group health plan premiums may be a tax deductible business expense.		
B. Employment					
Clothing			No. Not even itemized dry cleaning, cost of special shoes or workboots is allowable, but the Canada Employment Credit is available to cover these costs.		
Car Expenses			Yes, if Form T2200 is signed and auto log kept up for a representative period.		
Parking			Yes, if duties include working away from the employer's office to sign contracts on behalf of employer and Form T2200 is available.		
Lunches			Only if away on business for employer for at least 12 hours. Entertainment expenses may be allowed if you are a commission salesperson, for the purposes of entertaining your client.		
Office Supplies			Yes, if used up directly in your job and Form T2200 is signed by the employer.		
Long-Distance Calls			Yes, if made for business or employment purposes. However, monthly rental charges are not deductible unless a separate line is installed.		
Special Clothing			Generally no, unless unsuitable for street wear.		
Tools & Equipment			The self-employed may write off the cost of tools and equipment according to special rules; the employed taxpayer may not, with the exception of claims for auto, musical instruments or aircraft; also tradespeople and apprentice vehicle mechanics may claim cost of tools under a limited deduction.		
Licences & Bonding			Yes, these costs are deductible by both employed and self-employed persons.		

Figure 4.3			Business Component of Mixed-Use Expenses (continued)		

Expense	Do You Have Receipts?		Can You Claim the Expense? Talk to your tax advisor about these grey areas	Can You Use It?	
	Yes	No		Yes	No
Computers/Phones			Only the self-employed may write off the costs of these capital assets, including cost of acquisition (usually a capital expense) and interest costs.		
Interest Costs			The self-employed may claim the costs of interest paid on loans to finance their operating costs, equipment purchases and home workspace. Employees may write off only interest costs on auto, aircraft and musical instrument acquisitions, but not mortgage interest or other costs.		
Salary to Assistant			Yes, these costs are deductible by both the employed and self-employed. File Form T2200 for the employee.		
Office Rent/ In-Home			These costs are deductible by employed and self-employed. However, for employed taxpayers, there is never an allowable claim for mortgage interest or CCA. Unless you earn commissions you also may not claim property taxes or insurance costs.		
Training Costs			These may be deductible against business income or claimed as a tuition tax credit, if eligible.		
Accounting/Legal Fees			Yes, in certain cases, for employees, the fees must be paid to appeal an assessment of tax; or in cases where you were forced to establish rights to salary, wages or commissions owed to you.		
Income Tax Preparation			Not deductible by employees; however employed commissioned salespeople and the self-employed may make a claim; certain investors also.		
C. Investments Interest Costs			Yes, deductible if there is a potential for the earning of rents, interest or dividends. However, this is true only of loans used to acquire non-registered investments, TFSA not eligible.		
Safety Deposit Box			Yes.		
Management Fees			Yes, but not for registered investments.		
Accounting Fees			Only if accounting is a usual part of the operations of your property.		
Investment Counsel			Yes. For details, obtain CRA's IT-238.		
D. Self-Employment Operating Expenses			Yes, those expenses "used up" in the running of a business are 100% deductible if reasonable and incurred to earn income from a business with a reasonable expectation of profit. May create loss.		
Capital Expenses			No. Only a percentage of costs, known as Capital Cost Allowance, may be deducted, at the taxpayer's option, to write down a notional amount for wear and tear of the asset.		

or acquiesce in the filing or representation of a false statement or omission, a penalty equal to the greater of either $100 or 50% of the understated tax is imposed.

4. **Third-party misrepresentation:** Third-party tax or financial advisors who know or ought to reasonably know that a false statement is being made in a return are liable for a penalty equal to the greater of either $1,000 or the gross compensation that the advisor is entitled to receive for that particular tax-planning activity.

5. **Tax evasion:** The penalty for prosecution under summary conviction is a fine of not less than 50% and not more than 200% of the amount sought to be evaded, plus possible imprisonment of up to two years. The penalty for prosecution under indictment is a fine of not less than 100% and not more than 200% of the amount sought to be evaded plus imprisonment up to five years.

6. **GAAR:** General Anti-Avoidance Rules can be imposed in cases where the taxpayer circumvented the intent of the law in undertaking a series of transactions that resulted in a tax benefit. While there are no criminal consequences in such a case, the avoided tax plus interest must generally be paid. An avoidance transaction for these purposes is defined as:

   • One that does not have a bona fide business purpose, its primary purpose being to provide, directly or indirectly, in a tax benefit, or
   • A transaction that is part of a series of transactions in which the primary purpose is, as a whole, to result directly or indirectly in a tax benefit

Initiating Taxpayer Relief Provisions

Under its Taxpayer Relief Provisions, CRA can waive penalties and interest charges if the late filing or non-payment of an amount is beyond the taxpayer's control, resulting from circumstances such as natural or human-made disasters, personal hardship or CRA information that misled the public. Ask your tax professional to help you initiate a Taxpayer Relief request.

Voluntary Disclosures Program (VDP)

CRA encourages taxpayers to come forward and correct past omissions so that the taxpayers can be compliant with their legal obligations. Under the VDP, taxpayers who make a valid and complete voluntary disclosure would still have to pay the tax owing plus interest; however, CRA could provide relief from penalties and prosecution.

RECAP. YOU NEED TO KNOW:

1. How to read and use the Form T2125, *Statement of Business or Professional Activities*, to assist with your decision-making on tax deductible expenses

2. How to claim losses you are entitled to and use jurisprudence for comfort in the "grey areas"

3. How to link intent to earn income in the future with current costs and/or losses

4. How to classify expenses into proper tax deductibility categories

5. How to prepare a margin analysis to justify your commercial activities

6. How to audit-proof expenses that may require restriction, application to current or capital uses or proration for business/personal use

7. How to avoid penalties and interest for non-compliance and in hardship cases

YOU NEED TO ASK: Your tax advisor for help in writing off more of your expenditures by:

1. **Establishing intent:** Your expenditures will be deductible only if your activities are linked to a viable commercial activity. You must report your income and expenses by filing a tax return. (Otherwise, you could face the potential of being charged with gross negligence or tax evasion.)

2. **Legitimizing your claims:** Put yourself in the tax auditor's shoes. If there is any question that your activities may not be linked to a commercial activity, document the following:

   - Time devoted to the business
   - Distribution activities—presentation of works, products, services to the public
   - Time spent in marketing the goods or services of the enterprise
   - Revenues received
   - Historical record of profits

- Cyclical trends in the business
- Type of expenses claimed and their relevance to the business
- Business owner's qualifications to run the business successfully
- Business owner's membership in professional associations
- Growth of revenues, taking into account economic conditions and other market changes

All criteria are analyzed together to assess whether you are indeed running a commercial enterprise under which your expenses are deductible. Make sure your Daily Business Journal addresses these 10 factors. (See Chapter 3.)

3. **Establishing consistent revenue channels and streams:** Identify your unique product/service and income-earning process, your distribution channels, payment methods, pricing policies and gross margins by preparing detailed budgets and projections.

4. **Setting your profit margins to ensure profitability:** Ask your tax advisor to discuss this with you.

5. **Understanding expense restrictions:** Don't try to deduct more than two conventions per year, 100% of meals and entertainment costs or 100% of legal fees paid to acquire your office building. Scan relevant sources from CRA—such as Interpretation Bulletins, information circulars and tax guides—for important news about business deductions, or subscribe to an interpretive and instructional resource such as *EverGreen Explanatory Notes* from www.knowledgebureau. com.

6. **Establishing consistent bookkeeping practices:** Attach expense classification and verification statements to your hard-copy receipts to document intent and proration for personal use. As a minimum:

- Get receipts/invoices for all expenditures.
- Keep logs for cash expenses such as parking and payphones.
- Classify receipts/invoices (current, capital, restricted, prepaid).
- Enter into a bookkeeping system.
- File hard-copy documentation in folders/envelopes for retrieval.
- Keep a meticulous auto distance log.

7. **Finding the "low-hanging fruit":** Have you made expenditures that include a business component? If so, are you claiming the business portion of those expenses on your return? Try to turn every expenditure into a legitimate tax deduction.

8. **Preparing with foresight to challenge hindsight:** Before spending another dollar—ever—stop to consider, "Is this deductible?" Is there

a business purpose attached to the expense? If not, can there be? Document the business purpose. Remember, a tax auditor's interpretation about expense reasonableness comes with an unfair advantage—hindsight. However, the onus-of-proof rules can actually put the taxpayer in a position of power for two reasons:

- You have "vision" on your side—you can outline the potential for profit.
- You have "fairness" on your side—the courts have ruled it is unfair for an auditor to judge or second-guess business acumen. There aren't too many taxpayers who actually risk their resources to intentionally lose money. Rather, commercial viability must be considered at the time decisions are made.

For these reasons, you should pursue your rights under the law to claim every one of the properly documented business expenses you are entitled to, even those with mixed components of personal and business use.

9. **Establishing your rights to legitimate business losses, and fighting for them:** There is no legislated time limit for a "reasonable expectation of profit." If a tax auditor is looking at a period of only two to three years, he/she might be unreasonable to expect a profit from your business. Attaining profitability is often a slow process for songwriters, visual and recording artists, writers, farmers and others. Such taxpayers may take years to turn a profit (and be sure, CRA will be there then to take their share). Therefore it is most important for you to be able to establish legitimate operating losses that can be carried forward to offset future income. CRA will not deny you this right if you can show legitimate efforts to make a profit.

10. **Appealing with proper process:** If you are facing an unfavourable reassessment of tax, know your appeal rights and deadlines. Find out everything you can about the way CRA has taxed those in similar ventures. Ask your advisors for information about recent court cases that deal with the issues you face in growing your business. Be highly pro-active.

. . . .

CHAPTER 5

Simple Rules for Writing Off Asset Purchases

"Talent alone won't make you a success. Neither will being in the right place at the right time. The most important question is: 'Are you ready?'"
JOHNNY CARSON

KEY CONCEPTS

- Repairs and restoration of an income-producing asset to its original condition are 100% deductible as a current expense
- Costs of acquiring an asset with a useful life of more than one year must be "capitalized"
- Assets used to earn income in a business will often lose their value over time
- CRA allows a "permissive deduction" to account for this loss in value
- Capital Cost Allowance (CCA) is a deduction based on a declining balance method of accounting for depreciation of an asset on the tax return
- Taxpayers can choose to take this deduction, at their option

REAL LIFE: Jared enjoyed his work as a waiter while he attended university. During his days at The Happy Hunter Inn, he encountered many guests, one of whom was a local businessman, Allan Blair. Another was a local business-woman, Juanita Cares. The usual chitchat between server and client led to a number of interesting conversations. Jared was a computer whiz who special-ized in devising policies and procedures for businesses struggling with the ever-changing world of information and communications technology. Before he knew it, he was sub-contracting for Allan's company and Juanita's, and reaping the rewards of a job well done—further referrals.

Jared found himself, at year end, clearly in business, and with a major tax problem—where to start in gathering information about his income and expenses? After meeting with his accountant, he was surprised to learn his income records and deductions for operating expenses were in fairly good order.

To complete his tax return, what he needed were details about the assets he had acquired in his business: his computer, his office furniture, his desk, his car and his professional library.

THE PROBLEM

Jared's accountant didn't know it, but he was being somewhat exasperating to Jared. Going on about "Capital Cost Allowance," he was trying to save tax dollars on Jared's return by scheduling the assets he used in the business on the right tax form. Problem was, Jared had bought some assets new, some used, and his parents had given him the rest. Scheduling these business assets now involved not just receipting but also fair market valuations. How was he supposed to figure it out? He wasn't even sure what this "CCA" was all about!

THE SOLUTION

Jared's accountant did a wise thing—he sat Jared down and gave him a crash course in CCA, the deduction acknowledging wear and tear on business assets used to produce income. By knowing how assets are written off for tax purposes, he knew he would help Jared make wise tax-oriented decisions about spending his money in the future.

He also filled him in on some recent tax changes:

- **Small tools:** When it comes to small tools costing less than $500 and including things like instruments and kitchen utensils, linen, uniforms, dies, jigs or moulds, rental video cassettes and computer software, Jared can go ahead and write them off in full. The definition of these costs and how to handle them on the tax return was clarified in 2006 to specifically exclude electronic communications devices and electronic data processing equipment such as cell phones and PDAs. Prior to 2006, the dollar limit for full write-offs for these types of expenditures was $200.
- **Computer equipment (hardware and software):** In the Federal Budget of 2009, a temporary 100% CCA rate was introduced for eligible computer equipment, including software and hardware acquired from January 28, 2009, to February 1, 2011. The "half-rate rule" normally used to restrict tax write-offs in the year of acquisition will be waived, allowing a full deduction on eligible purchases in the first year that the CCA deduction is available.

- **Manufacturing and processing equipment:** An accelerated CCA is available for investment in manufacturing and processing assets purchased from 2008 until 2011. Jared's accountant told him that this is set of tax preferences the federal government likes to tweak as it reacts to challenges facing companies which compete in a global economy.

Jared was fascinated, and he was anxious to learn more about these terms and the tax consequences of the timing of his future asset acquisitions too.

THE PARAMETERS

An income-producing asset used in a business can be "written down" to acknowledge depreciation due to its use. No one really knows for sure what the value of an asset is at any given point in time. Value will be realized only upon disposition, when the owner sells the asset or disposes of it in another way, such as converting it to personal use or transferring it to a relative.

Therefore, determining the cost of wear and tear of assets during their use in business involves an educated guess. The Department of Finance has done some of that guesswork for you by prescribing special classes for various income-producing assets and establishing declining rates of depreciation resulting in a tax deduction called Capital Cost Allowance. CCA is a deduction that will reduce business income, subject to special rules.

For example, the recent tax changes you've already read about indicate that special rules exist for smaller expenditures, for certain types of equipment and for certain industries that the government wishes to stimulate through accelerated deductions. It is, in fact, not unusual to see adjustments to various CCA provisions with most annual federal and provincial budgets.

The CCA deduction can often be inadequately or incorrectly used by taxpayers, with the result that tax on business income is overpaid for several years because an important tax cost averaging provision was missed. Avoid such an oversight by observing the following parameters.

Timely Accuracy Is Important

CCA is known as a "permissive deduction." The claim is made at the taxpayer's option; however, there is a special rule the taxpayer must know about to manage the account properly right off the bat: Be sure to notify the CRA promptly if an error is made in claiming or deferring your CCA deduction. Doing so promptly is important because the adjustment period for permissive deductions like CCA is only 90 days after receipt of the Notice of Assessment or Reassessment. This is shorter than the normal adjustment period for errors and omissions, which is 10 calendar years for most other federal provisions. (Tax auditors have been known, however, to allow retroactive CCA claims when a file is audited.)

Capitalize Expenditures With Life Spans of More Than One Year

Generally, assets with a useful and enduring life—such as automobiles, trucks, machinery and buildings—are considered capital expenditures, scheduled for CCA purposes at time of acquisition. Their costs may not be written off in full in the same way that other operating expenses are. This is where many taxpayers make expensive mistakes.

Jared, for example, thought he could write off the full $3,000 he spent on his office furniture and professional library. Unfortunately, only a fraction of that expenditure would be allowed this year. However, he was delighted to find out that the full cost of the computer system would be deductible, thanks to new tax rules introduced specifically for those assets.

Capitalize Expenditures With Values Over $500

Even though small equipment and supplies may have a useful life of more than one year, if their value is under $500 they can generally be written off as operating expenses. This includes small tools or office equipment acquired on or after May 2, 2006. (Previously, the amount was $200.)

Know When Repairs Are Capitalized

If the repair of an asset adds to its useful life, the cost of the repair is generally added to the capital cost of the asset. If, on the other hand, the repair simply restores the asset to its original condition, the cost can be written off in full. For example, replacing the shingles that blew off a business premises during a windstorm would be fully deductible, whereas replacing the whole roof would be treated as a capital expenditure.

Know Your Basic CCA Rate Structure

CCA is a diminishing-balance method of claiming depreciation, used for tax purposes and applied to the capital cost of an income-producing asset. A fixed maximum percentage is applied against the balance of the capital cost of the asset remaining at the end of each year, and the result is the maximum CCA deduction that can be claimed to reduce business income. To arrive at this fixed percentage, assets of similar types are classified or "pooled" into specific classes for CCA purposes. Your tax advisor has a complete listing of asset classes and CCA rates, as do CRA's business guides. Or you can subscribe to *EverGreen Explanatory Notes* at www.knowledgebureau.com to keep current.

Certain Assets Are Exempt From the Half-Year Rules

Class 12 assets, a television commercial message, certain assets acquired from related persons and certain computer equipment are all examples of assets not subject to the half-year rule. As mentioned, these rules can change periodically and/or for limited periods of time, so consult your tax advisor about annual federal and provincial budget proposals when they are announced. The goal is to make timely decisions about your asset acquisitions.

Cost of Additions

The "cost of additions" of your assets for tax purposes includes federal and provincial taxes (GST/HST and PST) as well as freight charges. It gets a bit more complicated when the properties are acquired through a "deemed disposition," such as on the death of a taxpayer, or a "change in use" from personal to business. Deemed dispositions or transfers are valued at fair market value (FMV): what a willing buyer would pay a willing seller for the asset on the open market. Special rules apply when the amount received for the asset is inadequate (especially between related parties), when trade-in values are below FMV or when assets are disposed of at a superficial loss.

Know About the "Half-Year Rules"

When assets are acquired, the "cost of additions" is recorded on the CCA schedule, as outlined above. A "half-year rule" is then applied to most assets. That is, in the year of acquisition, the CCA rate can be applied only to half the cost of the asset.

Short Fiscal Years

Here is an important rule for start-up businesses: the CCA claim is generally prorated when there is a short fiscal year. This means that if you started your business on July 1 and had a December 31 fiscal year end, only 50% of the normal available CCA deduction allowed can be claimed. If you started your business on September 1, only one-third of the normal CCA deduction is claimable, and so on. The half-year rules, if applicable, must be taken into account as well.

Cost of Borrowing to Buy Assets

Interest costs to buy assets used in a business are tax deductible as an operating expense of the business. If there is a personal component to the use of the asset, the interest, like other related expenses including the CCA, must be prorated.

Many taxpayers don't know about this little rule: The taxpayer can choose to capitalize any annual financing fees paid for the assets simply by adding the cost on to the undepreciated capital cost of the asset. This allows the taxpayer to preserve more of those costs for future use, when profits are perhaps higher. To do so, the taxpayer must make an election under Subsection 21(3) of the Income Tax Act.

Calculating the CCA

Take a look at the CCA schedule used by the CRA (Figure 5.1). It's part of the Statement of Business or Professional Activities, previously discussed. You can readily see the requirements. Even if you won't be filing your own tax return, it is important that you understand the requirements as you contemplate the timing and consequences of asset acquisitions and dispositions throughout the year and as you are preparing your income tax records in the spring:

- Box 1: Enter the right class number
- Box 2: Enter the undepreciated capital cost (UCC) balance from last year
- Box 3: Record the cost of your capital additions, including taxes and freight, or record the FMV of assets converted to business use or given to you as a gift. Account for any personal use components in the detail boxes below.
- Box 4: Record your proceeds of disposition, but only up to the original cost noted on your CCA schedule when you acquired the asset,

Figure 5.1	Asset Tracking System for Tax Purposes

Area A – Calculation of capital cost allowance (CCA) claim

1 Class number	2 Undepreciated capital cost (UCC) at the start of the year	3 Cost of additions in the year (see areas B and C below)	4 Proceeds of dispositions in the year (see areas D and E below)	5* UCC after additions and dispositions (col. 2 **plus** col. 3 **minus** col. 4)	6 Adjustment for current-year additions 1/2 x (col. 3 **minus** col. 4) If negative, enter "0."	7 Base amount for CCA (col. 5 **minus** col. 6)	8 Rate %	9 CCA for the year (col. 7 x col. 8 or an adjusted amount)	10 UCC at the end of the year (col. 5 **minus** col. 9)

Total CCA claim for the year (enter this amount, **minus** any personal part and any CCA for business-use-of-home expenses, on line 9936 in Part 5 on page 2**)

* If you have a negative amount in this column, add it to income as a recapture on line 8230, "Other income," in Part 3 on page 1. If no property is left in the class and there is a positive amount in the column, deduct the amount from income as a terminal loss on line 9270, "Other expenses," in Part 5 on page 2. Recapture and terminal loss do not apply to a class 10.1 property. For more information, see Chapter 4 in the *Business and Professional Income* guide.

** For information on the CCA for "Calculation of business-use-of-home expenses," see Chapter 4 – "Special Situations" in the *Business and Professional Income* guide.

Area B – Details of equipment additions in the year

1 Class number	2 Property details	3 Total cost	4 Personal part (if applicable)	5 Business part (column 3 **minus** column 4)

Total equipment additions in the year `9925`

Area C – Details of building additions in the year

1 Class number	2 Property details	3 Total cost	4 Personal part (if applicable)	5 Business part (column 3 **minus** column 4)

Total building additions in the year `9927`

Area D – Details of equipment dispositions in the year

1 Class number	2 Property details	3 Proceeds of disposition (should not be more than the capital cost)	4 Personal part (if applicable)	5 Business part (column 3 **minus** column 4)

Note: If you disposed of property from your business in the year, see Chapter 4 in the *Business and Professional Income* guide for information about your proceeds of disposition.

Total equipment dispositions in the year `9926`

Area E – Details of building dispositions in the year

1 Class number	2 Property details	3 Proceeds of disposition (should not be more than the capital cost)	4 Personal part (if applicable)	5 Business part (column 3 **minus** column 4)

Note: If you disposed of property from your business in the year, see Chapter 4 in the *Business and Professional Income* guide for information about your proceeds of disposition.

Total building dispositions in the year `9928`

Area F – Details of land additions and dispositions in the year

Total cost of all land additions in the year	`9923`
Total proceeds from all land dispositions in the year	`9924`

Note: You cannot claim capital cost allowance on land.

Page 4 of 5

plus any capital improvements over time. Account for any personal use components in the detail boxes (Area B).

- Box 5: Subtotal
- Box 6: The adjustment box for your half-year rule
- Box 7: The figure upon which this year's CCA deduction is calculated
- Box 8: The CCA rate applied to this class of asset
- Box 9: CCA deduction (remember you can claim *any amount* up to a maximum of column 7 × column 8)
- Box 10: The UCC balance to be carried forward (column 5 – column 9)

Best bet: speak to your tax advisor first and have a Tax Savings Blueprint—your "what if" scenarios—prepared in advance of taking action on your CCA claim. Remember, you have a limited time within which to make adjustments to your claim should you wish to change your planning options.

Handling Dispositions

As important as it is to consult your tax advisor regarding capital acquisitions, it is also advisable to discuss the most advantageous procedure for disposing of assets and when to do so, as income inclusions or certain deductions can result *when all assets of a class are disposed of*. You want to be aware of any costly unintended consequences.

Remember that dispositions can occur not only due to sale, but also due to other circumstances such as the transfer of assets to another or to personal use, cessation of business due to death or emigration. In the latter instances, called "deemed dispositions," FMV of the asset must be determined.

The first consequence of asset disposition represents a potential cost to you: If the proceeds of disposition of any asset *exceed the cost of the asset*, **the result is a capital gain**. In that case, the gain is reported separately on the appropriate schedule for capital gains and losses on the tax return.

For CCA purposes, the proceeds subtracted from the undepreciated capital cost of the class cannot exceed the original cost of the asset (plus additions and improvements made during the year).

A second consequence involves dispositions of all assets in a class.

Dispositions of All Assets in the Class

While acquisitions and dispositions of assets to an existing pool of assets affect the undepreciated capital cost (UCC), it is usually when all assets in a class are disposed of that reconciliation of all the CCA claims made for the class will be made to reflect the actual increase or decrease in value of the assets in that class over time. When the proceeds of disposition of the last asset are subtracted from the class's UCC, you may have a positive or a negative result.

Understanding Recapture   If the proceeds of disposition are greater than the UCC of the class, your CCA claim made over the years has exceeded the actual decrease in value of the assets in the class. Therefore, the negative UCC must be added to your business income for the year. This is known as "recapture." Recaptured CCA results in an income inclusion, in full, in the year the disposition occurs. This "tax shock" is something that can often be planned for.

Understanding a Terminal Loss   If the proceeds of disposition are less than the UCC of the class, your CCA claim was insufficient to account for the actual decrease in value of the assets in the class. In this case, the ending UCC of the class may be taken as a deduction from your business income for the year. This deduction is known as a "terminal loss." This is easier to deal with but may affect other decisions, like whether or not to take an RRSP deduction, for example.

Certain asset classes—such as class 10.1, passenger vehicles—have slightly different rules. More on this below and in Chapter 6.

Patents and Licences

Innovators have some interesting rules to contend with in writing off their patents and licences. These are usually written off on a straight-line basis over the life of the patent or licence in Class 14. That is, if you paid $15,000 for a patent for a period of 15 years, the depreciation would be $1,000 a year. If the patent or licences have an unlimited life, they are classed as "eligible capital property." Three-quarters of the costs may be written off on a 7% declining balance. For all patents and rights to use patented information acquired after April 26, 1993, a CCA Class 44 is available with a 25% declining-balance rate. The taxpayer and his/her tax practitioner have some options with regards to claiming these rights, so detailed discussion in advance of the transaction is well advised.

Separate Classes for Certain Autos

Automobiles are generally classified in Class 10 at a CCA rate of 30%. "Motor vehicles" and like assets are pooled together in this class. An exception to the pooling rule applies to autos classified to be luxury or "passenger vehicles." Each such vehicle used for business purposes is placed into its own Class 10.1, which also features a CCA rate of 30%. However, there are deductibility restrictions on CCA, interest and lease costs. For example, since January 1, 2001, the maximum capital cost has been $30,000 plus taxes. This means that if you buy a $50,000 luxury or passenger vehicle, you can take a CCA deduction based only on a value of $30,000 plus taxes. The half-year rule also applies on acquisition of the vehicle *and in the year of disposition*. More on this in Chapter 6.

Separate Classes for Certain Buildings

Pooling is not allowed in cases where a taxpayer owns a number of rental properties, each with a capital cost of $50,000 or more. In such cases, each building is listed in a separate class (usually Class 1 at 4%). Where the taxpayer owns a condominium or row-housing structure, the aggregate cost of all the units in a building will become one class for each group of structures that costs $50,000 or more.

Land

Land is not a depreciable asset, so it cannot be scheduled for CCA purposes. That means the value of land must be removed from the purchase price in real estate transactions. Be sure to dig out your property tax assessment for this purpose or be prepared to produce other reasonable valuation. Also be aware there are special rules on accounting for the sale of land and buildings to ensure valuations are not weighted in favor of more advantageous terminal-loss write-offs.

Accounting for the GST/HST

A business registered to collect the GST/HST can apply to receive an "input tax credit" for the amount of GST/HST paid on capital assets in certain circumstances. This could have an impact on the "cost of additions." For example, assets classified as "Capital Personal Properties" for GST/HST purposes (those used 51% or more for business) qualify for a full input tax credit of GST/HST paid. Once received, such an input tax credit must *reduce* the capital cost of the asset used for capital cost allowance purposes. Therefore, it is important to keep track of ITCs received specifically for capital assets.

While your tax practitioner will likely do the calculations for you, you should understand the implications on your tax returns for decision-making purposes.

Streamlined Accounting Methods   Small businesses that do not track GST paid or received may use the "Quick Method" or "Special Quick Method" of remitting GST/HST amounts. Discuss the advantages and disadvantages of each method with your advisors.

TAX ADVISOR

It is very important for small business owners to plan asset acquisitions and dispositions carefully. Set up a tracking system, as shown in Figure 5.1, for your tax records. Note the important figures: your CCA deduction and the undepreciated capital cost (UCC). This UCC figure is what you'll base next year's CCA deduction on. It will be increased by any future additions or improvements and decreased by future dispositions.

Planning Opportunities Using the CCA Claim

One of the most important concepts to remember is that *CCA is always claimed at the taxpayer's option.* This allows you to tax cost average over time to get the best after-tax return for your money. Ask your tax advisor about options for making a CCA claim in the following circumstances:

- In year of acquisition
- In year of disposition
- When an asset appreciates in value
- When an asset depreciates more than the prescribed rate
- When business income is very low
- When net income is anticipated to be much higher next year
- When it is your goal to increase RRSP contributions
- When it is your goal to decrease CPP contributions

Buy vs. Lease

Prepare a Tax Savings Blueprint—"what if" scenarios—that gives you exact dollar outcomes to determine whether there are any tax benefits of buying an asset versus leasing it. There are two points to consider:

Your Marginal Tax Rate   Not only do you need to know that your income will support the leasing payments or interest costs, but you'll need to know the true dollar value of the deduction. Here's an example (Figure 5.2) using the acquisition of a motor vehicle with a marginal tax rate of 26%, assuming 100% business use.

Figure 5.2	Tax Cost Analysis: Motor Vehicles			

How?	Tax Provision	Write-off in Yr. 1	Write-off in Yr. 2	Dollar Value of Tax Write-off @ 26% MTR
Buy	CCA on auto total cost of $25,000*	$3,750	$6,375	Yr. 1 = $ 975; Yr. 2 = $1,658
	Interest on car loan @ 6%	$1,500	$1,350	Yr. 1 = $ 390; Yr. 2 = $ 351
Lease	Monthly leasing costs ($500)	$6,000	$6,000	Each year $1,560

* Year 1: 30% × $25,000 = $7,500/ $3,750. Year 2: UCC is $21,250 × 30% = $6,375

If this taxpayer took out a loan to buy the car, his tax write-offs in year one would amount to $3,750 + $1,500 = $5,250, and the real dollar value of those write-offs would be $975 + $390 = $1,365. Leasing the vehicle would bring a real dollar savings of $1,560. By leasing instead of buying, then, the taxpayer gets a benefit in the amount of $195 in Year 1.

In Year 2, there is no "half-year rule" on the asset acquisition. Therefore the real dollar value of the tax write-offs for CCA and interest is $2,009 for the purchase of the car versus $1,560 for leasing, so the CCA/interest claim is better.

One must also take into account, however, the cost and cash flow available under each option and your annual marginal tax rate. Have your tax advisor prepare a chart that looks like the one in Figure 5.3 to help you make the decision.

Which option makes the most sense for you?

Your Balance Sheet   Take into account the effect of asset acquisition methods on your balance sheet and the overall fiscal health of your business. Will a lender, for example, finance your leasing costs with an

Figure 5.3	Before- and After-Tax Earnings Chart

	Year 1	Year 2
Cash to be generated to pay for the car bought with a car loan:		
Interest amounts	$_____	$_____
Principal amounts	$_____	$_____
Total	$_____	$_____
Cash to be generated to pay for the leased car	$_____	$_____
Before-tax earnings required	$_____	$_____
After-tax earnings required	$_____	$_____

operating line? Or is it easier for the lender to provide you with a loan for a specific asset purchase? This will have a bearing on your decision-making as well as the tax implications.

RECAP. YOU NEED TO KNOW:

1. When to buy your capital assets to get the best "tax bang" for your buck

2. When to make adjustments for errors or omissions on your CCA claims

3. How to write off small tools and other equipment with costs under $500

4. When to capitalize repairs and maintenance, and when to expense the costs

5. What CCA rate will be applied to your asset acquisitions

6. When the half-year rule will be applied, and when it won't

7. What happens to your CCA deduction when you have a short fiscal year

8. When to expense and when to capitalize interest costs on loans for acquiring assets

9. How to account for any personal use component of assets

10. Special rules for writing off your computer and communication device costs

11. Why certain vehicles and buildings are reported in a special CCA class

12. How to account for the cost of land and building

13. Whether it's better to lease or buy your assets

14. How a Tax Savings Blueprint can help you assess your tax efficiencies—and deficiencies

YOU NEED TO ASK: Your tax advisor for help in making the right decisions in acquiring and disposing of capital assets by:

1. **Promptly reviewing Notices of Assessment or Reassessment from CRA:** Changes you wish to make to your claims for CCA have a time limit: adjustments can be made only within 90 days of receipt of the Notice of Assessment or Reassessment.

2. **Bringing details of your asset acquisitions and dispositions to your tax advisor each and every year**: This includes deemed acquisitions and dispositions.

3. **Properly classifying assets purchased:** 100% write-offs are generally not allowed on the purchase or improvement of assets with a useful life of more than one year. However, there can be exceptions, such as the temporary 100% CCA rate for computer equipment introduced in the Federal Budget of 2009. Discuss these rules with your tax advisor before you make your asset purchases.

4. **Scheduling the cost of improvements to assets:** Restoration of an asset to its original condition is expensed on your tax return (100% deductible). The cost of improving the useful life of the asset is generally capitalized (subject to CCA deduction). Take this into account when planning your cash flow.

5. **Classifying your assets correctly:** Make sure you know the CCA rate that will be applied to the new asset you are thinking of purchasing and whether there is an exception for the half-year rule. Why? If you are interested in a "no-surprises approach" to your business, you need to know your after-tax results *before* you buy.

6. **Prorating your CCA claim in the first year of business:** CCA rates and the half-year rule apply to businesses that are in existence for a full fiscal year. This means that a business that started mid-way through a fiscal year must prorate the calculated CCA claim by the number of days the business was operating.

7. **Capitalizing interest costs if your business is losing money:** This is a great way to preserve the costs for use in the future when income may be higher, thereby tax cost averaging.

8. **Disposing of all the assets of a class with tax efficiency:** Recapture will increase your net profits for tax purposes; terminal losses will decrease them. Do some planning to ensure ideal tax timing of dispositions, if this makes sense otherwise (i.e., if the buyer is co-operative).

9. **Updating for tax incentives:** The government often provides tax incentives for those who invest in new business assets. Review the latest interpretations of recent federal and provincial budget provisions with your tax advisor before purchasing new assets or consult *EverGreen Explanatory Notes*, available from www.knowledge bureau.com.

10. **Carefully tracking GST/HST paid:** If you are a GST/HST registrant, you'll be able to claim the cost of your taxes paid on an asset against your GST/HST remittances. This can give your after-tax cash flow an important boost.

11. **Prorating your maximum CCA deduction for any personal use of an asset.**

12. **Preparing a tax and cash-flow comparison of the costs before you make the decision to buy or lease an asset:** This is your Tax Savings Blueprint!

CHAPTER 6

Maximize Home Office and Auto Expense Benefits

"The person who makes no mistakes does not usually make anything."
WILLIAM CONNOR MAGEE

KEY CONCEPTS

- Common costs like operating your auto and home office may be tax deductible
- In each case, allocation must be made for any personal use component
- To satisfy a tax auditor, auto distance logs are required for a representative period
- Auto expenses break down into "fixed" and "operating" costs
- Autos are either "motor vehicles" or "passenger vehicles" for CCA purposes
- Home workspaces must be exclusively set aside and their size recorded
- A home workspace must be used as your principal place of business or regularly to see your customers
- Home workspace costs cannot be used to increase or create a business loss

REAL LIFE: Tom, a high school teacher, taught art and woodworking during the day and built beautiful furniture in his spare time. Over the years, as he perfected his craft, people would marvel at the eye-catching pieces in his home and beg him to consider designing and crafting something special for them too. Tom's hobby quickly flourished into a business with a potential for profit. In fact, he had visions of opening a furniture store one day, specializing in California-style pieces.

THE PROBLEM

At tax-filing time, Tom wondered about the $3,500 he had received for making a piece of furniture for his neighbours, the Smiths. Should he report the income? If so, are there expenses he can claim to offset his income? For example, can he claim the costs of setting up his workshop, his tools and the varnish he uses to finish the furniture? What about the trips back and forth to pick up supplies—are they deductible?

THE SOLUTION

As you know from prior chapters, tax deductions are legitimized by virtue of the fact that they are (1) reasonable and (2) incurred in a commercial activity that has a reasonable expectation of profit. In Tom's case, we need to first assure ourselves that his enterprise is not a hobby. According to CRA's IT-334:

> "In order for any activity or pursuit to be regarded as a source of income, there must be a reasonable expectation of profit.
> Where such an expectation does not exist (as is the case with most hobbies), neither amounts received nor expenses incurred are included in the income computation for tax purposes and any excess of expenses over receipts is a personal or living expense, the deduction of which is denied . . .
> On the other hand, if the hobby or pastime results in receipts of revenue in excess of expenses, that fact is a strong indication that the hobby is a venture with an expectation of profit."

Tom therefore begins by computing whether there is indeed an excess of income over expenses. Gathering receipts for operating expenses such as the varnish, paint, paint remover, brushes, etc. is easy. However, claiming his auto expenses and his home office expenses is trickier. Tom needs to know how to legitimize those real costs of doing business.

THE PARAMETERS

The specific deductions that any business may take should be made in the following order:

- Costs of goods sold
- Operating expenses
- Auto expenses

- Capital Cost Allowance
- Home office expenses

Home office or workspace expenses are claimed last, and there is a good reason for this, but first, a quick review. Cost of goods sold reduces gross profits on the Form T2125, *Statement of Business or Professional Activities*, to account for purchases of goods that will be resold. You studied that form and its various sections in detail, so you may recall that other operating expenses come next, things that are "used up" in the business: advertising, supplies, rent, salaries and so on. These amounts are 100% deductible and can be used to offset other income if the operating expenses exceed revenues for the year. You'll notice that auto expenses are claimed within that category. However, Capital Cost Allowance (CCA) is next, including CCA for auto expenses, which is claimed at the taxpayer's option depending on the results desired in the current year.

Therefore, in the case of a vehicle, a separate worksheet must first be prepared to separate out various categories of expenses you'll claim. See Figures 6.1, 6.2, 6.3 and 6.4 to compute "fixed" and "operating costs" based on the business use of the vehicle. Once these items are computed, the business owner and tax practitioner can decide whether to claim the deduction for CCA based on whether or not an operating loss already exists.

Next, take a close look at CCA available on other assets. Should the deductions be taken? It is possible that the owner may wish to create a larger tax loss if other income sources of the year, such as pension or interest income, are high, or if the owner wants to carry excess losses back to any of the prior three taxation years—a way to recover previously paid taxes. Alternately, the owner may wish to save the CCA deduction for a future date when income is higher.

Finally comes home workspace expenses. There is an important rule that accounts for their position at the end of the process: *you may not increase or create an operating loss by taking a deduction for home workspace expenses.*

TAX ADVISOR

There are special requirements when claiming common business expenses like the costs of running your car and maintaining a home workspace. It is most important that they are observed, as the deductions are both lucrative and frequently audited.

Automobile Expenses

Almost every small business owner claims auto expenses against the revenues of the business. However, this line is also the subject of more failures than any other in tax audits. The main tax-filing traps are ones taxpayers must assume responsibility for. They fail to keep receipts and a record of their travels.

Managing Your Auto Log

Be prepared to show the auditor how many kilometres were driven during a "representative" period of time in your fiscal year for both personal and business purposes. Most taxpayers have trouble keeping this log (see Figure 6.1), yet it's mandatory, and not keeping one will cause your claims to be reduced or disallowed completely. The rules for keeping the log have recently been relaxed. In the past, those claiming auto expenses were required to keep a log for the entire 12 months of their business year. Now you will likely want to choose a representative period that is your busiest time of the year. The CRA's new administrative policies do not specify an exact number of required logging days, but the time chosen should be a reasonable indictor of your driving routine for business and personal purposes. (If you keep a full year report, you can of course choose that representative deductible period more wisely.)

It's a good idea to record your business kilometres in your Daily Business Journal. Before you leave your home office, make sure you record your odometer reading. Then make a point of charting your business driving throughout the day. Often that means that the full day of driving is technically deductible.

What are not deductible are the distances you drive to pick up milk on the way home. That's personal driving, as is driving to and from work, unless, of course, you see a client on the way or the post office where you pick up your business mail is in the grocery store in which you buy the milk.

So it's important to isolate the personal portions of any of your driving in order to give the auditor an accurate picture of the business use of your auto.

Also allowed is a reasonable estimation of coin car washes and coin telephone calls (airports, bus terminals, hospitals, etc). When taxpayers fail to log these actual amounts, they usually end up underestimating their expenses.

Figure 6.1	Auto Log Summary

Month	Km Bus.	Km Pers.	Km Total	Gas	M & R	Park	Wash	Ins.	Int.	Other: (Explain)	$
Jan											
Feb											
Mar											
Apr											
May											
Jun											
Jul											
Aug											
Sep											
Oct											
Nov											
Dec											
Total											

REAL LIFE: Assume Guam, who is a self-employed hairdresser, drove 15,000 km this year for business purposes out of 20,000 km driven in total. His total expenses for the car were $7,500. Using the following formula, Guam would compute the tax-deductible portion of his expenses:

$$\frac{\text{Total Business Kilometres}}{\text{Total Kilometres Driven in Year}} \times \text{Total Expenses} = \text{Deductible Expenses}$$

$$\frac{15,000}{20,000} \times \$7,500 = \$5,625$$

The deductible amount is therefore $5,625.

Figure 6.2	Motor Vehicle Expenses, from CRA Worksheet

Chart A – Motor vehicle expenses

Enter the kilometres you drove in the tax year to earn business income	1
Enter the total kilometres you drove in the tax year	2
Fuel and oil	3
Interest (see Chart B below)	4
Insurance	5
Licence and registration	6
Maintenance and repairs	7
Leasing (see Chart C below)	8
Other expenses (please specify)	9
	10
Total motor vehicle expenses: Add lines 3 to 10	11

Business use part: $\left(\dfrac{\text{line 1 :}}{\text{line 2 :}} \right) \times$ line 11 : _____ = \$_____   12

Business parking fees	13
Supplementary business insurance	14
Add lines 12, 13, and 14	15

Allowable motor vehicle expenses: Enter the amount from line 15 on line 9281 in Part 5 on page 2.

Note: You can claim CCA on motor vehicles in Area A on page 4.

Chart B – Available interest expense for passenger vehicles

Total interest payable (accrual method) or paid (cash method) in the fiscal period	A
_____ $\times$ the number of days in the fiscal period for which interest was payable (accrual method) or paid (cash method)	B
$10*	

Available interest expense: amount A or B, whichever is less (enter this amount on line 4 of Chart A above)   \$_____

* For passenger vehicles bought from 2001 to 2008.

Chart C – Eligible leasing costs for passenger vehicles

Total lease charges incurred in your 2008 fiscal period for the vehicle	1
Total lease payments deducted before your 2008 fiscal period for the vehicle	2
Total number of days the vehicle was leased in your 2008 and previous fiscal periods	3
Manufacturer's list price	4

The amount on line 4 or ($35,294 + GST* and PST, or HST on $35,294), whichever is more

\$ _____ $\times$ 85% = ...   5

$\dfrac{[(\$800 + \text{GST}^* \text{ and PST, or HST on } \$800) \times \text{line 3}]}{30}$ ▶ _____ − line 2: _____ . . . . = _____   6

$\dfrac{[(\$30,000 + \text{GST}^* \text{ and PST, or HST on } \$30,000) \times \text{line 1}]}{\text{line 5}}$ . . . . = _____   7

Eligible leasing cost: line 6 or 7, whichever is less . . . .   \$_____

(Enter this amount on line 8 of Chart A above.)

* Use a GST rate of 5% or HST rate of 13% **after** December 31, 2007.
 Use a GST rate of 6% or HST rate of 14% from July 1, 2006 to December 31, 2007.

Your actual yearly vehicle expenditures are classified into two groups:

Operating Expenses

- Gas and oil
- Maintenance and repairs
- Tire purchases
- Insurance and licence fees
- Auto club premiums
- Car washes

Fixed Expenses

- Interest costs
- Leasing costs
- Capital cost allowances

The operating expenses are straightforward: keep the receipts, total them and claim a portion of the expenses based on your business use percentage, which you will calculate using your travel log.

The fixed expenses are subject to the proration as well; however, they are separated because there have been certain restrictions attached to them over the past several years. A significant development in tax law occurred on June 17, 1987. That was the day the Finance Minister announced the concept of "passenger vehicles." A passenger vehicle, in tax jargon, is also considered to be a "luxury vehicle." Tax write-offs for the fixed costs of passenger vehicles are limited to certain ceiling levels, a history of which is outlined in Figure 6.3.

If you buy a new car for $40,000 plus taxes, for example, your capital cost would be limited to a total of $30,000 plus federal and provincial sales taxes. If you leased a vehicle for, say, $900 a month, the most you could write off for tax purposes would be $800 a month plus federal and

Figure 6.3	Maximum Deductible Costs of Passenger Vehicle*		
Date	**Interest Costs**	**Leasing Costs**	**CCA**
After June 17, 1987 and before Sept. 1, 1989	$8.33 a day	$600 a month	$20,000
After Aug. 31, 1989 and before 1997	$10.00 a day	$650 a month plus taxes	$24,000 plus taxes
Jan. 1 to Dec. 31, 1997	$8.33 a day	$550 a month plus taxes	$25,000 plus taxes
Jan. 1, 1998 to Dec. 31, 1999	$8.33 a day	$650 a month plus taxes	$26,000 plus taxes
Jan. 1 to Dec. 31, 2000	$8.33 a day	$700 a month plus taxes	$27,000 plus taxes
Jan. 1 to Dec. 31, 2009	$10.00 a day	$800 a month plus taxes	$30,000 plus taxes

* Go to www.knowledgebureau.com for up-to-date information on maximum deduction ceilings for passenger vehicles.

provincial taxes. And if you paid the bank an interest charge on the auto loan, your maximum interest expense deduction would be limited to $10 a day or about $300 a month. Take these restrictions into account before making your buying decisions.

In fact, you might ask yourself if paying $40,000 for a car is really worth it since *it's not deductible!* To take that thought one step further: does it make sense to buy a new car at all? If, for example, a new car costs $40,000, but the same model, two years old, costs $25,000, what's the better decision? From a tax viewpoint, the used car makes more sense (but ask them to throw in a bumper-to-bumper three year warranty!).

If your car is not classified as a "passenger vehicle," it will be called a "motor vehicle" for tax purposes. That means the car is not subject to the passenger vehicle restrictions. A third category is the motor vehicle-automobile. In this sub-category, the value of the vehicle may exceed the passenger vehicle cost limits but have an allowable "use factor." For example, you can avoid the "passenger vehicle" restrictions with:

- A pick-up truck that seats one to three people used more than 50% of the time to transport goods or equipment
- A pick-up truck, sport utility or other van that seats four to nine people used 90% of the time or more to transport goods, equipment or passengers
- A farm truck used primarily (more than 50% of the time) to transport goods or equipment, or more than 90% of the time to transfer goods, equipment or people for the purposes of earning income
- A clearly marked police or fire response vehicle

Claiming Capital Cost Allowances (CCA) The CCA classification used for either a motor vehicle or a motor vehicle-automobile is Class 10, featuring a rate of 30%. You may have many different vehicles in this class provided each falls under the restricted value defined above. Acquisitions increase the value of the CCA pool, dispositions decrease the pool, and only when all the assets of the class are disposed of are there recapture or terminal loss consequences. See Chapter 5 for explanations of these terms.

A passenger vehicle is classified in Class 10.1, which also has a CCA rate of 30%. However, all Class 10.1 assets must be listed separately, rather than pooled together in one class. In the year of acquisition, the normal "half-year rules" apply to both Class 10 and Class 10.1. That is, only 50% of the normal capital cost allowance is claimed in the year of acquisition.

As mentioned earlier, a CCA deduction is always claimed at your option, so if your other business expenses are already high enough to reduce income to the desired level, you can choose to "save" the higher undepreciated capital cost to another year.

Dispositions   Keep in mind two more points regarding passenger vehicles:

- There is a "half-year rule on disposition" of a passenger vehicle. That is, you will be able to claim 50% of the capital cost allowance that would normally be allowed if you owned the vehicle at the end of the year.
- Terminal loss is not deductible and recapture is not reportable on Class 10.1 vehicles. This means you should keep a close eye on the value of your luxury vehicle and consider whether it makes sense to trade it in if the value drops too far below your allowable depreciated value.

In the case of Class 10 vehicles, there is no half-year rule on disposition of all the vehicles in the class. That is, the normal terminal loss and recapture rules apply to the self-employed. This is not the case for employees who write off the cost of their vehicles. These taxpayers may not claim a deduction for terminal loss when they dispose of their Class 10 assets.

More Than One Vehicle   Things can get somewhat complicated if you use more than one vehicle in the business. For example, let's say you own a florist business and have a delivery van, but you also use your personal vehicle to give quotes and make supply runs. In that case, the costs of the van would not normally be subject to prorations or restrictions, assuming it is used full-time for delivery of flowers. Use of the personal vehicle would obviously have a business component, which could be deductible if you kept distance records.

In fact, if you use your spouse's car occasionally for business affairs, keep track of the distance driven. Use those distance points to reduce your overall expenses. To be completely accurate, you can keep separate distance logs for each vehicle. This would enable you to claim a portion of annual costs, such as insurance, on both vehicles, as long as you don't claim more than one full claim on each vehicle.

Figure 6.4 shows what a typical auto expense worksheet looks like for filing purposes, with information taken from the distance log and saved receipts.

Figure 6.4	Worksheet for Deductible Auto Expenses

Distance Log:

Total kilometres driven to earn income	15,896
Total kilometres driven in the year	22,554

Operating Expenses

Gas and Oil	$1,527.00
Repairs/Maintenance	2,456.00
New Tires	1,298.00
Car Washes	150.00
Motor League Auto Club	65.25
Total	$5,496.25

Fixed Costs

Insurance	$1,250.00
License	48.00
Interest	752.00
CCA from schedule	4,700.00*
Total	$6,750.00

Total Auto Expenses

	Operating Expenses	$5,496.25
	Fixed Costs	6,750.00
	Total	$12,246.25

* This can be claimed in any amount up to $4700 at your option.

Personal Use Component	(3,615.13)
Deductible Auto Expenses	$ 8,631.12

Home Workspace Expenses

It is relatively easy to make the claim for home workspace expenses on the tax return. Whether you have a workshop in which you build furniture or a showroom for your Christmas wreathes and candles, keep your receipts for all utilities, mortgage interest, property taxes, insurance, maintenance and repairs for the whole home. Then prorate these costs by the fraction you obtain using the following equation:

$$\frac{\text{Square footage of home workspace}}{\text{Square footage of entire living area}} \times \frac{\text{Total Expenditures}}{\text{Allowed}} = \frac{\text{Deductible}}{\text{Portion}}$$

When computing the entire living area of the home, it is common practice to exclude bathrooms and closets. When allocating areas for a home with an unfinished or partially finished basement, include only the square footage of the areas that constitute "living area." That would usually include the area in which the wash is done but not unfinished areas or storage space.

If part of the home is used for the storage of business items, such as lumber for a carpentry business or boxes of goods for resale, this area would be added both to the home workspace area and to the entire square footage of the home. If a garage is used as a workshop, the square footage of the garage would be added to both the numerator and the denominator, and so on.

Total expenditures can include:

- Heating costs
- Electricity
- Insurance
- Maintenance

- Mortgage interest
- Property taxes
- Cleaning costs

These items are totalled for the year and then prorated according to the home workspace ratio. See Figure 6.5 for an example.

You need to know three more things to claim home workspace costs properly:

1. **You may claim home workspace expenses only if the space is used as follows:**

   - Exclusively to earn business income on a regular and continuous basis and for meeting clients, customers or patients, or
   - As the principal place of business of the individual

   To clarify, under the first criterion, one or more rooms are set aside solely or exclusively for income-producing purposes. This means the workspace can't be your living room or a desk in your bedroom unless you have a specifically defined, partitioned-off area.

Figure 6.5	Worksheet for Deductible Home Workspace Expenses

Home workspace ratio:

Home workspace area	250 sq. ft.
Living area of the home	2,400 sq. ft.

Operating Expenses:	Heating costs	$ 1,632
	Electricity	1,245
	Insurance	895
	Maintenance	1,496
	Mortgage interest	8,479
	Property taxes	4,532
	Total	$18,279

Calculation of Allowable Claim:

Total	$18,279	
Less personal portion	16,375	(2,150/2,400 × $18,279)
Allowable Claim	$ 1,904	

Furthermore, the space must be used to regularly meet customers at some level of frequency, which will be determined according to the type of business and individual facts of each taxpayer upon audit. Therefore, it is most important to keep a log of appointments to justify these claims.

For example, a chiropractor who has an office downtown where she sees patients as well as one at home would have to justify the home workspace claim by showing that clients regularly visited the home office for treatment. This is best done with a home workspace appointment log.

Another businessperson, a self-employed editor, for example, would not normally see clients in her home but would still be entitled to make a claim if the home workspace is her primary place of business.

Meeting this second criterion can be more difficult for some. For example, a plumber may make a legitimate claim for home workspace expenses despite the fact that he usually works away from home. Such a claim will be allowed if there is no other principal place of business to keep books, take appointments, prepare quotations and so on.

2. **You do not use the claim to increase or create an operating loss in the business:**

Example 1:	Operating profit before home workspace =	$3,500
	Home workspace expenses	$2,000
	Net profit	$1,500

This claim is OK as a loss is neither created nor increased.

Example 2:	Operating profit before home workspace =	$1,000
	Home workspace expenses	$2,000
	Net profit	($1,000)

This claim is not OK as a loss was created using home workspace expenses. The claim must be adjusted as follows:

	Operating profit before home workspace =	$1,000
	Allowable Claim for home workspace	$1,000 only
	Adjusted net profit	Nil
	Carry-forward of home workspace expenses	$1,000

The carry-forward amount can be used to offset business income next year, so be sure to review your tax records and use it up.

3. **You can and should audit-proof your home workspace claim:** Sketch out the office area and its relationship to the living area in the rest of the house. Keep this sketch in your tax files in case of a tax audit, to be used to justify the percentage of tax deductible expenditures that you have claimed. In all cases, expenses claimed as deductions must be reasonable.

RECAP. YOU NEED TO KNOW:

1. When a hobby becomes a business, so that home workspace and a portion of auto costs can be claimed on the tax return

2. Why it is important to claim operating expenses before making a CCA claim

3. How to keep a proper auto distance log for tax purposes

4. Which trips are deductible and which trips are considered personal in nature

5. How to track unreceipted costs like coin parking and car washes

6. Why your vehicle's fixed and operating costs are separated for tax purposes

7. The difference between a motor vehicle, automobile and passenger vehicle for tax purposes

8. How tax deductions differ for Class 10.1 assets on acquisition and disposition

9. How to claim expenses when you and your spouse have joint use of the car

10. The restrictions surrounding home workspace expense deductibility

YOU NEED TO ASK: Your tax advisor to help you compute car and home workspace claims to your best advantage by:

1. **Preparing a preliminary business statement:** If a profit motive is found to exist—i.e., income has the potential to exceed expenses—your hobby could very well constitute a viable business income source against which you can claim a series of deductions.

2. **Knowing how to order your deductions**: On your preliminary business statement for tax purposes, first claim cost of goods sold, then operating expenses, auto expenses, other capital cost allowances and finally home office expenses. Make claims in this order because CCA is claimed at your option, and home office expenses cannot be used to create or increase a loss. Once you know your net income level, you may wish to reduce your CCA deduction to use up your home workspace deduction first, particularly if you suspect you may be subject to recapture on your CCA claims in the future, or you may wish to carry both balances forward.

3. **Keeping an auto log:** It's mandatory for a tax audit, at least for a representative period of time.

4. **Keeping a log of cash expenditures for your car:** This includes coin car washes and parking meters. CRA allows a reasonable estimate, but a log will likely produce higher claims.

5. **Knowing your auto expense restrictions:** Fixed expenses like interest costs, leasing costs and capital cost allowances on your vehicle will be subject to restrictions if you exceed certain value limits. Check these out before making the decision to buy or lease.

6. **Sketching out your home office:** Make sure you can justify your home office claims by drawing a sketch of the office and how it relates in size to the rest of the living area of the home.

7. **Keeping an appointment log for your home office:** This is particularly important if you also have an office downtown, for example. You must use the home workspace either as the principal place of business or exclusively to earn business income on a regular and continuous basis for meeting clients, customers or patients.

8. **Remembering never to use home office claims to increase or create an operating loss:** They will be disallowed, and you may forget to claim the carry-forward of these expenses to income in future years.

CHAPTER 7

Profiles of the Self-Employed

"I do the very best I know how—the very best I can—and I mean to keep on doing so until the end."
ABRAHAM LINCOLN

KEY CONCEPTS

- Industry profiling is used by CRA to detect commonalities in small business reporting, for audit purposes
- Profile-specific tax provisions can help you maximize your filing options
- Members of partnerships face unique filing consequences on their personal returns, and special rules must be observed by those who are also spouses
- Artists and writers have unique time-specific tax consequences
- Child care providers can claim more of home and food costs
- Farmers benefit from unique averaging provisions
- RRSPs and spousal RRSP contributions can help with income splitting in retirement for self-employed couples
- Examining the latest tax proposals in the context of annual business planning is important

REAL LIFE: Marcie runs a babysitting enterprise out of her home. Her husband, Jim, is a full-time farmer. Both use their cars for business purposes, such as picking up supplies and meeting prospective clients. Between the two of them, keeping up with changing tax rules has been a challenge.

Marcie is a multi-faceted individual who helps out where she can. Daily she works in Jim's business as the bookkeeper, where she is paid a salary as an employee. She is also an accomplished singer/songwriter who specializes in writing children's songs. That's where her heart is. One of her pieces is being reviewed by a major record company and a television network.

Jim's start-up years were very lean. He is carrying forward unused losses of $38,000. This year was a banner year; unfortunately, world market activities have reduced pricing to such an extent that Jim is worried he won't be able to meet his commitments. He is now contemplating a partnership with a neighbour and/or the possibility of selling the farmland, which is extremely valuable, just to make ends meet.

THE PROBLEM

This couple already has an interesting tax situation, and with change on the horizon, a few more tax twists may be coming their way. Marcie is an employee but also runs two businesses of her own. Jim needs to maximize his tax write-offs now and in the future to pull out of his farming enterprise with the greatest success. They both need to keep an eye on securing their retirement, because the reality for the self-employed is that the responsibility for self-sufficiency now and later rests with you.

THE SOLUTION

Marcie and Jim should get advice from a qualified tax professional, who can look not only at the current year's after-tax results but also at the use of their tax filing "carry-over periods" to manage financial risk, secure retirement income, and pass along an estate to their children. In assessing future business decisions with the goal of building sustainable wealth, it is important for Marcie and Jim to know special tax rules for both the earning of profits and the appreciation of equity in their unique enterprises.

THE PARAMETERS

Many taxpayers are unaware that CRA's audit activities involve projects that test compliance for different groups of tax filers. This "profile approach" highlights differences in filing patterns for similar enterprises and targets areas where income appears under-reported or expenses overstated. CRA therefore requires you to identify your "industry code" right on your business statement. These codes are broken down into professions, services, sales, wholesales, construction, manufacturing and natural resource industries.

It's important that you and your advisor identify the taxpayer profile you and your business fit into and discuss what basic and industry-specific reporting rules you'll be required to follow based on special provisions outlined in the Income Tax Act; the latest federal and provincial budget proposals; and CRA's guides, forms and Interpretation Bulletins or Information Circulars for income tax and GST/HST filing purposes.

Your goal is to maximize your professional fees by understanding what questions you should be asking before you make financial decisions.

Next, it is important to flesh out your tax-filing profile with the circumstances specific to the way you run your business. For example, a self-employed editor would spend more on couriers or communications costs, while an in-home footcare specialist would likely claim larger amounts for auto expenses and medical supplies. Both taxpayers would likely file similar home office claims, though, and be subject to maximum fixed cost ceilings on their automobile values.

Both taxpayers would also want to overview their current tax-filing obligations in order to properly assess their RRSP contribution limits; life and disability insurance requirements; and other investment opportunities, like funding the new Tax-Free Savings Account.

They should discuss opportunities to split income in retirement by making spousal RRSP contributions or, in some cases, through the establishment of a Registered Pension Plan (RPP), a Retirement Compensation Arrangement (RCA) or an Individual Pension Plan (IPP) within a corporate environment.

Because entrepreneurs must be visionary and forward-looking in planning for their next income sources, delivering profits and retaining earnings for future investment purposes, it is a natural process for them to budget, forecast and carefully anticipate changes within their ventures. The self-employed taxpayer is in an excellent position to strategically explore and define plans for future retirement and investment income as a regular part of business planning. To gather the right information to do so, ask intelligent questions of professional advisors about recent tax changes that may apply to you. Then, present business budgets and cash flows in a logical, orderly way so that the advisor can do a better job for you quicker. When you both have a glimpse into your future planning, more tax savings opportunities arise.

This may seem like an over-extension of the tax filing process, but *it's an important one that will help you help yourself to better advice, and get more for your professional expenditures, too.*

Following is an overview of five different tax-filing profiles for unincorporated businesses: the sole owner shop, the business partnership, the self-employed artist/writer, the self-employed babysitter and the farming proprietorship. You will notice that each is subject to tax rules that are specific to the nature of the business. In addition, you'll see certain similarities in structuring the presentation of financial information that will "put it all together" for you in a framework in which you can easily ask questions and make decisions. This framework consists of:

- Methods of reporting income
- Deduction of operating expenses
- Computation of Capital Cost Allowances (CCAs)
- Computation of auto expenses
- Computation of home workspace costs
- Personal use allocation

Also check out Figure 7.1 for an example of this framework and tips about reporting various expenses that are tax deductible.

Sole Proprietorship

The buck stops here, and so does all responsibility for business performance and costs. To avoid late-filing penalties, unincorporated small business owners file personal tax returns (T1's) to report their business income before June 16 every year. That's right: the usual April 30 filing deadline is extended for the owners of proprietorships and their spouses, although it is not recommended that you wait until June 15 to file your tax returns, because if you owe money, *interest will be charged on the outstanding amount payable to CRA unless you pay it by April 30. Might as well file the return too!*

From landing the first contract to buying a new computer or hiring a first employee, small businesses have true grit—and true tax audit problems, if they don't conform to the rules. Income must be reported and deductions calculated on Form T2125, *Statement of Business or Professional Activities* (covered in Chapter 4), before subtracting home office and personal use to arrive at Net Income.

Consider the tax filing framework outlined in Figure 7.1 as you get started and remember:

- **Keep an eye on gross revenues:** If your gross revenues exceed $30,000, you'll need to register to collect and remit GST/HST in most industries. Speak to your tax advisor about the details of this obligation.
- **Time capital asset transactions carefully:** When you acquire assets with a useful life of more than one year that generally cost $500 or more, you must schedule them and claim CCA to account for depreciation for tax purposes. Also remember that consequences of disposition—terminal loss, recapture and capital gains—are all reported in the calendar year in which the transaction occurs. Timing your acquisitions and dispositions carefully allows you to "tax cost average" over time.

- **Keep an eye on tax changes:** Every federal and provincial budget and many periodic economic updates introduce new nuggets of tax "gold"—incentives for alert taxpayers and advisors. Be sure to discuss the following new changes and develop Tax Savings Blueprints ("what if" scenarios) to predict the effects of the changes on your family's after-tax results:

  – Tax brackets and most personal non-refundable tax credits are indexed to inflation every year. How much can you pay yourself and your family members on a tax-free basis every month? (This is discussed further in the next chapter.)

  – RRSP contribution maximums are rising. Is everyone in your family utilizing his/her RRSP contribution room to reduce taxes, using clawback zones to calculate refundable and non-refundable tax credits, and taking advantage of investment opportunities for any "redundant income" that can be invested in the RRSP to compound on a tax-deferred basis? Can tax savings from the RRSP then be moved into a Tax-Free Savings Account (TFSA) to earn even more, tax free?

  – Changes have been made to the taxation of dividends from large public corporations and highly profitable small business corporations. Are you aware of how to take advantage of these lower marginal tax rates on this income source? Do you understand the changes that are yet to come on the taxation of dividends? How much of your income should come from this source? How much should be received in the hands of family members?

  – Make tax adjustments on a timely basis. Correcting errors or omissions on the tax return is generally restricted to a 10-year period, a relatively recent change in the law few people are aware of. When you are on top of change—tax change, change in your business, change in your personal life—you position yourself to take advantage of every tax deduction and credit you are entitled to.

  – Other provisions have been expanded, such as CCA rules for computer write-offs and the extension of the non-capital-loss carry-forward period to 20 years.

  – The cash outlays for funding the Canada Pension Plan (CPP) increase every year as contributory earning levels change. Are you budgeted for this expenditure?

What other tax changes affect spending decisions in your proprietorship?

Figure 7.1	The Tax-Filing Framework of the Self-Employed

Transaction	Tax Tip
Income Reporting	Report income on the "accrual" basis. That is, include it in the taxation year in which it is earned. You will likely conform to a fiscal year ending December 31, unless there is a bona fide non-tax reason to have a non-calendar year end. In that case you can make a special election with CRA. In the first year of business, you could have a "short year": September 1 to December 31, for example. In that case, you'll need to prorate your deduction for capital cost allowance, and allocate expenses incurred during the time of business only (e.g., mortgage interest, property taxes and other annualized expenses).
Purchases of Goods for Resale	Keep opening inventory valuations handy, add purchases and deduct closing valuation balances to arrive at Cost of Goods Sold.
Operations	Classify all expenditures into either capital or operational groupings.
Entertainment & Meal Expenses	Mark reason for meeting, name of client on back of all receipts or on invoices. Most of these costs will be restricted to 50% deductibility.
Promotional Expenses	100% deductible. Any portion that qualifies for a charitable donation may be written off as a non-refundable tax credit or carried forward.
Communication Costs	Put assets with a useful life of more than one year into CCA classes, do not claim full costs of monthly phone rental unless you have separate business line installed. Long-distance business calls are deductible in full. The portion of air-time for cell phone, personal devices, or on-line time for internet use that relates to business income may be deducted.
Leasing, Equipment Repairs & Maintenance	All deductible in current fiscal year; year end is a good time for maintenance and repairs to reap tax rewards sooner.
Sub-Contracting	Deduct as fees 100%; ensure you can prove this is not an employer-employee relationship that should have been subject to source deductions.
Salaries, Wages, Bonuses, Vacation Pay	All deductible, as are employer's portions of CPP and EI. Make sure you make source remittances to CRA on time to avoid penalties.
Professional Fees	Fully deductible in the year incurred, except if on account of capital transactions, in which case they are deductible outlays on Schedule 3 when the capital asset is disposed of.
Home Office Set-Up	Separate it out from the rest of the house. Measure the square footage of the office and compare to the total square footage of the living area. Acquire Furniture (Class 8 @ 20% rate), Supplies (100% deductible) and Equipment (Class 8, 10 or 55). Keep all receipts for interest, utilities, etc.
Business Vehicle	Convert to business use by finding the Fair Market Value, if the vehicle was previously in use. Or, if new vehicle is acquired, determine the capital cost from the bill of sale. Start keeping a distance log. Save all receipts for operating/fixed costs.

Partnerships

A partnership involves a particular form of business organization that differs from a sole proprietorship in several ways. To begin, tax calculations are unique:

- A Statement of Business or Professional Activities is prepared for the partnership itself, as it is treated as a separate entity for personal tax purposes.
- The individual partners, who are allocated a share of the partnership income or losses, attach a copy of the partnership statements to their personal returns (again, assuming the partnership is unincorporated) and can then make an adjustment to the partnership's net income for the individual expenses of the business they each incurred outside of the partnership.
- Partnerships follow the same rules for claiming income and expenses that proprietorships do (although some professional partnerships can account differently for work in progress). However, unlike a proprietorship, a partner's interest in the partnership is itself a capital property that can be bought or sold, and the adjusted cost base of this interest must be recorded and tracked. The adjusted cost base is increased by income earned and capital contributed and decreased by losses incurred and cash draws. Because a partnership itself does not pay tax, most tax preferences—such as donations, certain resource expenditures and investment tax credits—are allocated from the partnership to the partners for claim on the partners' individual returns. Although no cash is involved, these allocations are treated as draws for tax purposes and also reduce the adjusted cost base of the partnership interest.

Partnership Assets   In general, capital cost allowance is claimed on partnership assets on the partnership's statements, so assets used should be scheduled by the partnership itself. Certain assets not owned by the partnership, such as an individual's vehicle, can be written off on each individual's income tax return. Capital gains or losses on the disposition of the partnership's assets are calculated by the partnership, and allowances are taken at the partnership level for eligible capital property. Speak to your tax professional about these rules before buying, selling or transferring assets in and out of a partnership or personally investing in assets used for partnership activities.

Adjustments for Individual Expenditures   Certain computations must be made at the *individual* rather than the partnership level:

- Charitable donations and political contributions made by the partnership must be claimed by the individual partner who made them. An adjustment is made to the adjusted cost base of the partnership interest in these cases.
- The individual partner's expenses for advertising, entertainment or expenses for the individual's auto, for example, can be used to reduce the partner's net income from the business on the personal tax return.
- Any GST/HST paid on such income-tax-deductible individual expenses qualifies for the GST/HST rebate on Line 457 of the personal tax return, provided the partnership is a GST/HST registrant.
- Interest expenses paid on money borrowed to acquire an interest in the partnership or for additional equity contributions must be deducted on a calendar-year basis; other expenses may be deducted either on a calendar year or in the fiscal period ending in a calendar year, depending on the business's fiscal year end.

Property that is transferred from an individual to the partnership may be transferred at FMV at the time of transfer, or at certain agreed upon amounts, by special election on Form T2059, *Election on Acquisition of Property by a Canadian Partnership*. However, where a transferor holds a right to acquire certain non-depreciable capital property whose tax cost is greater than its FMV, within 30 days after disposition, no loss may be recognized on the transfer. This must be deferred until the earliest of:

- A subsequent disposition of property to a person that is neither the transferor nor a person affiliated with the transferor
- A change in the property's use from income-producing to non-income-producing
- A "deemed disposition" due to a change of residence or change of taxable status

Generally speaking, if the partnership acquires the property at less than its capital cost, it is deemed to have acquired it at the capital cost. The partnership is deemed to have taken capital cost allowance equal to the difference.

Be sure you discuss with your tax advisor any transfers of assets from one business organization to another before the transfer so that you fully understand the tax consequences. This should also hold true when you enter into or leave partnership arrangements.

Partnerships Between Spouses   Where there is a bona fide partnership between spouses, the Attribution Rules* should not apply either on the business income or any subsequent capital gain. Each partner would report his or her share of the partnership income and any subsequent gain or loss on disposition of the business according to their partnership agreements.

However, CRA can and will adjust the partners' share of income, if they are not dealing at arm's length, to an amount the department deems "reasonable" under individual circumstances. This adjustment is outlined in the department's Interpretation Bulletin IT-231. Also note that income earned from funds transferred to a limited partner or a partner who is not actively engaged in the partnership will be considered income from "property" rather than business income, which would then be attributable back to the transferor.

To avoid the discretionary power of the Attribution Rules, one or all of the following conditions should be met:

- Both spouses are actively engaged in the business (time expended and expertise provided are taken into consideration).
- One spouse is actively engaged in the business, while the other invests his or her property in the business (except as discussed under limited partnerships above).
- Each spouse has invested his or her own property in the business, and the profits or losses are apportioned to these investments.

Before starting up a family business, it is a good idea to discuss with an accountant or lawyer what form of business organization the venture should take and to draw up specific agreements relating to ownership, remuneration, share of profits, etc. This will not only clarify the effect of Attribution Rules on your business but will also help you reap the highest after-tax return for your efforts. At the very least, establish firm agreements before starting.

---

* Attribution rules apply when an individual (usually the higher earner) transfers or loans property, directly or indirectly, to a spouse, common-law partner or minor child for that person's benefit. Resulting income is usually taxable to the transferor, although exceptions can apply. See further explanation in Chapter 9.

This is necessary for tax purposes and is in accordance with prudent business practice. You may wish to:

- Draw up a legal business or partnership agreement between husband and wife showing how annual profits and losses are to be split and how assets are to be shared on terminating the partnership or unincorporated business.
- Itemize which assets will be used in the business.
- Keep separate bank accounts for the business (never mix business funds with personal bank accounts).
- Keep strict and accurate records of all inventory.
- Allocate auto expenses between personal and business use.
- Keep accurate records of all income and expenses.

Finally, the leading cause of partnership dissolution is probably the inability of partners to get along. Whether you partner with your spouse, a neighbour or a colleague, it's most important to structure your entry and exit clauses in such a manner so as not to disturb the business enterprise.

Artists and Writers

Tax returns prepared for artists are also unique. The work of artists and writers may require much more time than an ordinary business to generate a profit. As a result of significant losses in court, CRA has agreed that continuous losses for many years alone are not sufficient to establish the absence of a reasonable expectation of profit in such ventures. Therefore, artists have recently enjoyed the application of losses against other income with more confidence at tax filing time.

In fact, a broader application of the tests for profit motive has been established to give direction not only to artists and writers but to other small businesses that need more time to establish profitability. Many of these creative entrepreneurs must also work at other jobs to finance their investment in their businesses in the meantime. CRA has recognized that other factors must be considered before ruling that the venture is a "hobby" or "sideline" only. Relevant factors include:

- The time devoted to the activity
- The extent to which the taxpayer has exhibited his/her work both in group and private exhibitions or the extent and nature of works published

- The extent to which the taxpayer is represented by private art galleries or art dealers or by publishers or the degree to which bona fide efforts have been made to have works published
- Planned or intended course of action, including recent sales of significance, plans for exhibitions, efforts to increase representation by galleries and dealers, recent commissions for work, work in progress, anticipated revenue for royalties and sale of book rights for movies, TV, etc., and receipt of government grants
- The taxpayer's efforts to promote the sale of his/her works
- Type of expenditures (i.e., whether a substantial portion of expenses is applicable to research, promotion and direct cost of works or, alternatively, whether the expenses are primarily those that would be expended irrespective of the taxpayer's art activities, such as office-in-home and auto expenses)
- The increase, if any, in the value of the artist's works as he or she progresses
- The taxpayer's qualifications (i.e., educational background, honours, awards, grants, etc.)
- The significance and growth of gross revenue, as well as the risk of loss
- External factors that may be affecting sales (e.g., economic conditions, change in the public mood, and bankruptcy of art galleries or publishers)
- Profit in prior years or continuous losses

When it comes to claiming certain operational expenses, CRA has accepted claims for the specific financial circumstances of the artistic community. For example, CRA has agreed that self-employed performing *artists may deduct the cost of music, acting or other lessons to develop their talent.*

Examples of other deductible expenses specifically for those artists and writers who are self-employed include:

- Accounting and legal fees
- Agents' commissions
- Cost of transportation, including board and lodging if the engagement is out of town, or the costs of transporting a large instrument or equipment
- Insurance premiums and repairs to instruments and equipment
- Cost of special make-up
- Cost of publicity photos
- Cost of video-taping or recording performances used for preparation or presentation

- Cost of repairs, alterations and cleaning of clothes used specifically in self-employment
- Cost of music, acting or other lessons for a role or part or for general self-improvement in the field
- Capital cost allowance on instruments, sheet music, scores, scripts, transcriptions, arrangements, equipment and wardrobe
- Office-in-the-home expenses
- Cost of industry-related periodicals
- Motor vehicle expenses

Where an artist is both an employed artist and a self-employed artist for part of the year, expenses can be allocated as follows:

$$\text{Total Allowable Expenses} \times \frac{\text{Time Worked as Self-Employed}}{\text{Total Time Worked}}$$

or any other reasonable allocation.

Artists and Their Inventory   Visual artists are allowed to exclude the value of inventory in computing income. Costs can be written off in the year they are incurred rather than apportioning such costs to particular works and claiming them when the works are sold.

Artists and Charities   It's also interesting to note that an artist is allowed to donate a work of art from inventory and, *without taking an income inclusion*, claim a tax credit for donations if the piece qualifies as a certified cultural gift.

In addition, artists who donate their works to charities may value such gifts *at any amount not exceeding fair market value, but not less than inventory cost*. This has the effect of creating income from which the charitable donations can be deducted and so requires some tax planning as this may affect other credits or investment opportunities.

Artists' Training, Grants and Awards   On the flipside, there are tax consequences when an artist is the recipient of certain benefits. For example, the value of workshops, seminars and other training programs provided to an artist who belongs to a national arts service organization will be taxable, as will prizes and awards received as a benefit from employment or in connection with a business. These amounts are not eligible for the scholarship exemption that is available to post-secondary students attending eligible programming at a designated educational institute.

Artists who receive a project grant that is considered neither business nor employment income may be eligible to claim offsetting expenses in one of two ways. They can choose to deduct reasonable expenses incurred to fulfil the conditions of the grant, supported by receipts, or they can claim the scholarship exemption,* but not both. In the latter instance, you'll note that the normal scholarship exemption provided for students who qualify for the education amount is not allowed unless the artist, too, qualifies for the amount.

Note that certain "prescribed prizes" received by an artist are not included in income at all. This includes prizes recognized by the general public and received after 1982 for meritorious achievement, like the Nobel Prize or Governor General's Literary Award.

Child Care Providers

This business profile is also an interesting one, because it offers an example of a self-employed taxpayer who has extensive "mixed use" claims (i.e., otherwise personal expenditures used primarily in a business environment), such as home workspace, food and toy costs.

As is the case for other proprietors, a child care provider may deduct various business expenses against income earned, including government grants. To report income earned and deductible expenses on the tax return, a record of all income received must be meticulously kept. As previously discussed, it is recommended that a separate bank account for such deposits be established.

When it comes to legitimizing deductions, keeping receipts of items purchased and used in the child care business is necessary as soon as the activities become commercial in nature, operated with a potential for profit.

When it comes to the deduction of home workspace costs, the dilemma often faced is this: "I use my whole home for the business when the children are here. How do I properly allocate the personal portion?"

If no one area is set aside exclusively for the business, portions of rent, mortgage interest, property taxes, utilities and repairs are deductible based on (1) the amount of floor space used in the child care busi-

---

* Scholarship exemptions were previously set at $500 and $3,000. For 2006 and subsequent years, the full amount of scholarships, fellowships and bursaries are excluded from income if an education tax credit is claimable.

ness and (2) *the number of hours the daycare centre is open,* as illustrated below:

$$\text{Total Operating Expenses of the home} \times \frac{\text{Square footage of home workspace}}{\text{Total square footage}} \times \frac{\text{No. of hours daycare is open in the year}}{\text{Total hours in the year}}$$

The result of this equation is the total deductible home workspace expense. Such claims must follow normal rules (i.e., home workspace costs must not increase or create a business loss).

Additional deductions for food, toys and supplies related to the business are also deductible. As well, a claim for capital cost allowance could be made for assets such as furniture, office equipment or a vehicle used in the enterprise.

Deductible Child Care Expenses:

- Accounting costs
- Advertising
- Art & craft supplies
- Auto expenses
- Bank charges
- Blankets
- Books
- Capital Cost Allowances (CCA)
- Diapers
- Employee expenses
- Entrance fees to parks, etc.
- Cost of field trips
- Food
- Household costs
- Insurance
- Postage
- Repairs
- Soap and shampoo
- Telephone/communications*
- Towels and toothbrushes
- Toys for the children
- Training courses
- Travel costs[†]

Food costs can be difficult to document. If all food consumed by the children is purchased separately, the full food bills can be deducted. However, in most cases, food is purchased at the same time for both family and business consumption. Therefore, in a separate book of account, the child care provider should keep a record of food items for the children and then prorate the total food bill accordingly.

Once all the applicable deductions are taken from child care income, it is possible that the taxpayer's net income, which is used in computing the spouse or common-law partner amount, is low enough for a full or

* Unless a separate business line is installed, the monthly rental on the personal phone is not deductible.

† Per-trip expenses may be claimed instead of keeping a detailed auto log if you use a vehicle only occasionally for business purposes.

partial claim by the higher-earning spouse. If net income is just over the threshold limits for those purposes, a Registered Retirement Savings Plan (RRSP) could be purchased for the self-employed spouse who has reported actively earned income last year. The results would be (1) a reduced net income, possibly creating a spouse or common-law partner amount claim for the higher-income earner, and (2) increased refundable tax credits such as the Canada Child Tax Benefit.*

Like other self-employed persons, the child care provider can begin making contributions to the Canada Pension Plan based on net income from the business. Hopefully any tax saving identified from the RRSP contribution can assist in funding this cost, or potentially additional savings in a TFSA or for the purchase of an insurance policy.

When issuing receipts, the child care provider should break down how much money the parents paid for children under seven and those over six so that parents can take advantage of higher allowable deduction limits for preschoolers.

Farmers

The income from farming is considered to be business income, subject to the same tax-filing provisions applicable to other businesses. Farmers who are not AgriInvest/AgriStability (formerly Canadian Agricultural Income Stabilization) participants use Form T2042, *Statement of Farming Income and Expenses*, to report income and expenses from farming activities. (Those who are AgriInvest/AgriStability participants in Alberta, Ontario and Prince Edward Island use Forms T1163 and T1164 instead of Form T2042, and all other provinces use Forms T1273 and T1274.)

Most of us think of farmers as those who raise cattle or other domestic animals or who grow grain. However, other activities considered "farming enterprises" include the tillage of soil, maintenance of race horses, bee-keeping, operation of wild game reserves, nursery or greenhouse businesses, fruit growing, raising poultry, fur farming, growing Christmas trees and even raising fish. Here's what farmers need to know to make sure their offsetting expenses are deductible.

Filing Methods   Persons who are in the business of farming or fishing may use the *cash method* of accounting to compute their income. This method calculates income actually received during the year and reduced by expenses actually paid during the year. They also have the

---

* This RRSP contribution should be made in addition to a contribution by the higher-earning spouse, who will reap a higher marginal return from his/her contributions due to income level.

option of reporting income using the *accrual method*, where income is calculated as it becomes receivable and expenses are deducted as they become payable.

Once a farmer elects to file a tax return using the cash method, all subsequent returns must be filed in a similar manner, and a formal request to change must be made to the Director of the local Tax Services Office. In the case of a partnership, each partner must elect to have the income from the farming or fishing business reported using the cash method. This means that all partners must file a tax return in the year of election.

Instalment Payments   Farmers are required to pre-remit tax in instalments, but only once a year, on or before December 31, based on two-thirds of estimated tax for the current year. Canada Pension Plan contributions are also required on net farming income and should be factored into the instalment payments.

Reporting Farm Expenses   Farm expenses are reported on Form T2042/T1163 and can include the following:

- Building and fence repairs
- Capital cost allowance on assets owned, claimed at your option
- Cleaning, levelling and draining land
- Crop insurance, GRIP and stabilization premiums, as well as NISA administration fees
- Interest on farm loans, mortgages and vehicles
- Insurance on farm buildings and, in certain cases, life insurance policy premiums (that is, only if the policy was used as collateral for a business loan)
- Machinery expenses including gas, diesel fuel and oil, repairs, licences and insurance
- Mandatory inventory adjustments included in income last year
- Memberships and subscription fees
- Motor vehicle costs, prorated for any personal-use component
- Livestock purchased
- Professional fees
- Property taxes
- Office supply costs
- Optional inventory adjustments included in income last year
- Rent for land buildings or pastures
- Salaries, wages and benefits, including employer's contributions, for family members

- Small tools that cost less than $500
- Utility bills for farm buildings
- Seeds, plants, feed, supplements, straw and bedding, pesticides, veterinary fees and breeding fees
- 50% of meals and entertainment costs

Home Workspace Expenses   Certain household expenses can be claimed as business expenses on the tax return under the general provisions for home workspace expenses. These include heat, electricity, insurance, maintenance, mortgage interest, property taxes and other expenses, prorated for the business/personal-use portions and subject to the restriction that no loss can be increased or created using home office expenses.

Communication Costs   Long-distance calls that are personal in nature may not be deducted. If you have a separate business phone, circle all personal calls on every monthly phone bill and use the rest of the bill as a deduction. If there is no separate phone, the monthly rental charge is usually considered a personal expense. You can also deduct the portion of your air-time costs of a cellular telephone or on-line charges for Internet access that reasonably relate to operation of the farm.

Deductible Wages for Spouse   Salaries paid to a spouse or common-law spouse in a family business are fully deductible, provided the following factors are in place:

- The work was required to be done, was actually done and would otherwise have required the hiring of a stranger
- Wages were reasonable and actually paid and documented

All persons employed by spouses must have Employment Insurance (EI) premiums withheld and remitted as well as Canada Pension Plan (CPP) premiums (if the employee is not receiving a CPP retirement benefit) and, of course, income taxes. A T4 slip must be issued under normal rules.

Employment by a person who controls 40% or more of the issued voting shares is not insurable under the Employment Insurance rules; neither is employment of a spouse unless the remuneration is tax deductible under the Income Tax Act (see comments below), nor is an unreasonably high salary. These tax provisions can make a considerable impact on the incomes of farmers and owners of small businesses. In effect, both spouses can earn income in their own right, allowing for legitimate income splitting within the family.

Wages Paid to Children   The same general rules apply to children's wages (that is, reasonable wages must be actually paid for services that were necessary in producing income and that would otherwise have required outside help). The employer must also contribute a portion of the premiums paid by the child to Employment Insurance (and, if the child is 18 or over, CPP) on the source deductions remittance form. The employer's portion is a deductible expense.*

Remember these important points when paying your children:

- If you pay your children by cheque, the CRA will accept your cancelled cheque as a legitimate receipt.
- Receipts signed by the child are required if you pay cash.
- If you give your child livestock or grain in lieu of money for the payment of wages, the child must report the value of this livestock or grain on his/her tax return as income. In order to claim the wage expenses, you will be required to include in your gross sales income the value of this property given to your child.
- The value of board may not be claimed as an expense if supplied to any child who is dependent upon you for support.

Source Deduction Remittances for Small Business   Those employers with average monthly withholding amounts of less than $1,000 for the second preceding calendar year and who have no compliance problems in either their withholding account or GST/HST account for the preceding 12 months may choose to remit their source deductions withheld from employees on a quarterly rather than a monthly basis. These remittances would be required on March 31, June 30, September 30 and December 31. The remittances are due the 15th of the month following the end of each quarter.

Vehicle Costs   As you have learned, the most important part of claiming any vehicle expenses is to keep a distance log, which can document your total business driving for a representative period of time during the year if your vehicle was used both for personal and business driving. The

---

* In some cases, EI premiums are not payable for family members. To determine whether you should deduct these premiums, complete Form CPT1, *Request for a Ruling as to the Status of a Worker Under the Canada Pension Plan and/or Employment Insurance Act*. Those who deduct premiums by mistake can recover overpayments for only 12 months in retrospect.

size of deductible expenditures for your vehicles depends on how many you have and what they are used for. Restrictions on certain expenses apply to passenger vehicles.

Farm trucks or vans, on the other hand, are "motor vehicles-automobiles" that will be exempt from these restrictions if they are designed to carry the driver and two passengers and are used primarily (i.e., more than 50% of the time) to transport equipment or goods, or if the motor vehicle is used 90% or more of the time to transfer equipment, goods or passengers for the purpose of earning income.

Group receipts in categories before you compute deductible totals. All of the following expenses are deductible: gas and oil, interest on loans (subject to restrictions for passenger vehicles), insurance, licence renewal costs, tires and repairs, lease payments (again, restrictions may apply to passenger vehicles), auto club premiums, car washes, parking and tolls. By keeping all receipts in order and faithfully maintaining a distance log, you will maximize your deductions and minimize the time required to file your return. Joint owners of a motor vehicle cannot collectively deduct more than one owner could.

Ineligible Expenses   Expenses not allowable include:

- Replacement or improvement of assets (these must be capitalized)
- Principal payments on borrowed money, including repayments of a loan for tile drainage
- The value of animals that have died during the year (when they are purchased, the cost is written off as an expense)
- Expenses for a personal garden or upkeep of livestock gifted to children

Inventory Valuations   To combat the fluctuations in income that a farmer may experience, the role of his/her inventory is an important one in determining net income each year. That is because CRA wishes to avoid tax loss reporting in cases where expenditures have been made to increase inventory size. There are two inventory provisions for the farmer. One is optional, the other mandatory.

MIA   CRA won't just let you write off operational losses from a farm if you have purchased inventory on hand. A Mandatory Inventory Adjustment (MIA) must be made. The effect of this provision is to reduce the cash loss a farmer may experience in one tax year by adding in the market value of inventory on hand at year end. Amounts included in income must be deducted the following year, thereby reducing income earned from operations in that year.

OIA   A farmer has a further opportunity to average income and losses over the years by electing to make an Optional Inventory Adjustment (OIA). Such an adjustment, which adds the fair market value of all remaining inventory (less the MIA provision) to a farmer's income, will further reduce a farmer's remaining cash loss in one year and then be deducted from income the next. The definition of inventory for these purposes may encompass all inventory on hand including livestock owned, cash crops, fertilizer, chemicals, feed, seed, fuel, etc. Proper management of this provision can save the farmer thousands of dollars over the years.

Certain Prepayments   Under the cash method of reporting income, amounts are generally deducted when paid. However, a deduction for prepaid expenses can be made in advance, but only for the current year and one more year. The portion of amounts paid for tax years that are two or more years after the actual payment must be deferred and deducted in those future years.

To be deductible, the amount is required to have been paid in a preceding tax year and cannot be deductible in computing income of the business for any other year.

Land Improvement Costs   Expenditures, such as clearing land and constructing unpaved roads, are deducted as a current expense by farmers. A farmer may claim less than the full cost of these expenses in the year they are incurred. He or she will be allowed to carry forward and use the remaining undeducted amounts in a subsequent year. This is significant to farmers who have little or no net income in the year the expenditure is made because it allows the deferral of the write-off to a year when there is taxable income. As well, the cost of laying or installing a land drainage system is deductible, whether it is composed of tile or other materials.

Livestock Income Tax-Deferral Program   Here's a little-known tax saver. A tax-deferral program exists for farmers who deplete their breeding herds of grazing livestock because of drought conditions. Farmers are required to include the proceeds received for the forced destruction or sale of breeding animals in income. However, an offsetting deduction may be taken to defer tax on such proceeds to the next tax year. Qualifying areas will be determined every year upon recommendation by the

Minister of Agriculture and Agri-Food. Ask your tax advisor to brief you on this year's prescribed areas.

Loss Deductibility   CRA groups farm losses into three categories:

- **Losses from a full-scale farming operation:** A farming operation is considered "full-scale" if the taxpayer spends all of his/her time and effort in the operation of the farm, and farming is the chief source of income. These losses are deductible in full against other income the taxpayer may have.
- **Losses from part-time ventures:** Farm losses claimed against other income when it is clear that the taxpayer's chief source of income is not farming.
- **Hobby farms:** Farm losses claimed against other income when it is questionable whether a business actually exists. These losses are not deductible at all, because the activities are considered to be a hobby.

    The tax department will look at a number of factors in determining that a viable operation exists. These guidelines are also useful in determining whether other business ventures have a reasonable expectation of profit.
- **Gross and net income from the farming operation:** This includes the amount of capital invested and a close look at the cash flow of the business.
- **The size of the property used for farming:** Your losses may be disallowed if:
  - Your property is too small to offer any hope of profit.
  - You have made no attempt at farming or developing your land.
  - You have no intention of using more than a fraction of the land over a period of years. There must be potential for profit that you can document and justify with cash flow statements and budgets for the future.
- **Qualifications of the taxpayer:** Losses will generally be allowed if:
  - You have farming background experience and spend most of your time on the operation during the busy months.
  - You make commitments for the future expansion of the farm.
  - You qualify for some type of provincial assistance.
  - You personally are involved to a large degree in the operations.
- **Other sources of income:** Generally speaking, if your chief source of income is from other sources, losses may be restricted or disallowed. If you are forced to earn income elsewhere in a bad year, full losses may be allowed if it can be proven that farming is still your chief

source of income and that it is your intention to continue spending most of your time and money on the farm.

- **Future business plans:** Be prepared to show how your farm will be maintained and developed in future years.

Restricted Farm Losses   Farmers whose chief source of income is not from farming are currently restricted to a maximum farm loss write-off of $2,500 plus one-half of the next $12,500 for a maximum of $8,750. This means that a loss of $15,000 or more will qualify for a write-off of $8,750.

Also be aware that if you have a capital gain, perhaps from farmland sold during the year, interest or property taxes that were included in any restricted farm losses of prior years that have not yet been deducted *may be used to reduce the capital gain* but not to create or increase a capital loss on the sale of the farmland.

This provision of the Income Tax Act is the subject of numerous court cases. Farmers argue that they are in the full-time business of farming and therefore should be allowed full loss deductibility while CRA argues that the chief source of income is not from farming and therefore losses should be restricted. The circumstances of the farming operation, as outlined above, together with the farmer's ability to show potential for profit for enterprises that are clearly commercial in nature should assist taxpayers.

Value of Accounts Receivable   A taxpayer is required to include the value of accounts receivable in income in cases where (1) a Canadian resident ceases to carry on the business of farming and becomes a non-resident; (2) a Canadian resident ceases to carry on a farming business in another country and becomes a non-resident; and (3) a non-resident ceases to carry on a Canadian farming business after July 13, 1990. In such cases, inventory will be considered disposed of at its fair market value.

Farmers and the GST/HST   Farmers should enquire about becoming GST/HST registrants because most supplies produced by farmers are zero-rated; that is, no GST/HST is charged by the farmer on the sale of supplies. However, in the case of "zero-rated" supplies, a GST/HST input tax credit can be claimed to recover GST/HST paid on purchases incurred in producing those supplies. Examples of zero-rated supplies are livestock used to produce wool or food, grains, seeds (not garden seeds) and fodder crops, share cropping and unprocessed fish.

Special Capital Cost Allowance Classes and Rates for Farmers   Most items of farm equipment can be considered as depreciable assets, subject to a variety of prescribed classes and rates. Generally, they fall into Class 1 (4% for buildings), Class 8 (20% for non-motorized equipment), Class 10 (30% for motorized equipment) or Class 50 (55% for computer equipment).

For a complete list, see CRA's *Farming Income Guide*. Farmers who buy certain pollution-control manure-handling equipment—including pads, liquid manure tanks, pumps and spreaders—may qualify for special accelerated CCA rates. Contact the Minister of the Environment for more details.

Also note that the cost of paving roads must be added to Class 17, which has an 8% rate. Casing and cribwork for a waterwell as well as the cost of the system that distributes water, such as the pump, pipes and trenches, will all be capitalized in Class 8, which has a 20% rate.

Eligible Capital Properties   Farmers who own milk and egg quotas have what is known as an "eligible capital property," which is a property that has a lasting economic value and therefore must be written off over time. To do so, a special account is set up—the cumulative eligible capital account—and 75% of the value of the quota is recorded here. The annual allowance that is claimed against other income is 7% of this amount.

However, a CEC allowance deduction is allowed only if there is a positive balance in the account. Any negative balance would have to be reported as income, consistent with the capital gains inclusion rate.* If the property is qualified farm property eligible for the $750,000 Lifetime Capital Gains Exemption, qualifying income amounts will be reported on Schedule 3, Capital Gains and Losses, to enable the deduction.

Capital Gains Exemption

The $750,000 Lifetime Capital Gains Exemption may be used on the gains generated by the disposal of shares of the capital stock of a small business corporation owned by the individual or partnership related to him or her. A small business corporation is a Canadian-controlled private corporation in which all or substantially all of the assets are used in an active business carried on primarily in Canada. The shares must be owned by such an individual through the 24 months immediately prior

---

* For business years ending after October 17, 2000, 2/3 of the gain is included in income. The original purchase of ECP was originally factored by 3/4 for determination of the pool addition (2/3 times 3/4 is 1/2).

to the disposition. During the holding period, more than 50% of the FMV of the corporation's assets must have been used in an active business.

Those who own qualifying farm property may also make the claim for farm property acquired after June 17, 1987, including real property owned by the taxpayer, spouse or child for at least 24 months immediately before sale. A gross revenue test must be met; that is, in at least two years prior to disposition, gross income earned by the individual from active farming operations must exceed net income from all other sources. Second, all or substantially all of the fair value of the farm assets must be used in active business operations for at least 24 months prior to disposition.

On farms acquired before June 17, 1987, the $750,000 Lifetime Capital Gains Exemption will be allowed if the farmland and buildings were used in an active farming business in Canada in the year of sale and *for at least five years prior to the disposition.*

Consult your tax advisor about meeting the qualifications to enable a future tax-free gain of farming property held by your family.

Family Farm Rollovers   A tax-free rollover of farm assets, including the farmland, depreciable properties and eligible capital properties, will be allowed on transfers to the spouse, children or grandchildren. This means that no capital gain or loss, terminal loss or recapture will generally arise on the tax return of the transferor. However, to qualify, the property must have been used principally in an active farming business, and the child must have been a resident of Canada immediately before the transfer.

The meaning of "child" has been extended to include persons who, before reaching age 19, were under the control and custody of the taxpayer and dependent upon him/her. This could include nephews, nieces and in-laws. The cost of acquisition of the property is equal to the deceased's deemed proceeds of disposition.

When transfers occur due to death, the property must be transferred to the child within 36 months. In either case, transfers can be valued at an amount between ACB (adjusted cost base) and FMV (fair market value). Also see Figure 7.2 for rules surrounding depreciable property.

As well, farm rollovers from a child to a parent would be allowed in cases in which the child dies leaving a surviving parent.

Property eligible for such transfers includes property leased by a taxpayer to the family farm corporation. A special election is available to transfer depreciable property on death (including buildings, equipment or other depreciable property used in business). This may be done in *any amount between the fair market value of the property and its undepreciated*

Figure 7.2	Transfer of Farm Assets

Asset	While Living	At Death		Transfers to Spouse or Child
Equipment	At any amount between FMV and transferor's undepreciated capital cost	$\dfrac{\text{FMV of asset}}{\text{FMV of all assets in that class}}$	$\times$ $\dfrac{\text{UCC of all assets}}{\text{in that class}}$	Special Election: The lower of Capital Cost Or $\dfrac{\text{Capital Cost of Asset}}{\text{Capital Cost of all property in same class}} \times \dfrac{\text{UCC of all in same class}}{}$ Or FMV if transferred to spouse, Or an amount between FMV and special election for transfer to child
Land	At an amount between the fair market value and the transferor's ACB	At the adjusted cost base immediately before death, or any amount between ACB and FMV		

Note: The deceased's legal representative may choose to transfer property at any amount between its FMV and ACB or UCC before death, if this is to the advantage of the estate. The property must have vested indefeasibly within 36 months of date of death.

capital cost at the time of transfer. Eligible Capital Property (ECP) can be transferred at any amount between FMV and:

$$4/3 \times \text{Cumulative Eligible Capital*} \quad \times \quad \frac{\text{FMV of Property}}{\text{FMV of all Eligible Capital Property}}$$

Careful planning of disposition and acquisition cost values allows the farm family to maximize use of the capital gains exemption on transfer as well as any capital and non-capital loss provisions to minimize tax now and in the future.

Note that a farmer who transfers shares of a family farm corporation or interests in a family farm partnership at fair market value to his/her child who then disposes of it before attaining age 18 will be subject to the Attribution Rules on farm income earned. That is, the farming income must be reported by the adult transferor.

---

* Only on the sale of assets are adjustments made to income in order to adjust for the capital gains inclusion rate in effect at the time of sale.

The same Attribution Rules hold true in cases where a spouse disposes of the property during the farmer's lifetime, except this time attribution applies to the capital gain or loss.

Also note that these rollover rules apply to fishers on or after May 2, 2006, as does the Capital Gains Exemption on dispositions of qualifying property.

Construction Industry

Businesses whose principal activity is construction must ensure they record the name, the amount paid, and the identifier number (Business Number or Social Insurance Number) of their subcontractors. The due date for reporting this information is six months from the end of your reporting period of the year following the end of fiscal year of the business.

Contractors who pay subcontractors must file Form T5018, *Summary of Contract Payments*. They are also encouraged to send a T5018 information slip to each subcontractor. Alternatively, the information may be reported on a line-by-line basis in a column format with the appropriate summary information.

Only payments for services in excess of $500 per year need be reported. Payments primarily for goods need not be reported unless there is a total annual service component of $500 or more.

THE TAX ADVISOR

It is important to communicate effectively with your tax advisor throughout the year. Use a Tax Compliance Action Planner (see Figure 7.3), which records required periodic tax-filing milestones throughout the year on your Daily Business Journal for your particular business profile. Your tax accountant can help you customize this plan.

Equally important is the construction of your five-year Business Profile Overview (see Figure 7.4). This statement charts your record of income, expenses, before-tax profits and after-tax cash flow over five fiscal years to help you understand the growth patterns of your business as well as key decisions to make with your professionals to average taxes down to their lowest possible level over time. The key is to know your tax filing compliance milestones. Along the way, you'll keep more of the first dollar you earn by looking at your legal obligation to arrange your affairs within the framework of the law to pay the least taxes possible on your business profits, your personal investments and your personal family taxes.

Figure 7.3	Tax Compliance Action Planner				
Month	**Week 1**	**Week 2**	**Week 3: 15th**	**Week 4**	**Week 5: 30th**
January	RRSP contr. Mo. end review File TD1 form/ T1213 Jan. 30 interest on interspousal loans	Payroll Accts. Payable	Remit Source Deductions, GST for Dec.	Payroll	Final Quarter Review
February	RRSP Contr. Overview T4s, T5s, T3s Mo. end review	Payroll Accts. Payable	Remit Source Deductions, Prepare to remit tax return	Payroll, RRSP Top Up, Mail or Distribute T4 Slips	
March	RRSP Contr. Mo. end review	Payroll, Accts. Payable	Remit Source Deductions, Instalments	Payroll Mail T3 Slips	Appointment with Tax Advisor re tax return
April	RRSP Contr. Mo. End review	Payroll, Accts. Payable	Remit Source Deductions, GST for 1st quarter	Payroll T1 Filing Deadline	Ist Quarter Review; File tax return if you owe money

Continue planner for the months of May through December

RECAP. YOU NEED TO KNOW:

1. What industry profile your business falls into for tax audit purposes

2. When a business is required to register to collect the GST/HST

3. What the latest tax changes are regarding your tax filing profile

4. How partners are taxed in the partnership and on the personal return

5. How partnerships between spouses are affected by Attribution Rules

6. What specific rules apply to artists and writers when claiming expenses and losses

7. Rules surrounding scholarship exemptions, particularly for artists

8. The nuances surrounding home workspace claims for child care providers

9. How loss deductibility, income averaging, the requirement for tax instalments and taxation of asset dispositions differ for farmers

Figure 7.4   Business Profile Overview

Business Name: _____

Type Of Business:

Proprietorship   Owner: _____

Partnership   Partners: _____

_____

Corporation _____ Date of Incorporation _____ Costs: _____

Business Plan:

Source of Revenue:	Year 1	Year 2	Year 3	Year 4	Year 5
Total Income					

Operating Expenses:	Year 1	Year 2	Year 3	Year 4	Year 5
Total					
% Of Income					

Profits:	Year 1	Year 2	Year 3	Year 4	Year 5
Total					
% Of Income					
Taxes Payable					
After-Tax Retained Earnings					

Obstacles Forecast: _____

_____

10. How income and losses are averaged around annual tax filing milestones to provide business owners with the retained earnings they need to live and invest for the future

YOU NEED TO ASK: Your tax advisor for help setting up your industry filing profile by:

1. **Summarizing your business activities:** Develop a business plan that has a focus on tax efficiency. This will help you and your advisor make decisions about your form of business organization and family income splitting opportunities while meeting audit requirements. However, mostly this focus will maximize your cash flow.

2. **Choosing the right method of reporting income:** Make sure you choose the correct reporting method when you start your business and that you know the exceptions to the rules. Farmers and very small businesses may use the "cash method" of reporting income, for example. Most other businesses must report their income on the "accrual basis." Special provisions may be available for certain professionals and those who qualify for a variety of reserving provisions. Discuss this concept with your tax advisor.

3. **Planning the deduction of operating expenses:** Remember that most operating expenses are 100% deductible against revenues of the business. In the case of husband and wife teams, it is most important to show that personal living expenses are not claimed against business income. (Farmers, for example, should make adjustments for food taken for personal consumption to ensure only business portions of the cost are deducted.)

4. **Planning to write off tax losses:** CRA has made a practice of scrutinizing certain industries more thoroughly than others when it comes to writing off tax losses. This is particularly true of the farming community. Discuss the loss-filing rules applicable to your industry profile with your tax advisor.

5. **Knowing why you could be chosen for audit:** CRA has profiled certain industries to identify those participating in the Canadian and the global underground economy. International efforts have focused also on money laundering and Internet commerce. Special investigative projects have included:
   - Independent couriers
   - Subcontractors in construction and home building

- Unregistered car salespeople
- Home renovations including carpet installers
- Direct sellers
- Mechanics and auto body repairers
- Service industry workers (waiters, waitresses, bellhops, etc.)
- Those selling goods on Internet portals like eBay (eBay sellers who have not yet reported their commercial transactions should seek out voluntary disclosure opportunities to avoid penalties.)

If you are in a high-risk group, be sure to put your affairs in order, as the probability of audit is higher in those identified industries.

. . . .

CHAPTER 8

How to Put Your Family to Work and Write It Off!

"See it big, and keep it simple."
WILFRED PETERSON

KEY CONCEPTS

- You can hire your family members to work in your business and make it deductible
- It is important to know the difference between an employee and a contractor
- Amounts must be paid for work actually completed
- Payments must be reasonable and in line with what you would pay a non-related person
- Hiring should be formal, with contracts in place
- Proper payroll procedures must be in place, including T4 slip processing
- Remittances of statutory deductions must be made
- Tax withholdings should be minimized to maximize your investments
- Taxable and tax-free perks add value to employment contracts

REAL LIFE: Raj and his wife, Vasi, were happy to live in Canada. They had emigrated from their native India the year before and in January of the new year opened their own business—an Indian restaurant. Vasi did the cooking with her sous-chef daughter, Tara, while Raj and his son, Ram, played host and waiter, respectively. After their first quarter in business, the books showed a small operating profit. However, the proprietorship showed no deductions for wages for family members, and Raj wondered if he could reduce his tax liability by paying his family members. Was this possible? How would he justify payment of wages and the work of the family retroactively?

THE PROBLEM

Most new businesses in Canada have something in common—usually the whole family pitches in to get the business established. While it is legal to pay your family members to work in your small business and deduct the amounts from your profits, be careful to avoid the common mistake Raj made. He didn't keep the documentation required to show that family members were actually working in the business, and worse, he didn't actually pay them. Therefore, at tax time, he'll be unable to write off any salary or wage expenses retroactively. However, for the future, Raj and his family are poised for significant tax savings through income splitting.

THE SOLUTION

Family members can be hired as hourly employees, wage earners, subcontractors, commission salespeople or any other position you would hire a stranger for. You can pay them salary, wages, gratuities, overtime, premium hours, banked time, retroactive earnings, salary, bonuses, commissions, advances, draws, gifts, severance, sick leave, vacation pay, wages in lieu of notice or a number of taxable or tax-free benefits.

However, a simple rule must be followed in hiring and remunerating your family members: *treat the process of hiring and paying them in the same manner as if you were hiring a stranger.* All the paperwork must be in place, including the signing of employment contracts or sub-contracts, or the keeping of time cards to support hours worked. Without the paperwork, not only will it be impossible to write off the amounts paid to your family members, but you'll also miss out on an important tax saver: the ability to legitimately split income amongst family members.

The establishment of formal payroll records, however, can only happen once you have determined whether you have an employer-employee relationship with your family members who work in your business. If you do, certain statutory source deductions must be made from gross pay and remitted to the government on a regular basis.

You should also know that there are a number of important tax-savings opportunities that you can utilize in designing compensation packages for your employees, including family members. In fact, you should consider implementing a primary objective in structuring all compensation packages for your employees: *Put as many after-tax dollars in your employees' pockets as soon as possible, but ensure they keep more of the first dollars they earn.* There are many ways to do this, including the minimization of taxes withheld at source.

THE PARAMETERS

The following parameters should be observed in order to deduct amount paid to family members working in your small business:

Formalize Hiring Practices

When a business hires an employee, generally the employee is given a role description, a rate of pay or salary level and a statement of expectations that can include termination, confidentiality and non-compete clauses. When a business hires a sub-contractor, the self-employed person generally submits a proposal to the business to perform a certain task that has a start and end period and an agreed-upon invoice price.

In a family business, such formalities are often dropped or forgotten about. This is bad business in several respects, including HR management and business succession planning. From a tax point of view, these formalities are especially important, as CRA will scrutinize such "non-arm's-length" transactions to ensure that no inappropriate family income splitting is taking place. (A non-arm's-length relationship generally exists when one deals with someone related by blood, marriage or adoption.)

To legitimize your deduction for amounts paid to family members, you will want to meet the following criteria for CRA:

- The work was actually performed by your relative
- The work was necessary and would have otherwise required the hiring of a stranger
- The amounts paid were comparable to what would have been paid to a stranger for the same work
- The amounts paid were reasonable in relation to the relative's age and experience
- The amounts were paid in pursuit of business profits

It is a very good idea to establish a human resource guide or a policies and procedures manual in which your human resource policies are outlined, including things like job descriptions, job postings, employer-paid training, sick leave and vacation policies, sexual harassment and bereavement policies, and so on. Such a document will show CRA that you are running a serious, for-profit business, treating all employees—related or not—with consistency.

Employed or Self-Employed?

This is an important question, as the business owner will have certain obligations to meet by law if the relationship is one of employer-employee or "master-servant."

CRA defines an employer-employee relationship as

> "a verbal or written agreement in which an employee agrees to work on a full-time or part-time basis for a specified or indeterminate period of time, in return for salary or wages. The employer has the right to decide where, when and how the work will be done. In this type of relationship a *contract of service* exists."*

When a family member works in the business as an employee, the owner must therefore do the following:

- Make statutory deductions from gross pay for contributions to Canada Pension Plan (CPP), Employment Insurance (EI) and income taxes. These must be remitted usually once a month, although very small businesses have the option to remit each quarter. Children under 18 need not contribute to the Canada Pension Plan, and those over 70 (except in Quebec) or in receipt of CPP benefits need not contribute at all.
- Prepare a T4 slip for each employee and issue it by the end of February each year.

Salary paid and any "employer portion" of CPP and EI are tax deductible to the employer.

Where a family member works as a sub-contractor to the business, a "business relationship" is said to exist. CRA defines a business relationship as

> "a verbal or written agreement in which a self-employed individual agrees to perform specific work for a payer in return for payment. There is no employer or employee. The self-employed individual generally does not have to carry out all or even part of the work himself. In this type of relationship, a *contract for service* exists."*

In this case, the family member who is a sub-contractor invoices the business, which pays the amount in a timely fashion (usually within 30

---

* CRA publication: Employee or Self-Employed?

days). By the way, the invoiced amount is fully deductible by the business owner.

The sub-contractor who is unincorporated must then calculate and remit CPP premiums via the income tax return at year end and, in some cases, via quarterly tax instalment payments.

In addition, if the sub-contractor earns more than $30,000 in gross fees billed, GST/HST registration may be required. Take this into consideration in deciding whether your family member is better off working for you as an employee or as a sub-contractor.

In order to properly pay those who work in your business, you will need to know whether the relationship you have is a contract *of* service or a contract *for* service. The big issue for CRA is the remittance of source deductions, required for all employees. You will be fined if your sub-contracting brother-in-law is found to actually be an employee of yours. This could be expensive.

There are four basic factors CRA will look at if the distinction is unclear:

1. **Control:** The degree of control exercised by the payer will help to define the relationship with the person doing the work. If the payer has the right to hire or fire; controls the payment of wages and how much is to be paid; and decides on the time, place and manner in which the work should be done, including hours of work and the assessment of work quality, generally there is a strong indication of an employer-employee relationship. Additional factors include control of the list of clients of the business and the territory covered, as well as training and development.

2. **Ownership of assets and tools:** If the payer supplies the equipment and tools required to perform the tasks of the job and pays for repairs, insurance, rental, fuel or other costs of operation, generally an employer-employee relationship is considered to exist.

3. **Risk of loss:** The payer is generally considered to be the employer if he/she assumes the financial risk for the company, including the responsibility for covering operating costs like office expenses, salaries, insurance coverage, freight and delivery, rent, bad debts, damage and promotional expenses. Those who receive remuneration without financial risk—that is, salary is paid in full regardless of the health of the business—would generally be considered to be employees.

4. **Integration:** This final factor involves the worker's viewpoint. If the worker is not dependent on the payer and simply integrates the job done for the payer into his own business activities, the worker is

likely self-employed. To strengthen this position, it is important to show that the self-employed person has other jobs lined up with other suppliers. However, if the job done for the payer is actually integrated into the payer's commercial activities to the extent that the worker is connected with the employer's business and dependent on it, likely an employer-employee relationship exists.

Taken together, these four criteria will generally help you to determine whether an employer-employee relationship exists.

REAL LIFE: Marina works in her husband Paul's construction business, doing the books. She has a home office; she answers the phone and prepares the books on the computer that Paul bought for her. He has asked her to be in the office available for calls from 9 a.m. until 2 p.m. every day, but Marina often spends all day there, handling correspondence, invoicing and other odds and ends. Paul is her only payer.

In this case, there is a very strong likelihood that Marina will be considered Paul's employee. He has acquired and written off the equipment she needs to do her job; he controls the place and time she works; and she has no other clients. Marina should be filling in a time card to post her hours worked, or Paul should have her on an employment contract if salary is being paid. He should issue a T4 slip at year end and make periodic source remittances for CPP, EI and income tax.

If Paul were one of several clients for whom Marina was keeping books, if she purchased her own equipment and tools and if it could be shown that she assumed the risk of paying overhead and responsibility for the contracts she bid and won, Marina would likely be considered self-employed. Marina would then become a supplier of Paul's and submit invoices to be paid, usually within a 30-day period.

In that case, CRA would require that Marina do at least four things:

- Self-report her income on her tax return
- Make CPP premium contributions via the tax return at the end of the tax year
- Pay tax instalments if she owed CRA more than $3,000 in the current tax year and the immediately preceding year
- Register to collect GST/HST if her gross earnings exceeded $30,000

Payroll Procedures

Once you have determined you have an employer-employee relationship with family members, you'll have to put payroll procedures in place. The basic payroll equation you must follow is shown in Figure 8.1.

As you can see, gross pay can comprise three remuneration types: cash and taxable benefits, which are reported on the T4 slip, and tax-free benefits, which are not. From this gross pay, the employer may take one of two types of deductions:

- Statutory deductions—those required by law—which are CPP, EI and income tax deductions
- Non-statutory deductions, which can include deductions for union dues, registered pension plans, charities and other deductions at the option of the business.

After deductions, the net pay can be given to the employee in cash or by cheque, deposited directly to the employee's bank account, held or advanced.

10 Steps in the Payroll Cycle:

1. Collect information about the employees' gross pay for the period on the payroll journal.
2. Determine the CPP and EI premiums payable by looking up the gross earnings in the CRA guide books or on CRA's Tables on Diskette (TOD).
3. Determine the amount of taxes to be withheld based on CRA's Form TD1, *Personal Tax Credit Return*, or Form T1213, *Request for Reduction*

Figure 8.1   The Basic Payroll Equation

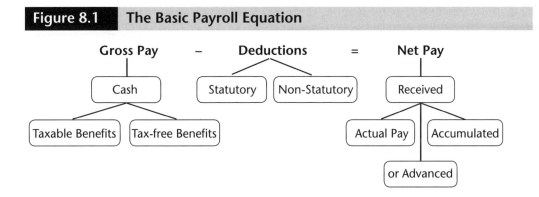

in Source Withholding, or other specialized forms filed with you by the employee. Correct withholding is most important to ensure the largest after-tax dollar goes to the employee first. You will want to withhold the correct amount of tax required by law but no more. This is discussed further below.

4. Calculate net pay on the payroll journal and double-check all figures.

5. Calculate the employer's portion of CPP and EI.

6. Calculate the total employer CRA remittance required for the current period for total income taxes withheld, CPP premiums withheld plus employer's portion, and EI premiums withheld plus employer's portion.

7. Total the CRA remittance for the period. Write the cheque for the remittance.

8. Prepare the bookkeeping journal entries for the payroll:
   - To record the payment of the payroll
   - To record the withholding amounts as a liability

9. Write the payroll cheques and double-check all against the payroll journal before distributing the cheques to employees.

10. Prepare a new payroll journal for the next pay period, carrying forward all year-to-date accumulated figures.

Employer's Obligations for the CPP

Hiring an employee can be a costly undertaking for a small business because the employer must make contributions to the Canada Pension Plan and Employment Insurance in addition to the deductions that are taken for the employee's contributions.

In the case of the Canada Pension Plan, the employer must match the employee's contributions. CPP premiums do not have to be deducted for those who are collecting certain benefits from the CPP or who make less than $250 in a calendar year in agriculture, forestry, trapping, fishing, hunting, horticulture or lumbering employment, and work less than 25 days in the same year. Other exceptions include employment of a child under 18; casual employment for purposes other than normal trade or business; employment of a teacher on exchange from a foreign country; a person employed in a disaster rescue operation; residence benefits of clergy; severance pay or death benefits. For a complete list, see CRA's *Employers' Guide—Payroll Deductions and Remittances.*

A \$3,500 basic exemption is allowed. That is, if your employee earns less than \$3,500 for the year, no CPP premiums are payable. If your employee earns \$6,500 for the year and is over the age of 18, CPP premiums must be contributed on earnings of \$3,000 (\$6,500 – \$3,500). You should also know that in the following circumstances, CPP premiums will be prorated:

1. The employee is under the age of 18
2. The employee is over the age of 70 (except in Quebec)
3. The employee has started to receive a retirement or disability benefit from the CPP
4. The employee is deceased

In the last three instances, CPP premiums are payable until the month of the event. CPP is remitted for teenagers in the month after they turn 18.

When overdeductions occur for CPP or EI, you can file Form PD24E, *Application for a Refund of Overdeducted CPP Contributions or EI Premiums*. This form is used when deductions were made but not required (as in the circumstances above) or when there was an error reading the contribution tables. However, when there is a deduction in excess of the maximum amounts required for the year, this form should not be filed. Rather, CRA will notify the employer when the T4 information return is assessed at the end of the year. Also, when overdeductions are made in a current calendar year, you may simply reduce the next remittance rather than complete the refund application form.

Employer's Obligations for the Employment Insurance (EI) Fund

As with the CPP, both the employer and the employee must contribute EI premiums to the fund. However, there are certain exceptions to the rules for remittance, according to the *Employers' Guide - Payroll Deductions and Remittances*, which is a document employers and their bookkeepers should review at least annually or whenever there is a change in income tax rate or bracket structure. The guide states that

"even if there is a contract of service, employment is **not insurable** and therefore not subject to EI premiums in the case of:

- casual employment that is not expended for your usual trade or business;

- employment when you and your employee do **not** deal with each other at arm's length. Two categories are addressed here:
  - *Related persons:* those connected by blood relationship, marriage, common-law relationship or adoption. Where the employer is a corporation, the employee will be related to the corporation when she/he is related to a person who either controls the corporation or is a member of a related group that controls the corporation.
  - *Non-related persons:* an employment can be non-insurable if it is apparent from the circumstances of employment that the parties were not dealing with each other in the way arm's-length parties normally would;
- when a corporation employs a person who controls more than 40% of the corporation's voting shares;
- employment that is an exchange of work or services;
- employment by an employer in agriculture, in an agricultural enterprise or in horticulture when:
  - the person receives no cash remuneration; or
  - works less than seven days with the same employer during the year;
- employment of a person connected with a circus, fair, parade, carnival, exposition, exhibition or other similar activity, **except** for entertainers, if that person:
  - is not your regular employee; and
  - works for less than seven days in the year"

It is wise to request a ruling when you have any doubts about the requirement to deduct EI premiums for family members or other non-related employees whose circumstances of employment are unusual. Do so by completing Form CPT1, *Request for a Ruling as the Status of a Worker Under the Canada Pension Plan and/or Employment Insurance Act*. Avoid overpaying EI premiums, as they are expensive (1.4% times the employee's contribution) and recoverable for only 12 months in retrospect if paid in error.

Remember also that Form PD24E, *Application for a Refund of Over-deducted CPP Contributions or EI Premiums*, can be filed when EI premiums in excess of the maximum were made for a year in cases where an employee controlled more than 40% of the corporation's voting shares or was not engaged in insurable employment.

Overpayments that are made because an employee works for several employers during the year will be recoverable by the employee by filing an income tax return at year end. However, the employer gets stung here: there are no refunds for you, even if your employee has already maxed out contributory earnings with another employer. You also do not have the choice to stop contributing to the fund because the maximum was already reached for the employee with another employer.

Reduce Tax Withholding—File TD Forms

As an employer, always be vigilant about designing compensation packages that are tax efficient. Start by helping your employee invest more of the first dollar earned—before tax withholding—rather than the last. To ensure that only the correct amount of tax is withheld, your employee must complete Form TD1, *Personal Tax Credit Return,* for the federal government and for the province of residence to report personal tax credit entitlements. Employees who are paid commissions and who claim tax deductible expenses against these may choose to complete Form TD1X, *Statement of Commission Income and Expenses for Payroll Tax Deductions,* instead of Form TD1. Also, note that fishers complete Form TD3F, *Fisher's Election to Have Tax Deducted at Source.*

In some cases, tax withholding can be reduced further by filing Form T1213, *Request for Reduction in Tax Withholding* (see Figure 8.2).

Your employee should initiate the filing when there are additional deductible expenditures during the year that do not show up on the TD1 form. This would include RRSP contributions not deducted from pay by the employer; child care expenses; tax deductible support payments; employment expenses on Form T777, *Statement of Employment Expenses;* carrying charges and interest expenses on investment loans; loss carry-overs; allowable business investment losses; or other items like significant charitable donations or rental losses. Supporting documentation must be attached.

Form T1213, which results in a "Letter of Authority" permitting you to withhold less tax, is not required. That is, you can reduce tax withholding without formal permission if you are otherwise making tax withholdings for any of the following items, which are tax deductible for your employee:

- Employees' contributions to a registered pension plan (RPP)
- Union dues
- Contributions to a retirement compensation arrangement (RCA) or certain pension plans
- Contributions to a registered retirement savings plan (RRSP), provided you have reasonable grounds to believe the contribution can be deducted by the employee for the year

Figure 8.2	**How to Reduce Tax Withholding at Source**

Canada Revenue Agency   Agence du revenu du Canada

REQUEST TO REDUCE TAX DEDUCTIONS AT SOURCE FOR YEAR(S) ——————

- Use this form to ask for reduced tax deductions at source for any deductions or non-refundable tax credits that are not part of the Form TD1, *Personal Tax Credits Return.*
- All your income tax returns that are due have to be filed and amounts paid in full before you send us this form.
- You usually have to file this request every year. However, if you have deductible support payments that are the same or greater for more than one year, you can make this request for two years.
- Send the completed form with all supporting documents to the Client Services Division of your tax services office. You can find the addresses on our Web site at **www.cra.gc.ca/tso** or by calling us at **1-800-959-8281**.
- We will notify you in writing within four to eight weeks whether or not we approve your request.

Identification

First name	Last name	Social Insurance Number

Address

City	Province or territory	Postal code	Residence	Telephone Business

Employer Name	Contact person	Telephone and fax numbers

Address

Request to reduce tax on

☐ Salary   ☐ Lump sum – if lump sum, give payment amount and details (for example, a bonus or vacation pay)

$ _____

Deductions from income and non-refundable tax credits

Registered retirement savings plan (RRSP) contributions .... $ _____
- Give details or a copy of the payment arrangement contract
- Do not include contributions deducted from your pay by your employer

Child care expenses .... $ _____
- Give details on a separate sheet

Support payments .... $ _____
- Attach a copy of your court order or written agreement and Form T1158, *Registration of Family Support Payments* (if not previously filed);
- Recipient's name and social insurance number:

Employment expenses .... $ _____
- Attach a completed Form T2200, *Declaration of Conditions of Employment,* and Form T777, *Statement of Employment Expenses.*

Carrying charges and interest expenses on investment loans .... $ _____
- Attach a copy of statements from the lender confirming the purpose and amount of the loan(s) and the interest payments to be made in the year

Other (for example, charitable donations or rental losses) .... $ _____
- Attach all supporting documents. Use a separate sheet to give details if necessary.
  Specify: _____

Total amounts to be deducted from income $ _____

Subtract income not subject to tax deductions at source (interest, net rental or self-employed income)   – _____

Net amount requested for **tax waiver** $ _____

Certification

I request authorization for my employer to reduce my tax deductions at source based on the information given. I certify that the information given is, to the best of my knowledge, correct and complete.

_____   _____
Signature   Date

T1213 (04)   (Français au verso)   Canada

File the Letter of Authority with your payroll records. This is a great way to bring the benefits of a tax refund directly into your employees' pocketbooks every two weeks. It can help them save on a tax-deferred basis by investing the freed-up tax withholdings into an RRSP, thereby building wealth faster in a tax-deferred manner while averaging into the marketplace all year long.

Remember, a tax refund is a bad thing. Don't overpay taxes within the family. Make that money work for you all year long. You are required to pay only the correct amount of tax and not one cent more.

Pay Tax-Free Perks to Your Employees

A host of tax-free benefits can be paid to your employees, and in some cases your family members. Figure 8.3 provides a checklist of benefits common to small businesses:

Figure 8.3	Tax-Free Perks for Employees and Family
Tax-Free Benefits	**Description**
Wedding or Christmas Gifts up to $500, for arm's-length employees— maximum of two	Not taxable, as long as the gift is not in cash or near-cash and is awarded to an arm's-length employee. Maximum of two non-cash gifts and two non-cash awards. Effective 2010, there is no limit to the number of non-cash gifts or awards as long as aggregate is under $500 annually; however, this policy does not apply to related persons.
Discounts on Merchandise	This status will not extend to cases where the merchandise is purchased below the merchant's cost. A commission received by a sales employee on merchandise acquired for the employee's personal use is not taxable, nor is a commission received by a life insurance salesperson for the acquisition of his/her own policy.
Subsidized Meals	Not taxable if the employee is charged a reasonable amount that covers the cost of food, its preparation and service.
Uniforms and Special Clothing	Payments made by an employer for laundering special uniforms or for reimbursement of the employee's expenses in laundering uniforms will not be taxable to the employee.
Recreational Facilities, including memberships to social or athletic clubs	Pools, gym, exercise rooms or fees paid to be members of a social or athletic club qualify as a tax-free benefit to the employee, if it can be shown such a membership is primarily to the advantage of the employer. See IT148 and IT470.
Moving Expenses if the move was required by the employer	• Cost of movers to move and store household effects • Cost of moving the family including all travelling expenses • Cost to move personal items such as a car or trailer • Reasonable temporary living accommodations in the new work location if the new residence is not ready

Figure 8.3	**Tax-Free Perks for Employees and Family (continued)**

	• Charges for alterations to furniture and fixtures that were part of the old home
	• Costs of cancelling a lease
	• Costs of discharging a mortgage
	• Legal fees and transfer taxes to buy a new home
	• Long-distance charges incurred to sell the former residence plus costs of keeping up the old residence after move if efforts to sell are not successful
	• Costs of house-hunting trips to new location
	• Charges and fees to disconnect telephone, TV aerials, water, etc.
	• Costs to connect and install utilities, appliances, and fixtures from old home
	• Costs of auto licences, inspections and drivers' permit fees if owned at former residence
	• Costs to revise wills or other legal documents if necessary because of move
	• Certain losses on selling of home: The first $15,000 plus one-half the amount over $15,000
Premiums Paid under a private health services plan.	See IT339, which describes private health services plans. Premiums paid to private health services plans are not taxable to the employee. Also be aware that premiums paid by proprietors now qualify as a tax deduction, provided certain conditions are met. The proprietor must be actively engaged in the business; self-employment income must comprise at least 50% of the individual's total income for the year or the individual's income from other sources may not exceed $10,000. As well, a maximum deduction of $1,500 for each individual and his/her spouse and $750 per child will be allowed, unless there is at least one qualifying non-related employee. In that case, amounts are based on the lowest cost of equivalent coverage for non-family members.
Employer's Required Contribution to Provincial Health and Medical Plans	Remittances to certain provincial Health Insurance Plans are considered to be employer levies and so are not taxable.
Attendant Costs	For the assistance of a mentally or physically challenged employee who works in your business. This provision, together with the next one, can go a long way in helping families who support employment of a disabled relative in the family business on a tax-assisted basis.
Transportation to and from work of blind or severely impaired employees	Also includes costs of parking near the work location. A great way to help your disabled relative find a rewarding and productive work position and absorb the costs of attending the jobsite as well.
Employee Counselling Services	Not taxable if for mental or physical health or for re-employment or retirement. Therefore you can have your company pay for your relative's re-employment services once it's time for the person to move on.

Figure 8.3	Tax-Free Perks for Employees and Family (continued)
Employer-Paid Training	Courses taken by the employee that enhance the employer's business activities will be received by the employee tax-free. This is a great way to enhance your employee's resume, but may not apply to relatives (see IT470).
Board and Lodging at a Remote Work Site	See Form TD4 to establish tax-free status on employer-paid board and lodging and transportation at a special worksite.
Subsidized School Services in remote areas	If employer provides free or subsidized school services. This tax-free benefit will not extend to a payment of an educational allowance made directly to the employee unless the allowance covers away-from-home education of a child who is in full-time attendance at a school using one of Canada's official languages. The school must be only as far away as the nearest community to the remote worksite in which there is a suitable school.
Loyalty Programs	Frequent flyer points earned on business are no longer required to be included in employee's income as long as: points are not converted to cash; the plan is not indicative of a form of remuneration; or the plan is not for tax avoidance purposes.
Overtime Meals and Allowances	Beginning in 2009 no taxable benefit will arise if the value of the meal is reasonable (up to $17), employee works two or more hours before or after regular shift, and the overtime is infrequent and occasional in nature.

Note: Employers may be required to remit GST/HST on certain taxable benefits. Effective 2010, the non-taxation of free or discounted transit passes provided to family members of transit employees is a taxable benefit.

As you can see, you can arrange your family's remuneration in such a way that much of it is tax-free by maximizing opportunities to use RRSP deductions and making a point of paying at least a portion of your family's remuneration with tax-free perks. Speak to your tax advisor about the possibilities for the coming year.

TAX ADVISOR

When hiring any employees, including relatives and family members, do the following:

Set Up an Employment Contract   This will help you determine factors of remuneration. Make sure the contract has the following components:

- Identifies the parties to the agreement
- Outlines the duties of the employee

- Outlines the remuneration
- Outlines vacation pay and sick leave policies
- Outlines how changes to the contract will be recorded
- Outlines non-competition agreement
- Outlines confidentiality agreement
- Outlines termination procedures
- Outlines how notices are to be given to each party
- Outlines the binding effect of the contract
- Outlines arbitration procedures (optional)

Your legal representative may suggest other standard clauses to include in all employment contracts. It is important to put your family members on the same legal footing as others hired in your business. For this reason it is a good idea to have every employee sign a contract.

Keep Time Cards for Hourly Staff   You may wish to devise a time card that looks something like the one in Figure 8.4 and then have your bookkeeper summarize the hours.

Figure 8.4   Sample Time Card

Employee Name _____ Emp. No. _____

Week of _____

Day	Time		Tot Time	Time		Tot Time	Time		Tot Time	Time		Tot Time	Tot Reg Hrs	Other Tot Hrs	Total Time
	In	Out		In	Out		In	Out		In	Out				
Sun															
Mon															
Tue															
Wed															
Thu															
Fri															
Sat															
Total															

Keep Formal Payroll Records   These should be summarized in a payroll register with the following components for hourly wage-earners:

- Regular hours, rate of pay, total pay for this period and cumulative
- Overtime hours, rate of pay, total pay for this period and cumulative
- CPP, EI and tax deductions for this period and cumulative
- Total deductions for this period and cumulative
- Net pay for this period and cumulative
- Cheque number

Prepare Payroll Source Remittances   These should generally be monthly but can be quarterly if the source deductions owed are less than $1,000 a month. These remittances are made on a special form that will be forwarded to you regularly by CRA.

Prepare a T4 Slip   One should be prepared for each family member, by February 28, for the prior calendar year.

Preparing the Income Tax Return   Write off the gross wage expenses and the employer's portion of CPP and EI premiums paid for employees during the year.

Proprietors remember: one-half of the CPP/QPP payable on the self-employment earnings will be a deduction in the calculation of Net Income on the tax return (line 222). The remainder will still be written off as a non-refundable credit.

For more information about in-office certificate bookkeeping, payroll, managerial accounting and tax preparation courses in which you may wish to enroll your family members to help in your family business, visit www.knowledgebureau.com.

RECAP. YOU NEED TO KNOW:

- How to employ family members on a tax compliance basis, including document need, actual performance and reasonableness of the remuneration
- How to assess the difference between an employee and a contractor for compliance purposes
- What the filing deadlines are for source remittances and T4 slip preparation
- When to deduct and pay CPP and Employment Insurance premiums

- How to reduce tax withholding payments to account for your employee's tax deductible expenses, refundable and non-refundable tax credits
- How to provide tax-free benefits to your staff and manage perks that are taxable
- How to recover overdeductions made to the CRA for CPP and EI remittances

YOU NEED TO ASK: Your tax advisor for help in setting simple steps to make family payroll costs deductible by:

1. **Paying your family members as you would a stranger:** Put them on the payroll, make sure the work is actually done and pay the relative the same as you would pay a stranger for the same work.

2. **Discussing the difference between a sub-contractor and an employee**: Do you have a contract *of* service, or a contract *for* service? In the former case, you have an employer-employee relationship. Take stock of who has control of the relationship, who owns assets and tools, who bears the risk of financial loss for non-performance and how the job integrates with the business itself.

3. **Understanding the basic payroll equation:** Gross pay, which can include cash and/or taxable benefits, should be clearly defined on each employment contract and thought through with the help of a tax and a legal advisor.

4. **Making compensation tax-efficient:** You can do this by minimizing withholding taxes on RRSP contributions or by adjusting for child care deductions, moving expenses, loss carry-forwards or other deductions or credits the employee may have. You can also endeavour to pay the employee as many tax-free perks as possible.

5. **Making statutory deductions:** You'll be helping to create a tax-assisted pension income source in retirement when you contribute to the CPP. EI contributions need careful consideration—will benefits be payable if your family members are unemployed? Remember, the employer's portion of CPP/EI premiums is tax deductible to you. Be sure to make those contributions on time to avoid interest and penalties. Your income tax remittances can be reduced using forms TD1 and T1213. Check it out; then invest more money sooner to secure your own future.

6. **Contributing to private health insurance plans for family members:** Here's a tax-free perk for the family that's deductible to the business owner, provided that certain conditions are met. For example, there are maximum deduction limits if your workforce is composed primarily of family members.

7. **Subsidizing your employees' meals, giving discounts on merchandise, and paying for athletic club memberships:** These are great tax-free perks you can give to family members to improve their lifestyle and career paths.

8. **Making sure the young contribute to an RRSP as early as possible:** Teens should contribute 18% of their earnings, up to an annual maximum. This is a great way to build long-term, tax-assisted wealth quickly for your teenager.

9. **Giving the whole family a raise with income splitting:** Make sure you calculate the tax benefits of formalizing the work your family does to help grow your small business.

10. **Maximizing TFSA deposits:** Make sure every adult family member contributes company bonuses or other monetary gifts to their own Tax-Free Savings Account (TFSA). However, because there are no Attribution Rules associated with the TFSA, it may make sense for family members to revisit investment ordering in the context of family wealth management. For more information, see two certificate courses from the Knowledge Bureau:

    - Tax Efficient Investment Income Planning
    - The Elements of Real Wealth Management

CHAPTER 9

Often-Missed and Little-Known Family Tax Deductions

"The only true failure lies in failure to start."
HAROLD BLAKE WALKER

KEY CONCEPTS

- Business owners are in the unique position of controlling the first dollar earned, before taxes.
- This starts with minimizing tax withholdings or instalment payments.
- Next, know how to claim often-missed and little-known personal tax deductions to save more money and build wealth faster.
- Take a team approach: paying less tax as a family begins with the use of each individual's "tax-free zone."
- Master income splitting opportunities: avoid the Attribution Rules.
- Multiply the eggs in your family basket and reinvest your surplus income.
- Start with an annual Tax-Free Savings Account (TFSA) deposit.
- Then make maximum individual RRSP contributions.

REAL LIFE: The Hamptons of Elm Street are a typical Canadian family. Husband Tom works as an employee for a computer consulting firm. He earns $85,000 a year and has a company car at his disposal, which adds a taxable benefit of $5,000 to his income every year. Wife Helen stays home with the family but has a part-time craft business she runs out of their home, grossing $25,000 annually. Daughter Suzanne, a happy 14-year-old (yes, that is a bit unusual), babysits every afternoon for the neighbours. She earns $3,500 annually. Son Cal, a 16-year-old volleyball star at his high school, has a part-time job at the local hamburger joint on weekends. His gross earnings are $8,200 annually.

There are numerous changes about to happen in the Hampton household. Tom is considering one of two career moves. He can stay in his current position with no additional perks or benefits, but a big comfort zone. Or he can take a new training course to get a management promotion within his company and renegotiate his contract for cash and/or benefits.

Helen is on the verge of a major expansion in her business. She needs help in production and distribution and is just about ready for a bookkeeper as well. She estimates her gross revenues next year could jump to over $50,000.

Suzanne has just received word of a remarkable opportunity. She is an up-and-coming pianist. She has been asked to tour with a professional production company over the summertime. She would be earning $3,000 a month and living with a chaperone. Her living expenses would be covered.

Cal, showing signs of young entrepreneurship, has decided to take some extra courses after school to shore up his computer skills. He wants to buy a car (doesn't every 16-year-old?) and has been looking for a few more hours at work.

This is one productive family, with all kinds of economic activity being generated. Each individual, as well as the family unit as a whole, has the potential to get more from those economic activities by minimizing tax on earned income and also by maximizing the tax benefits received for as many of their expenditures as possible. The problem is they don't know it and, as a result, overpay their taxes, not just every year, but over a period of years. *Taken together, those often-missed and little-known tax deductions and reductions can amount to a small fortune.*

THE PROBLEM

While it is important to think about every individual's contribution to the income and capital that funds needs and wants, it is when we consider the family unit as a whole that the tax system provides many incentives to arrange affairs within the framework of the law to pay the least taxes possible.

If the Hamptons could plan their affairs as a tax-wise economic unit, chances are their combined productivity would multiply significantly over time. When this happens, more dollars become available for investment purposes—and that's how you build wealth. Further, it's never a good idea to have all the family's eggs in the business basket. Diversifying investments with surplus profits or income can help the family manage risk.

Knowing more about making your expenditure choices tax deductible is particularly important so you can keep your taxable income as low as possible. The more time you have to grow the resulting tax savings within various investment vehicles available to you, the richer you'll be. It's that simple. Problem is, very few families fully take advantage of these opportunities.

THE SOLUTION

Business ownership is the lead source of millionaires' wealth in Canada (26%) and globally (37%).* Of Canada's roughly 230,000 millionaires, 70% are over the age of 50 and one-third are over 70, so they will soon be transferring their primary source of wealth to the next generation—an estimated $1.2 trillion in assets.

Will your family be among those who become millionaires in the next several years? It's very possible. Remember, it takes just as much time and effort to think big as it does to think small. When you think big— on tax savings, that is—you will have a very good chance of joining the ranks of Canada's top earners and wealth creators.

To do this well, a strategy and structure for wealth accumulation, growth and preservation is required so that the investment of your significant resources of time and money transition as intact as possible to the next generation.

That's because, taxes are a big eroder of wealth, both as you are earning the income and later when you tap into your accumulated wealth for retirement or succession purposes. So you need to plan to protect that wealth with the investment choices you make.

The process of understanding how to create more after-tax wealth begins with your annual tax filing obligation. Thank goodness for the tax filing deadline! (Yes, I'm serious!) For many families, filing a tax return is the most significant financial transaction of the year; one that forces people to think about their financial planning strategies at least annually.

Suzanne and Cal, for example, should be as aware as their parents are of current tax brackets and rates their income is subject to. They should know how to take this information into account when they plan the use of their time and money. If this family gets together to combine its opportunities, powerful momentum can result. *In the end, what matters is what you keep.*

Here is what you need to know: to become wealthy, one must accumulate capital. To sustain wealth, one must keep a firm eye on the taxes paid on both income and the accumulated assets to be passed along during a human lifecycle.

---

* Capgemini SA and Merrill Lynch & Company, *National Post*, June 2006.

Capital accumulation is accelerated when more of the first dollars you earn go into your family's collective pockets *sooner*. That's more difficult than it sounds for some. Most employees, for example, don't see the first dollars they earn. Many dollars leave—right off the top—to reside in the coffers of government, through required withholding taxes. To make matters worse, most employees are owed a tax refund when they file their annual tax returns. Some are happy about these "forced savings." But a tax refund is really an interest-free loan you give to government, rather than making an investment in your future. This is not a very good strategy for managing your time and money, especially if you believe you need to take responsibility for your own future.

The impact of overpaying your taxes every year is big. Just multiply the annual tax overpayments made by the whole family over the course of each person's 40 years or so of working life and you will quickly understand that a very big nest egg has dissipated. That's where vigilance over withholding taxes—and the size of your tax refund (a bad thing, now you know)—is important. *Remember: you are obligated to pay only the correct amount of tax and no more.*

Some tax tips are therefore in order: First, know that income taxes become payable when taxable income is "realized" or generated for tax purposes. Second, those who are asset-rich, as well as those in business for themselves, can often choose when that realization will occur. *And when it comes to taxes, timing is everything.*

That's why you need to consider the tax consequences of your financial decisions all year long and discuss the before- and after-tax results of those decisions with your tax and financial advisors regularly. That's called tax planning, and tax planning is for everyone at every income level. You know you're doing well when you pay the least taxes possible annually, over a period of years with individual tax cost averaging. *But it's when the family team gets involved in the process that you significantly multiply your economic power.*

THE PARAMETERS

Family tax-planning activities should include the following:

- **Everyone makes money:** Start by creating enough income in the hands of each family member so that everyone uses up his/her "Tax-Free Zone." This is the Basic Personal Amount on the annual tax return. It is available to everyone, and when you add to this deductions and credits specific to individual circumstances, that Tax-Free Zone grows.

- **Minimize income realized for tax purposes:** Do so to avoid the next tax bracket and the higher marginal tax rates that come with it.
- **Invest with tax efficiency:** Consider TFSAs, registered and non-registered investments (in that order).
- **Diversify the sources of income you earn in the family.**
- **Split income with family members** to leverage Tax-Free Zones and the lower tax rates available to lower income earners.
- **Stay onside the Attribution Rules:** Otherwise, they may reverse your income splitting efforts.
- **Stay on top of little-known and often-missed tax credits and deductions available to your family:** You'll eek out even more tax savings at filing time and ask better questions of your tax advisor.

Following are some basic tax-planning parameters the Hamptons could discuss with their tax advisors to take advantage of the seven parameters above.

Create Income to Maximize Tax-Free Zones

Tax-Free Zones are levels of income Canadian taxpayers can make without paying any taxes at all. This includes a calculation of total deductions and various non-refundable tax credits available for each family member and the family unit as a whole:

Basic Personal Amounts Those with taxable incomes below the Basic Personal Amount (BPA) will pay no taxes.* This annually indexed amount has risen to over $10,000 per person on the federal tax return. This means that a four-member family can earn over $40,000 tax free annually. Therefore, when planning compensation to be paid from family business or investment income, it's important to pay enough to use the BPA, as most unused personal tax credits do not carry forward from one year to the next.

Other common personal amounts that recognize the increased financial obligations of families include amounts for spouse or common-law spouse, an "equivalent-to-spouse" claim, amounts for infirm dependants over 18, age and disability amounts, amounts for those who are caregivers, medical expenses and charitable donations.

See Figure 9.1 for a summary of personal amounts.

---

* However, proprietors may be liable for their portion of CPP premiums on income earned over $3,500—the CPP exemption level.

Figure 9.1	Summary of Personal Amounts for 2008–2009

Personal Amounts		2008	2009
Basic Personal Amount	Maximum Claim*	$9,600	$10,320
Age Amount	Maximum Claim*	$5,276	$6,408
	Reduced by net income over*	$31,524	$32,312
Spouse or Common-Law Partner Amount	Maximum Claim*	$9,600	$10,320
	Reduced by net income over	$0	$0
Eligible Child under 18		$2,038	$2,089
Amount for Eligible Dependants	Maximum Claim*	$9,600	$10,320
	Reduced by net income over	$0	$0
Amount for Infirm Dependants	Maximum Claim*	$4,095	$4,198
	Reduced by net income over*	$5,811	$5,956
Pension Income Amount	Maximum Claim	$2,000	$2,000
Adoption Expenses	Maximum Claim*	$10,643	$10,909
Caregiver Amount	Maximum Claim*	$4,095	$4,198
	Reduced by net income over*	$13,986	$14,336
Disability Amount	Basic Amount*	$7,021	$7,196
	Supplementary Amount*	$4,095	$4,198
	Base Child Care Amount*	$2,399	$2,459
Tuition and Education Amounts + Textbook Tax Credit	Minimum Tuition	$100	$100
		$400	$400
	Full-time Education Amount (per month)	+$65†	+$65†
		$120	$120
	Part-time Education Amount (per month)	+$20	+$20
Medical Expenses	3% limitation*	$1,962	$2,011
Refundable Medical Expense Credit	Maximum*	$1,041	$1,067
	Base Family Income*	$23,057	$23,633
Canada Employment Amount	Maximum*	$1,019	$1,044
Children's Fitness Tax Credit	Maximum*	$500	$500

* These amounts are indexed (and some adjusted per legislation).
† Textbook credit.

Create More Tax-Free Zones with RRSP Room   A taxpayer who earns $10,000 in qualifying "earned income" accumulates 18% or $1,800 in RRSP contribution room. There are two things you need to note here:

- Family members who are not taxable by virtue of the Tax-Free Zone must still file a tax return to accumulate RRSP contribution room on their qualifying income sources.
- In the following year, the Tax-Free Zone will be increased by RRSP contributions made. In our example, then, using the RRSP opportu-

nity and the available Basic Personal Amount, each family member could make about $12,000 a year—$1,000 a month—*and still pay absolutely no taxes*. (However, this also depends on the province of residence, so check it out with your tax advisor.)

Further, the RRSP reduces "Net Income" on the personal tax return, which is a figure used to determine the size of other refundable and non-refundable tax credits available to supporting individuals for their family members. This is an investment that just keeps giving back, so *you really can't afford not to make it*.

TFSA Contribution Room Creates Tax-Free Income   The best kind of money is free money, and here is a great opportunity to get your hands on some. Taxpayers must file a tax return to create "unused TFSA contribution room"—the ability to contribute annually to the Tax-Free Savings Account. While the contribution to the account is not tax de-ductible, an investment here will build earnings—interest, dividends and capital gains, for example—on a tax-free basis. Over time, that's a significant family wealth builder that cannot be ignored. Every adult in the family should have a TFSA and contribute to it annually and consistently. The maximum contribution is $5,000 (plus indexing) per adult in the family.

More Tax Freedom with Deductions and Non-Refundable Tax Credits   Now you know that every taxpayer, including the low-income earners of the family, should strive to increase their Tax-Free Zones and/ or reduce on each individual's tax return with an RRSP contribution in order to create new tax savings.

Minimize Income Realized for Tax Purposes

Once Tax-Free Zones are established and maximized, it's important to minimize the income that will be subject to tax. You have learned that one way to do this is to reduce your gross business income with deduct-ible expenditures to arrive at net business income.

This principle holds true when reporting other income sources you earn throughout the year to arrive at your income for tax purposes. You will want to reduce that overall income subject to tax within the context of tax "preferences" available (i.e., different tax rates on varying income sources, together with available tax deductions and credits). In short, from a "big picture" point of view, it's important to know how much tax you'll pay on the next dollar of income that's earned and when those taxes need to be paid.

The next dollar you earn could push you or your family members into a new tax bracket, subject to a higher tax rate. Take this into account as you plan income levels for both your active income sources, your pension withdrawals and the passive income your family will earn from investments. It helps to make decisions about what income levels to generate for each family member together with your tax and financial advisors. In fact, these decisions can be as important as asset allocation within an investment portfolio in determining your ultimate family worth.

At the time of writing, the following federal brackets and rates were in effect:

2009 Federal Tax Brackets and Rates

Up to $10,320	0
$10,321 to $40,726	15%
$40,727 to $81,452	22%
$81,453 to $126,264	26%
Over $126,264	29%

Tax brackets are indexed according to increases in the consumer price index, so you'll want to keep current on changes by speaking to your tax advisor and/or checking www.knowledgebureau.com for any news.

When we covered tax brackets and rates in earlier chapters, we urged you to consider a Tax Savings Blueprint—a series of "what if" scenarios to calculate your tax efficiencies annually. We are now suggesting that you expand your blueprint to include the family unit as a whole and investment income as well as business income.

Your big opportunity as a business owner rests with your ability to work with the first dollar you earn (remember, employees must usually invest with after-tax dollars as their withholding taxes come off the top). Because the first dollar earned comes straight to you, you can plan your own compensation and investment strategies as well as those of your family with more control over earnings and when they are generated for tax purposes. If you believe money invested today will be worth more tomorrow, you will want to save and invest more now and defer tax as far into the future as possible.

Decisions to Be Made   How much income is required to be "realized" for tax purposes in order to take advantage of tax-free zones and taxation preferences on various income sources so that you can better fund your lifestyle and invest for the future? How much tax can you avoid now to take advantage of the time value of money? Here are some suggestions for using the power of your business structure to make decisions:

- Make sure the business pays for any expenditures that are tax free or tax deductible: Make sure that everyone in the family keeps receipts for travel, meals, school-related items, work-related expenditures, etc. It's possible some, if not all, of those receipts are tax deductible. Sometimes those items can be received from the company on a tax-free basis. In other cases, such as free or discounted travel passes provided for an employee's family member, amounts received will be considered a taxable benefit to the employee.

  Tax law and administrative policy constantly evolve, so it pays to keep on top of this. For example, did you know about the following tax-free benefits that can be provided to employees, including your relatives who work in the business?

1. **Loyalty programs (frequent flyer points):** Starting in 2009, the CRA will no longer require frequent flyer points earned while flying on business to be included in an employee's income so long as three conditions exist:
   - The points are not converted to cash
   - The arrangement is not an alternate form of remuneration
   - The arrangement is not for tax avoidance purposes
   Where an employer controls the points (e.g., via a company credit card), the employer will continue to be required to report the fair market value of any benefits received by the employee as income on the employee's T4 slip when the points are redeemed.

2. **Overtime meals and allowances provided to employees:** Beginning with tax year 2009, no taxable benefit will arise if:
   - The value of the meal or meal allowance is reasonable (a value of up to $17 will generally be considered reasonable)
   - The employee works two or more hours of overtime right before or right after his or her scheduled hours of work
   - The overtime is infrequent and occasional in nature. Fewer than three times a week will generally be considered infrequent or occasional. If overtime occurs on a frequent basis or becomes the norm, CRA considers the overtime meal allowances to be a taxable benefit since they start taking on the characteristics of additional remuneration.

3. **Travel within a municipality or metropolitan area:** Starting with tax year 2009, allowances paid for an employee to travel within

the municipality or metropolitan area may be excluded from income if the allowance is paid primarily for the benefit of the employer, such as when the principal objective of the allowance is to ensure that the employee's duties are undertaken in a more efficient manner during the course of a work shift.

Discuss the options you have for tax-free compensation through perks and benefits or through the deductions available on the tax return to offset employment income, itemized later in this chapter.

- **Split individual income sources receivable over two tax years:** For example, if you are going to pay out lump sums like retiring allowances or bonuses, make an RRSP withdrawal or sell capital assets, try to spread out the income over two tax years if possible. This should allow you to tax cost average by avoiding marginal tax rate spikes. You will learn more about this shortly.
- **Keep an eye on investment income sources too:** There is much you can do to make sure your tax-efficient business income blends well with income created by your investment portfolio. For example, you can plan to offset capital gains generated in the year with prior year capital losses incurred. However, this requires the review of your investment portfolio on a regular basis, preferably with both your tax and financial advisors. It's always good when you can find a team of professionals who can work together with you to maximize tax-efficient income generation opportunities.

Remember too that when you have "redundant income" from the business, it may need to be retained for future investments in capital assets or in the human resources you need to expand. But if you decide to put it into investment accounts, work with financial advisors who understand your business structure and can help you plan income tax deferrals in tune with your goals for the business enterprise.

In short, understand your "income mix" for tax purposes. Don't generate more taxable income than what's required to meet your immediate cash flow needs and your plans for retirement income. Invest the rest, tax efficiently. To do so you'll need to know more about investment income sources and how to blend them with your business income.

Invest with Tax Efficiency

People who are in business for themselves must take care of their own futures. That's why those often-missed and little-known family tax deductions we've been talking about are so important. You need to have a heightened awareness of the size of your after-tax dollar so you can save and invest for the "rainy days" in your business and, of course, for your own future needs and wants. Business owners who understand the budgeting and forecasting process for their business enterprises can easily apply those skills to their family's income and wealth planning requirements.

Together with their tax advisors, astute business owners anticipate "redundant income" and invest it tax efficiently, as soon as possible. It is in fact possible to plan salary and other income levels in advance to generate just the right amount of money to fund an orderly investment process. Depending on your family and business structure, the following three categories of investments and the order in which you make your deposits should be discussed in detail with your tax and financial advisors at least annually:

1. **Tax-Free Savings Accounts (TFSAs):** The name says it all. Invest here first if you have no earned income for RRSP purposes; second if an RRSP will provide you with an opportunity for double-digit tax savings; or third after RESPs and RDSPs if the government granting structures attached to those plans are important to you. Use these savings for emergencies if you need to (as TFSA contribution room is never lost) or as a "parking lot" within which you accumulate the funds you need for other specific future purposes (remember, your earnings will compound on a tax-free basis here).

   A good example is pension income savings. If you have both employment and business income and belong to an employer pension plan, you may be precluded from making RRSP contributions because of your Pension Adjustment (PA) amount. Likewise, if you have contributed the maximum to your RRSP—18% of earned income—and want to do more to supplement your retirement savings on a tax-assisted basis, the TFSA gives you a good opportunity to tap into yet another tax-deferred savings opportunity.

   The TFSA also provides retirees a place to continue to shelter investment earnings when they reach age 71 and are required to withdraw taxable retirement benefits from their RRSP accumulations. Reinvestment of some of those amounts into a TFSA will allow those tax-paid dollars to grow again—faster—in a tax-sheltered TFSA account as opposed to a non-registered account.

2. **Registered accounts:** Shelter as much of your taxable income as possible with RRSPs, RDSPs, RESPs and RRIFs as a way to reduce taxes and tax cost average. Find out first whether you are eligible to con-

tribute to an RRSP—the most often-missed tax saver for people with actively earned income from business or employment. Then identify the tax savings you'll earn by making your RRSP contribution and move those into the next best sheltered investment vehicle for your family's needs.

3. **Non-registered accounts:** To get your taxable "income mix" just right year over year, you'll want to work with your tax and financial advisors on your taxable income plan for each family member before the end of each calendar year—your most effective time for such planning.

   After creating the right amount of income from active sources like employment or business income to invest in the registered accounts described above, you will have the opportunity to next place your savings into non-registered accounts that generally earn taxable interest, dividends or capital gains.

   Interest earnings are taxed at the highest marginal rates, as there are few deductions we can use to offset those earnings, with the exception of carrying charges like interest costs, investment counsel and safety-deposit-box fees. But when it comes to dividends and capital gains, the tax filing results can be more advantageous, as you will see below.

Diversify Income Sources Earned by Family Members

Income from varying investment sources stemming from your investments in non-registered accounts can have an effect on family Tax-free Zones, as shown in Figure 9.2, excerpted from The Knowledge Bureau's *EverGreen Explanatory Notes*.

You will notice that ordinary income like employment, pension and interest income will attract higher marginal rates of tax than dividends and capital gains. Your after-tax results also depend on your province of residence. This illustration highlights marginal tax rates on various income sources in the province of British Columbia, the best province in the country in which to earn dividend income. In fact, at certain tax brackets we see a "negative tax" in which the dividend tax structure creates a reduction in taxes owing on other income of the year.

Depending on where you live in Canada, the earning of dividend income can provide a substantial Tax-Free Zone. In some provinces, you can earn well in excess of $30,000 in dividends before paying any tax. However, in the case of dividend income, remember that the dividend gross up will affect Net Income on the personal tax return (Line 236).

Figure 9.2	Federal and Provincial Marginal Tax Rates for 2009			
	Ordinary Income	**Capital Gains**	**Small Corp. Div.**	**Eligible Div.**
BC Up to $10,320	0%	0%	0%	0%
$10,321 to $17,845	15.0%	7.25%	2.08%	−5.75%
$17,846 to $35,716	20.06%	10.03%	2.03%	−15.81%
$35,717 to $40,726	22.70%	11.35%	14.08%	−1.83%
$40,727 to $71,433	29.70%	14.85%	15.21%	−0.38%
$71,434 to $81,452	32.50%	16.25%	18.71%	3.68%
$81,453 to $82,014	36.50%	18.25%	22.71%	9.48%
$82,015 to $99,588	38.29%	19.15%	25.95%	12.07%
$99,589 to $126,264	40.70%	20.35%	28.96%	15.57%
Over $126,264	43.70%	21.85%	32.71%	19.92%

This is the figure upon which other deductions, refundable and non-refundable tax credits are based.

So to make sure all your deductions and credits are claimable, you need to be careful not to overweight your dividend income in certain cases. For example, if you choose to earn dividends only from your small business corporation, you will miss maximizing the CPP and RRSP contribution room you'll build by taking a salary.

You may find that the grossed-up dividend will artificially increase other provincial "taxes" in the form of user fees, expenditures like nursing home per diem rates, pharmacare deductibles or other user fees based on the results of your federal tax return.

Recently two tiers of dividends were introduced in Canada: eligible and ineligible as shown in the table below. For "eligible" dividends paid after 2005, a revised dividend gross-up and dividend tax credit mechanism applies. Most dividends paid by public corporations resident in Canada will be eligible under this scheme, as will certain dividends from Canadian-Controlled Private Corporations (CCPCs) taxed at the general rate. Where the dividend is eligible, the gross up is 145% of the actual dividends, and the dividend tax credit is 19% of the grossed up amount (for the 2009 tax year). The result is that the marginal tax rate on such dividends is substantially lower.

There are, however, changes on the horizon when it comes to the taxation of eligible dividends, as outlined in the table below, indicative of budget proposals in effect at the time of writing:

Year	Dividend Gross Up	DTC Rate (of gross up)
Eligible Dividends		
2009	45%	27.50%
2010	44%	25.88%
2011	41%	23.17%
After 2011	38%	20.73%
Ineligible Dividends		
2009	25%	13.33%
2010	25%	13.33%
2011	25%	13.33%
After 2011	25%	13.33%

These changes have been anticipated as corporate tax rates have been reduced in recent years. Discuss with your professional advisors the effects of these foreseeable changes on your personal tax and investment planning.

Ineligible dividends represent those paid from business profits that were subject to the small business deduction, which is available to qualifying small business corporations. For business owners, it's important to consider whether to create a bonus to keep corporate profits under this small business deduction level, particularly if retirement income planning with eligible and ineligible dividends is part of the discussion. Income projects now and in the future can help with these decisions.

The earning of capital gains can also increase your Tax-Free Zone. Capital gains result when an income-producing asset is disposed of for more than its original cost, plus additions and improvements. They are taxed extremely advantageously in that accrued increases in value are never taxed until disposition. Then, on disposition, only 50% of the capital gain is included in income. Therefore, if the taxpayer's only income of the year is from a capital gains disposition, the capital gain could be twice the Tax-Free Zone (that is, with the Basic Personal Amount at just over $10,000, capital gains of $20,000 will be tax free).

To earn a taxable capital gain, the taxpayer must dispose of an asset in one of the following ways:

- Through the actual sale of the asset
- Through a "deemed disposition," which can occur:
  - When one asset is exchanged for another
  - When assets are given as gifts
  - When property is stolen, destroyed, expropriated or damaged

- When shares held by a taxpayer are converted, redeemed or cancelled
- When an option to acquire or dispose of property expires
- When a debt owed is settled or cancelled
- When property is transferred to an RRSP or other trust
- When the owner of the property emigrates
- When the owner of the property changes the asset's use from business to personal
- When the owner of the property dies

Split Income Earned by the Family

Business owners are in a unique position to take advantage of a number of ways to split income with family members to create the lowest overall household tax cost over a period of time. You have learned that business income can be split by paying family members who work in the business. For example, if Tom reported all the money earned in the family (let's say $126,700), the family tax liability would be just over $36,000 (depending on province of residence). Assume, however, that $25,000 of this is earned by wife Helen and $8,200 by son Cal, both of whom work in the family business. In that case, the actual family liability is less than $27,000, a difference of more than $9,000 a year. Multiply this by Tom and Helen's approximately 40 productive working years, and you have tax savings of over $360,000, assuming no changes in earnings or tax structure. That's too large a number to ignore in your planning.

As you can see, family income splitting is a very important financial skill. In fact, when you couple income splitting with wise use of RRSP contribution room, many families could be earning part-time income completely tax free, qualifying for more refundable tax credits like the Child Tax Benefit, investing more money on a tax-free basis in a TFSA, and increasing cash flow to pay down non-deductible credit card or mortgage debt faster with the resulting savings.

It all adds up to more wealth, sooner, for you and your family.

Other ways to split income depend on the various operating structures and your income sources. For example:

- Incorporated business owners can sprinkle dividends—retained earnings of the company—to various shareholders, who can be family members.
- The use of family trusts can further enhance your ability to distribute earnings and capital to beneficiaries.

- Those who withdraw funds from an eligible private pension plan can split retirement income with their spouses under certain conditions.
- Those who reach the age of 60 can split their CPP benefits with their spouses in some cases.

To do all of this well requires the help of a tax professional. But to begin, you must be well versed in the "Attribution Rules," which seek to prohibit taxpayers from avoiding taxation by transferring income from the higher earner to the lower earners in order to reduce or avoid taxation. These rules will be discussed in more detail in the next section.

Stay Onside With the Attribution Rules

Money transferred by one spouse (the higher earner) to another (the lower earner), who then invests the sums in a non-registered account and earns interest, dividends or capital gains, will result in attribution of earnings back to the higher earner for tax purposes.

In the case of minor children (those under 18), interest or dividend income resulting from the investment of gifts or transfers of money will generally be attributed back to the transferor. Resulting capital gains remain taxable in the minor's hands. There are other exceptions to the Attribution Rules and some precautions to be aware of.

For family business owners, the exceptions begin with salary or wages paid to a spouse or children according to the rules outlined earlier. As you have learned, those earnings are properly taxed in the hands of those family members who actually did the work and at a fair and reasonable wage or sub-contract agreement.

Precautions are in order when dividends or management fees from a corporation owned by a parent are paid either directly or through a trust to minor children. Those amounts are taxed at the highest marginal rate on the child's return. Talk to your tax advisor about this "kiddie tax."

When other sums are transferred to a spouse or children, the tax consequences can be more complicated because of the Attribution Rules on income transferred to a spouse or children. Please review the following rules to ensure you have a good understanding of this concept for decision-making purposes.

Definition of Spouse   To understand the Attribution Rules, you must be aware of the definitions of "spouse" and "common-law partner":

- A *spouse* is a person of the same or opposite sex who cohabits with the taxpayer in a conjugal relationship as a legally married couple.
- A *common-law partner* (same or opposite sex) is someone who co-habits with the taxpayer in a conjugal relationship for at least 12 continuous months, or who lives with the taxpayer and has a child in common (through birth or adoption), or who has control and cus-tody of the taxpayer's child and that child is dependent on them for support.

Note that since January 1, 2001, the following rules have existed:

- "Spouse" will refer only to those legally married.
- A retroactive election is possible for 1998, 1999, and 2000 for same sex couples to be considered common-law partners if this is to the couple's advantage.

Invest in TFSAs for All Family Members   Attribution Rules can be avoided altogether when investments are made in a TFSA for family members. Here's what you need to know about investing in this plan:

- **Age limitation:** Contributions can be made by/for those who have attained 18 years of age and are residents of Canada. There is no up-per income limitation.
- **Earned income limitation:** Unlike making an RRSP investment, there is no earned income limitation.
- **Contribution deductibility:** Contributions to the TFSA account are not deductible.
- **Earnings accumulate on a tax-free basis:** This includes interest, dividends and capital gains.
- **Contribution room**: Every TFSA holder can contribute a maximum of $5,000 per year, and this amount will be indexed after 2009, with rounding to the nearest $500. Withdrawals (distributions) from the fund will create new TFSA contribution room in an amount equiva-lent to the withdrawal.
- **Carry-forward room:** Unused contribution room can be carried for-ward on an indefinite carry-forward basis. You can take money out, in other words, spend it on whatever you want, and then put it back in later because the TFSA contribution room has been preserved.
- **Withdrawals:** Distributions of both earnings and principal are tax exempt.

- **Excess contributions:** When you contribute more than your annual maximum, you will incur a penalty tax of 1% per month until the amounts are removed. (The government understands that you'll think this is a very good thing.)
- **Purpose:** Recipients can take money out for whatever purpose they wish and create new TFSA contribution room, which means they can put it back in to grow when the withdrawal need is met and new savings are achieved. This will be welcome news to grandparents in particular.
- **Income testing not affected:** Income-tested tax preferences like Child Tax Benefits, Employment Insurance Benefits or Old Age Security pensions are not affected by earnings in the plan.
- **Attribution Rules:** There is no Attribution Rule attached to the new TFSA, allowing parents and grandparents to transfer $5,000 per year to each adult child in the family for the rest of their lives. In addition, one spouse may transfer property to the TFSA of the other spouse without incurring attribution. Have grandparents, aunts and uncles gift into the TFSA, which they can also do without attribution.
- **TFSA eligible investments:** The same eligible investments as allowed within an RRSP will apply to the TFSA. A special rule will prohibit a TFSA from making an investment in any entity with which the account holder does not deal at arm's length.
- **Interest deductibility:** Interest paid on money borrowed to invest in the TFSA is not deductible.

Create Income From a Spouse's Business   You can avoid Attribution Rules when you lend your spouse the money needed to start a small business, as the subsequent profits and losses of the business will be taxed in the hands of your spouse. Capital dispositions, however, would be taxed in your hands.

Pay a Wage or Salary to Your Spouse or Children Who Work in Your Business   As you know, you can avoid attribution here too, as your children will report the income on their tax returns and create RRSP room; you report the amounts paid as a legitimate deduction from your business income.

Managing Joint Accounts   *Always document income in joint accounts and from the sale of principal residences in order to maximize income splitting opportunities.* The interest earnings generated from money held in a joint account will be taxed according to the ownership of the principal. That is, if the husband earned 90% of the principal, he would report 90% of the earnings. If 100% of the money in the account came from the wife's inheritance, however, 100% of the earnings will be reported by her.

Let's say a husband and wife married in their early twenties. The wife worked for a couple of years before staying home to raise a family. She contributed $5,000 toward the $10,000 down payment of their first home, which was 50% of the equity. On the sale of that home, the family made a $25,000 tax-free gain. (Remember, gains on the principal residence are tax exempt.) This money was reinvested in a larger principal residence that was later sold, this time for a $50,000 tax-free gain. This happened two more times during this couple's marriage. Today, they have sold their last home and moved into a rented condo to maximize their travel opportunities. They have $250,000 in a joint account, the accumulated principal and gains from the tax-free appreciation of their various principal residences. In this case, subsequent investment earnings can be properly split between husband and wife, because the wife's participation in the original transaction can be traced.

Invest Lower Earner's Money   When low earners receive income, they should invest rather than spend it. It can make perfect sense, for example, for those who receive proceeds from a tax-exempt life insurance policy, an inheritance, a GST/HST credit or tax refund, for example, to reinvest those sums to generate tax-free investment earnings if possible. Use the TFSA for those purposes if the recipient is an adult, or consider maximizing tax-free zones for dividends and capital gains discussed earlier. Otherwise, investments by low-income earners generate tax at lower marginal rates, so it usually makes sense for them to invest while the higher earner buys the groceries.

Invest in Your Own RRSP   With the introduction of pension income splitting rules, taxpayers can now elect to split periodic income received from an RRSP or RRIF (Registered Retirement Income Fund) once age 65 is reached. This is a very good tax savings provision, though not quite as good as the opportunity for those who receive retirement pension income from a superannuation or company pension plan. (Those folks can income split at any age.) Business owners should discuss corporate investments in Registered Pension Plans (RPPs), Retirement Compensation Arrangements (RCAs) and Individual Pension Plans (IPPs) to meet tax efficiency goals by sheltering more of their earnings now and by tapping into tax preferred retirement benefits later.

Invest in Spousal RRSPs   Despite the lucrative pension income splitting rules described above, investing in an RRSP for your spouse under the spousal RRSP rules can still be a very good way to invest to avoid the Attribution Rules and split income in retirement. This provision allows you to make an RRSP contribution for your spouse based on your own RRSP earned income *and* take the deduction on your return too. To do so, you must have actively earned income, and resulting RRSP contribution room, in a prior year. You can find out what your RRSP contribution room is by looking at last year's Notice of Assessment or Reassessment.

Earnings within the spousal RRSP will not be taxable until there is a withdrawal, and then the withdrawn amounts are taxed in the hands of the spouse. It may make sense, for example, to start drawing money from the spousal RRSP for pre-age 65 retirement fun first if you are both under age 65 and your spouse is in a lower tax bracket.

But be careful. If the withdrawal is made within three years of the last contribution to any spousal RRSP, the principal will be taxable to the contributor (i.e., you). Beyond this, withdrawals are taxed to the spouse. A little loophole can be used when the RRSP accumulations are transferred to an RRIF. In such cases, minimum withdrawals under the RRIF rules will not be subject to the Attribution Rules when those payments come from a spousal RRSP.

So it's important to speak to your tax advisor first, as you are planning your retirement early in life, to set up RRSP contributions for both spouses that position you to split income in retirement so you can keep more to have memorable times together with.

Invest in a Child's RRSP   You can gift your child money to invest in his/her own RRSP. Resulting investment earnings will be tax sheltered until the child withdraws the money from the plan. However, the child must have "earned income," which creates RRSP contribution room. To register this with CRA, the child must have actively earned income and filed tax returns to report the income every year. Be sure to report all earnings from part-time work like babysitting, lawn care, snow shovelling, etc.

Invest in an RESP for the Child   Education savings are always a priority for families, so it's good to know that not only are taxes on earning generated in the plan tax deferred but also that an investment in a Registered Education Savings Plan for a child under 18 will generate a Canada Education Savings Grant (CESG) from the federal government. Twenty percent of your contribution to a maximum of $500 will be granted each year. The maximum CESG is usually achieved when you put away $2,500; however, an enhanced grant is available at rates of 40% and 30% of the first $500 invested, in cases where family income levels are lower. A Canada Education Savings Bond is also available to encourage very low earners to participate in the plan.

Earnings within the RESP accumulate tax free, as mentioned, and if the child chooses to withdraw the funds later to attend a designated educational institute, the earnings and CESG grant will be taxable in his/her hands. Often that means tax-free distributions to the student. Speak to your tax and financial advisor about the immediate return you'll reap on your investment via the CESG, and then try to make a contribution *at the end of every year* to maximize savings opportunities with the CESG.

Invest in an RDSP for the Disabled   A new savings plan was introduced in 2008 with the specific purpose of accumulating funds, on an attribution-free basis, for the benefit of a disabled person and his/her ability to fund a retirement lifestyle. The Registered Disability Savings Plan (RDSP) functions in very much the same way as RESPs do, in that the government provides generous matching grant structures to enhance the earnings potential in the plan. Speak to your tax and investment advisors about the details:

- **Eligibility:** Any person eligible to claim the Disability Tax Credit can be the beneficiary of an RDSP, and the plan can be established by the individual or by an authorized representative. Anyone can contribute to an RDSP—neither the beneficiary nor the contributor need be a family member. This makes the RDSP a very significant vehicle for community philanthropy.
- **Tax treatment:** Contributions are not deductible, but income earned accumulates in an RDSP tax free. Contributions withdrawn from an RDSP are not taxable, but all other amounts—accumulated investment income, grants and bonds—are taxable in the hands of the beneficiary as withdrawn.
- **Contributions:** There is no annual limit on contributions, but lifetime contributions cannot exceed $200,000. Contributions are permitted until the end of the year in which the disabled beneficiary turns 59.
- **Withdrawal of funds:** The beneficiary must start to withdraw funds from the RDSP in the year he or she turns 60. Maximum annual withdrawal amounts are established based on life expectancies, but an ability to encroach on capital is also possible. Only the benefi-

ciary and/or the beneficiary's legal representatives can withdraw amounts from an RDSP. Contributors can never receive a refund of contributions.

- **Canada Disability Savings Grants (CDSG) and Canada Disability Savings Bonds (CDSB):** The federal government provides generous matching contributions depending on family income level and amounts contributed. Family income is calculated in the same manner as it is for Canada Education Savings Grant purposes except that in years after the beneficiary turns 18, family income is the income of the beneficiary and his/her spouse or common-law partner. There is a lifetime maximum of $70,000 that will be funded under the CDSG, and an RDSP will not qualify to receive a CDSG from the year in which the beneficiary turns 49.

  When it comes to the Canada Disability Savings Bond, unlike the CDSG, there is no requirement that a contribution be made to a RDSP before a savings bond contribution is available. The maximum annual CDSB contribution is $1,000, and this is earned where family income does not exceed about $21,000. The CDSB amount is phased out completely when family income is just under $40,000. (These amounts are indexed annually.) There is a lifetime maximum of $20,000 for CDSBs. Like the CDSG, CDSBs will not be paid after the beneficiary of the RDSP turns 49.

Grant Interest-Bearing Loans to Family Members   Spouses can lend money to each other, use the funds to generate investment earnings and have those earnings reported for tax purposes on the return of the debtor, provided that the loan bears a commercial rate of interest and that the interest is paid at least once a year, no later than 30 days (January 30) after the end of the calendar year. The higher earner must report that interest on his/her return.

This is an excellent way to split investment earnings on accumulated capital, particularly if the prescribed interest rates, set quarterly by CRA, are low. You will want to bring this up with your tax advisor whenever you review your quarterly instalments or when significant changes occur within your portfolio (i.e., significant contributions or losses are anticipated).

Transfer Dividends to Spouse   If your spouse's income is so low that he/she is not taxable but has earned dividend income (and the offsetting dividend tax credit, which will be going to waste in the absence of taxes payable), the higher earner can elect to transfer that dividend income and the dividend tax credit to his/her return, if a tax advantage results. The catch is that the transfer must create or increase the spousal amount claimable for the lower earning spouse. The benefits, if any, will depend on the size of the transferor's income. This is a situation where a number of "what if" scenarios should be considered with the help of your tax advisor.

Invest Child Tax Benefits Received　The Canada Child Tax Benefit (CCTB), the Universal Child Care Benefit ($100 a month for each child under age six) and provincial Child Tax Benefits received for a child may be invested in an account held in trust for that child. If the money is untainted by birthday money or money that should be attributed to another adult, resulting interest, dividends or capital gains will be taxed in the child's hands. These benefits are discussed later in more detail.

Invest Gifts From Grandparents Who Live Offshore　The Attribution Rules can be avoided on money received from non-resident grandparents or other relatives, provided the money is held in trust for the child and not used by adults for any other reason.

Accumulate Tax-Free and Tax-Deferred Income Within Life Insurance Policies　Usually it costs little to invest in a child's life insurance policy, and this can grow to a lucrative tax-free pension or estate in some cases. Speak to your insurance advisor about this.

Know the Taxation of Income and Assets on Death of a Spouse　While the Attribution Rules can create hurdles for you during your lifetime, CRA does show a bit of consideration at time of death. For example, life insurance policy proceeds are received by beneficiaries on a completely tax-free basis. (The time to arrange to pay for such a policy is when you are healthy. Look into it now.)

In addition, taxable assets can be transferred to your spouse on a tax-free basis. This includes accumulations within an RRSP, RRIF, other annuities, as well as the transfer of assets held outside a registered plan. In the latter case, the assets may be transferred to the spouse at the adjusted cost base calculated for the deceased, at fair market value (which means the capital gain, if any, is reported on the final return of the deceased, if this is advantageous) or at any amount in between. Be sure to maximize use of any available capital losses on the final return.

Transfers of assets to children are usually at fair market value in death as in life, with the exception of certain farming assets. Transfers of RRSP/

RRIFs to dependent children may also qualify for a tax-free rollover even if there is a surviving spouse. But you should receive tax advice before filing the final returns of a deceased taxpayer and, better still, in anticipation of your tax status, well before death.

Buy Lottery Tickets Jointly   If all else fails, don't forget to buy those lottery tickets jointly too. Earnings on the resulting investment of your tax-free windfall could then be split in the future between the winners.

Now that your total income mix is as tax efficient as possible, let's move to the filing of the personal tax return and the categories of deductions you should ask your tax advisors about to make sure as many of your expenditures as possible are deductible.

Find and Maximize Deductions and Credits

If you have made good decisions throughout the year about the type of income sources to realize for tax purposes and how to leverage and invest your savings on a tax-efficient basis, then when it comes time to file taxes, you must put a plan in place to find and maximize family tax deductions and credits. That begins with a meeting with your tax practitioner—no more dropping off the shoe box of receipts and heading for the door!

Challenge your advisors to help you understand what tax deductions and credits are new this year and how they might fit in with what's new in your family's personal, investment and business affairs. Remember that there are two types of tax reducers available on your tax return, and you should know the value of each to better plan what you'll do with the savings in your investment portfolio:

- Tax deductions
- Tax credits

Tax Deductions   The value of a tax deduction is directly proportionate to your marginal tax rate. If your marginal tax rate on income is 22%, each tax deduction you can find will reap a tax saving of 22 cents on the dollar. If your marginal tax rate is 45%, each deduction is worth 45 cents on the dollar. The higher your income, the greater the value of a tax deduction.

There are three types of deductions to look out for at tax filing time:

- Deductions that reduce your Gross Income to arrive at Total Income
- Deductions that reduce Total Income to arrive at Net Income on Line 236 of your personal tax return
- Deductions that reduce Net Income to arrive at Taxable Income on Line 260

Deductions That Reduce Your Gross Income to Arrive at Total Income   These are the specific expenses paid that offset taxable income sources before including the income on your return. They can include items like wage loss replacement plans (reduce the gross taxable amount by premiums paid into the plan), research grants (arrive at Net Income for tax purposes by reducing the grants by direct expenses incurred), capital gains (reduce the gross gain with outlays and expenses to generate the disposition) and business income (proprietors are taxable on Net Income) to allow you to arrive at the total income. See Figure 9.3 for details.

Deductions That Reduce Total Income to Arrive at Net Income   This is probably the most important line on the tax return as Net Income determines the level of tax payable before deducting non-refundable and refundable tax credits on the return. Ask your tax advisor about your ability to claim the following tax deductions:

- Registered Pension Plan deductions from Box 20 of T4 slips or Box 32 of T4As
- Registered Retirement Savings Plan deductions
- Saskatchewan Pension Plan deductions
- Union, professional or like dues
- Child care expenses, as computed on Form T778
- Disability supports deduction
- Business investment losses
- Moving expenses, as computed on Form T1-M
- Deductible child/spousal support payments
- Carrying charges on your investments, like interest and safety-deposit-box fees
- Exploration and development expenses
- Deductions for one-half of CPP contributions for a self-employed taxpayer
- Other employment expenses, including artist's and musician's expenses

Figure 9.3	Deductions That Reduce Total Income on Line 150

Income Source	Deductions Allowed	Documentation Required
Employment Income on Line 101*	Up to $1,000 received by volunteer emergency services personnel is tax-exempt.	None, except a properly completed T4 slip.
Net Research Grants on Line 104	The cost of out-of-pocket expenses incurred in the research process.	A statement itemizing list of expenses.
Wage Loss Replacement Benefits	The cost of premiums paid by the employee since 1968 can offset this income.	Obtain a statement from your employer to verify this amount.
Rental Income	Operating expenses of running the revenue property, including capital cost allowance. Some restrictions apply.	Records of all income receipts, operating expenses, auto logs, and capital acquisitions and dispositions, mortgage fees and payments, etc.
Taxable Capital Gains	Costs of outlays and expenses including brokerage fees and appraisal fees.	All income reports from brokerage houses and sale of other properties including cost of improvements; expense receipts.
Support Payments	Total amount is reduced for child maintenance if pursuant to agreement made after April 1997.	Court order or written agreement or election to consider child support non-taxable.
Other Income	The first $500 of income from scholarships, fellowships, bursaries is tax exempt; however it is 100% exempt if the student qualifies for the education credit; also the first $10,000 of death benefits received from a deceased's employer recognizing the deceased's contributions or unused sick benefits. In the case of retiring allowances, rollovers into an RRSP qualify for an RRSP deduction; sometimes a deduction for legal fees is allowed if the taxpayer had to fight to establish rights to the severance.	Keep all supporting documentation for any income sources reported here, including payments for serving on a jury, RESP distributions, payments out of a retirement compensation arrangement, interest earned on loans made for investment purposes to lower-earning family members, annuity payments not reported as pension income.
Self-Employment Income from unincorporated small businesses, professional practices, commission sales agents, farmers or fishermen.	All reasonable operating expenses incurred to earn income from a business with a reasonable expectation of profit, including a deduction for Capital Cost Allowance on business assets.	All supporting income deposit records, receipts and logs for all business expenditures and asset acquisitions and dispositions.

* Note the Canada Employment Amount will also be available to address the costs of employment, as will the Amount for Public Transit Passes. Check this one on Schedule 1.

- Cleric's residence deduction
- Other deductions on Line 232, including legal fees incurred to collect salary and wages owed to an employee; to establish a right to a retiring allowance; to enforce payment of maintenance amounts previously established as payable; and to appeal an assessment of tax, interest or penalties under the Income Tax Act, Employment Insurance or Canada Pension Plan
- Clawback calculation of Employment Insurance or Old Age Security

Deductions That Reduce Net Income to Arrive at Taxable Income

- Employee home relocation loan deduction per your T4 slips
- Securities options deduction as itemized on your T4 slips
- Other payments deduction for social assistance, worker's compensation or federal supplements
- Limited partnership losses of other years
- Non-capital losses of other years
- Net capital losses of other years
- Capital gains deduction
- Northern residents' deductions
- Additional deductions for vows of perpetual poverty, net employment income from the United Nations and its agencies, income exempt under tax treaty and alimony or child support received from a U.S. resident.

Tax Credits

There are two types of tax credits.

Federal Refundable Tax Credits include the Canada Child Tax Benefit, the Goods and Services Tax Credit, the Working Income Tax Benefit and a host of provincial refundable tax credits. Both spouses must file a tax return to receive these amounts, as the credits are dependent on your net family income. Those age 19 and over should file to recoup their own Goods and Services Tax Credit by filing a tax return at age 18.

Non-Refundable Tax Credits, on the other hand, are the allowances the government makes for personal circumstances that warrant consideration under the tax system. These were covered earlier in our discussion of tax brackets and rates.

The federal amounts are found on Schedule 1 of the T1 General Return and provide the same benefit to all taxpayers, regardless of income level.

Similarly, the provincial amounts found on the individual provincial tax calculation forms yield the same benefit for all taxpayers. Some recent additions to the list include the following:

- **Canada Employment Credit:** This credit recognizes the costs of work-related expenses such as driving to and from work, lunch and dry cleaning. It amounts to just over $1,000 annually, as it is indexed to CPI inflation.
- **Children's Fitness Tax Credit:** Up to $500 in eligible fees paid for children under 16 to participate in eligible sports and physical activity programs became available starting in 2007.
- **Pension Income Credit:** For those eligible private pension recipients age 65 (or those under 65 receiving eligible pension income), a tax credit of up to $2,000 is possible when qualifying income is received periodically.
- **Amount for Public Transit Passes:** Beginning in 2006, families can claim a credit for monthly or annual Public Transit Passes on the tax return of each individual who purchased one. Receipts are required in order to claim the credit. However, there are special benefits to being a business owner who hires family members when it comes to this expense. Starting in tax year 2010, CRA's policies regarding transit passes provided to employees will be as follows:
  - Passes for the exclusive use of the employee will be tax free
  - Free or discounted passes for the use of the employee's family (who are not working in the business) will be a taxable benefit Either way, it's a good idea to get the business to pay for the passes.
- **Tuition, Education and Textbook Tax Credit:** This credit recognizes the cost of textbooks for post-secondary students and is claimed, beginning in 2006, as part of the tuition and education credit, based on a monthly allocation, depending on whether the student is in full-time or part-time attendance.

Other changes are covered later in the book and should be discussed in detail with your tax advisor. For a complete annual federal and provincial budget summary, see www.knowledgebureau.com. It's free and provides a good starter script for your discussions.

You should know that many tax credits are "income-tested" and can be "clawed back."

Clawback Zones

For taxpayers in income ranges between approximately $10,000 and $125,000, a variety of "clawback" provisions exist to return the benefits of certain tax preferences to government as income rises. The effect of this is that low to middle income earners often have a higher marginal tax rate compared to those at top income levels, who do not qualify for these social benefits. It is therefore most important that those family members who find their income within a clawback zone work every legal angle to reduce Net Income. Top choice is the RRSP, if you are age eligible and have the required earned income sources. Discuss these clawback zones with your tax and financial advisors to see if you can reduce them within the family unit to increase your tax efficiencies and your social benefits. For recent clawback zones, visit www.knowledgebureau.com.

THE TAX ADVISOR

Having understood the basic parameters surrounding the claiming of tax deductions and credits, you will now want to know and implement a few strategic tax plans with your professional advisors:

Create New Capital Monthly   Minimize your tax withholdings on your employment income. Remember that a tax refund is a bad thing— pay only the correct amount of taxes each month and invest the difference. Review your tax withholdings on form TD1 and T1213 as previously discussed. If possible, have your employer make RRSP contributions directly to your RRSPs from your gross income earned, thereby getting you the benefit of your tax refund right away. Also, if you pay tax by instalments, minimize your quarterly tax obligations by anticipating income levels, tax reductions and credits for this tax year. Discuss these very important issues with your tax advisor and ask for a Tax Savings Blueprint specifically aimed at minimizing tax prepayments.

Pay Off Non-Deductible Debt   Credit card balances attract very high interest rates. A smart way to reduce these costs is to make an RRSP contribution (monthly or annually), reap your tax savings and then pay off your personal credit cards and their non-deductible interest costs.

Turn Non-Deductible Debt Into Deductible Debt   Borrow for investments placed in non-registered accounts; the interest on such loans will be deductible. (Please note that the interest paid on money borrowed to invest in TFSAs, RRSPs and RESPs will not be deductible.) Opening a home-based business and claiming home office expenses will make your mortgage interest costs partially deductible, or you can borrow against the equity in the home, place investments in non-registered accounts and then write off the interest on the loan. Discuss these options with your tax advisor.

Maximize RRSP Room for All Family Members   The first way to do this is to file a tax return each and every year in which there is "earned income," which includes:

- Salary or wages before the deduction of Employment Insurance, Canada Pension Plan or RPP contributions, employee contributions to a retirement compensation arrangement or the cleric's residence deduction.

PLUS:

- Income from royalties from a work or invention of which the taxpayer was the author or inventor
- Net research grants
- Supplemental unemployment insurance benefits
- Employee profit-sharing plan allocations
- Net rental income
- Taxable support payments or repayments included in income, including support payments received by a common-law spouse
- Net income from carrying on a business where the taxpayer is actively engaged in the daily operations, either alone or as a partner
- After 1990, income received from a CPP/QPP disability benefit

LESS:

- Refunds of salary, wages or research grants
- Union dues or professional dues paid
- Other employment expenses
- Current-year losses from carrying on an active business
- Current-year net rental losses
- Support payments deducted or repaid
- Any amount included in business income that represents the excess negative balance from dispositions of eligible capital property over and above recaptured deductions previously taken

Once earned income is known, the figure is multiplied by 18%. The result is then compared to the maximum dollar limits for the tax year. The lesser of the two is used in the calculation of the RRSP deduction claimable on Line 208.

Tax Planning Is for Everyone—Ask Your Advisors for Help at Tax Time   To maximize all tax savings opportunities your annual tax filing routine affords you, discuss tax efficiencies for every family member with your tax advisor at tax time. Some talking points follow regarding children and those who earn income.

Make Plans for Tax-Efficient Savings for Minors

- Save income attributed to the child (like Child Tax Benefits or the Universal Child Care Benefits) in a separate bank account, untainted by gifts or other transferred funds from adult relatives. Resulting earnings are taxed in the hands of the child.
- Invest a child's employment or self-employment earnings, then have the higher-income earner in the family pay for consumer goods. Resulting investment income is either not taxed at all (if income falls under the Tax-Free Zones) or taxed at low rates.
- Make sure the minor files a tax return. Actively earned income sources from part-time jobs, including work in the family firm, qualify for the building of RRSP room, which can be of assistance in reducing tax or maximizing tuition/education credits later.
- Gifts may be made to a minor child; however, until the child turns 18, resulting earnings in the form of dividends or interest are taxed back to the adult. The only exception to this rule is the earning of capital gains, which can accumulate in the hands of the child.
- Contribute to an RESP for your minor children in order to take advantage of the Canada Education Savings Grant and tax-deferred accumulations of earnings.
- Start investing in a TFSA for each child once he/she turns 18.

Tax Planning Strategies for Net Incomes Under $126,000

- Income deferral, diversification and income splitting opportunities are vital in this income range. Find ways to legitimately transfer income to lower earners in the family.
- These income ranges are in the "clawback zones," where marginal tax rates can increase dramatically as social benefits are clawed back through the tax system. This includes the value of the Age Amount,

Canada Child Tax Benefits (CCTB), GST Credits, OAS receipts and EI Benefits.

- Maximize RRSP contributions first to reduce the high marginal tax rates clawbacks sting you with. Then utilize all tax deductions to reduce Net Income, including full RRSP room, to avoid clawbacks of refundable tax credits.
- Maximize child care expense claims (up to $7,000 for children under the age of 7, $4,000 for those age 7 to 16 or over age 16 and mentally or physically infirm, and $10,000 for any child for whom a disability amount is claimable). Special provisions are available for students.
- Separated couples may wish to revisit old taxable support payment agreements in light of generous new federal/provincial Child Tax Benefits (CTB), particularly if recipient and payer are both in the lowest tax brackets. Enhanced Child Tax Benefits could bring more tax relief than the support payments deduction.
- Consider earning more taxable dividends or capital gains in your investment portfolio.
- Maximize non-refundable tax credits like medical expenses and charitable donations.

Tax Planning Strategies for Net Income Over $126,000

- Always make your maximum RRSP contribution, then contribute to a TFSA for each family member. Remember that you can fully avoid attribution on TFSA investments.

  Consider investing in an Individual Pension Plan (IPP) or Retirement Compensation Arrangement (RCA) to shelter more of your earnings over and above the RRSP contribution maximum.
- Plan to average realized taxable income in business and investment portfolios and consider adding Labour Sponsored Tax Credits and flow through shares to your portfolio. Remember that capital gains transferred to charities result in a charitable donation receipt and no tax consequences on the gains themselves.

Shelter and Split Private Pension Income

Once you are ready to take a taxable pension by converting RRSP accumulations to an RRIF (Registered Retirement Income Fund) or annuity, you should decide what income level you will want to create with your withdrawals, being mindful of Tax-Free Zones for the lower-earning spouse and tax bracket levels for the higher earner. It is generally best to withdraw the money from a sheltered plan in the hands of the lower earner first, to bring income up to either the Tax-Free Zone, if the person has no other income, or at least to within the upper limit of the first tax bracket.

However, with the introduction of pension income splitting, a lucrative new opportunity arises for you to reduce the taxes you will pay on your retirement savings. Speak to your tax advisors about the election to split your RRSP/RRIF retirement benefits.

Remember, a tax-free rollover of unused RRSP accumulations to a surviving spouse is possible upon the death of the first spouse. However, remaining amounts are taxable when the second spouse dies. Therefore, it is often more tax effective to realize RRSP income during your lifetime, especially when both spouses are alive, as tax brackets and rates can skyrocket when large RRSP accumulations are added to the final return on death.

Tax Planning for Taxpayer's Death

- As a regular part of tax and financial planning activities, individuals should prepare a tax projection every year to anticipate tax liabilities should unexpected death occur, particularly if there are valuation changes in the non-registered investment portfolio or the value of the business itself. Most business owners are poorly prepared for succession, sometimes because they think they are invincible but mostly because they fail to anticipate how soon to start their succession planning activities.
- Life insurance policy requirements should be closely reviewed to cover potential tax liabilities and for the purposes of leaving a tax-free estate to the family.
- TFSA/RRSP/RRIF beneficiary elections should be made and wills updated to ensure hassle-free rollover of assets to the proper beneficiaries.
- Remember, RRSP/RRIF accumulations of the second surviving spouse may be subject to tax upon that person's demise. This generally means the estate will lose almost half of its accumulations to tax. Perhaps that survivor, who may be at a lower tax bracket in life, should consider generating the tax on the registered funds by withdrawing and reinvesting funds in a non-registered account or possibly a universal life insurance policy.
- Bring forward unused capital/non-capital loss balances for use on the final return.

- Discuss planned giving for those whose estates are adequate and already cover family concerns. Remember, capital gains tax exemptions are available for donated shares from public companies.

No Such Thing as a "Stupid Tax Question"

Tax rules are always changing; so are personal lifecycles. Be prepared to ask your tax advisor lots of questions about the latest tax changes for your family members and discuss how they relate to lifecycle changes—births, deaths, marriages, divorces, new careers, new businesses, etc. Your goal is three-fold:

1. **To reduce taxes in the current year** by claiming every often-missed and little-known tax deduction that applies to you and your family
2. **To recover overpaid taxes from prior years** because you may have missed some of those items
3. **To plan to save taxes in the future** on a tax-efficient basis

You have learned a great deal about those three objectives in this chapter. But to really win on the tax planning side, make an attempt to understand current economic and political trends in order to recognize the impact of those trends on family tax filing profiles. Be sure to read federal and provincial budget summaries every year. You can do so at **www.knowledgebureau.com**.

Recover, Correct and Amend

When you find out about those often-missed, little-known family tax deductions, which you may not have claimed in the past, be sure to recover the tax benefits you may have missed. Perhaps you have missed filing a tax return completely. Or maybe you have a guilty conscience about the overstated deductions or under-claimed income on your return. If so, tap into CRA's Taxpayer Relief Provisions. That is, you can apply to recover missed tax deductions and credits, file missed returns or amend returns for most provisions over a period of 10 calendar years, provided you forward an adjustment request (use Form TI-AD) outlining the error or omission and attach supporting documentation. Your tax advisor can help you with this and explain the process. In the meantime, consult the check list of Tax Savers for tax adjustments on prior filed returns in Figure 9.4.

ACTION PLAN: Summary of Often-Missed and Little-Known Family Tax Deductions and Credits

Take a moment now to work through our family tax write-off check list in Figures 9.4, 9.5 and 9.6.

For specific tax deductions allowed to investors and seniors, use the check list in Figure 9.5 to double check Grandpa and Grandma's prior-filed returns.

For specific tax deductions for those reporting income from self-employment, use the check list in Figure 9.6. Review business statements and the personal tax return itself to ensure the points in the check list have been claimed in the past and are supported by receipts.

RECAP. YOU NEED TO KNOW:

- How to maximize each family member's Tax-Free Zone and marginal tax rates
- How to diversify income sources and accumulate capital in an order that offers maximum tax efficiency
- How to split income with family members, staying onside with the Attribution Rules
- How to make decisions that help you maximize new taxation rules for dividends and capital gains
- How to maximize tax deductions, refundable and non-refundable tax credits
- How to avoid the clawback zones
- How to pay off non-deductible debt and make debt deductible
- How to use tax planning strategies all year long to reduce income taxes for each individual and the family unit as a whole
- How to take the savings you find by making sure you claim all your deductions and turn them into investments that generate a tax-efficient retirement income and sustainable wealth for your family in the future

Figure 9.4	Check List of Tax Savers* for Tax Adjustments on Prior Filed Returns

Tax Deductions

❑ RPP Contribution
❑ RRSP Contributions for each family member
❑ Elected split pension amount
❑ Union or professional dues paid
❑ Child Care Expenses paid
❑ Disability Supports Deduction
❑ Business Investment Losses
❑ Moving Expenses
❑ Spousal Support
❑ Child Support (agreements before May 1, 1997, or certain specific purpose or third party payments)
❑ Carrying Charges and Interest Expenses
❑ Exploration and Development Expenses
❑ Employment Expenses
❑ Cleric's Residence Deduction
❑ Repayments of Employment Insurance
❑ Repayments of Old Age Security
❑ Repayments of Worker's Compensation
❑ Payments of Legal Fees for objecting to an assessment or appeal under the Income Tax, EI, CPP or QPP legislation, collection of late child support payments, collection or establishment of a right to retiring allowances or pension benefits
❑ Repayments of retiring allowances or Canada Pension Plan benefits
❑ Repayments of refund interest paid by CRA
❑ Refunds of undeducted RRSP contributions made after 1990 and received in the tax year
❑ Deduction for CPP contributions on self-employment or other earnings

Tax Credits

Non-Refundable Federal Credits

❑ Claim for Basic Personal Amount
❑ Claim for the Age Amount (65 & older)
❑ Claim for Spousal Amount
❑ Claim for Eligible Dependant Amount
❑ Claim for Eligible Child under 18
❑ Claim for Infirm Dependant over 18
❑ Claim for the Pension Income Amount
❑ Adoption Expenses
❑ Claim for the Caregiver Amount
❑ Claim for the Disability Amount (be sure to obtain a Form T2201 signed by the attending medical practitioner)
❑ Claim for Tuition/Education and Textbook Amount
❑ Claim for Student Loan Interest Amount
❑ Claim for the Canada Employment Amount, Amount for Public Transit Passes, Children's Fitness Amount
❑ Claim for Transfers from Spouse, including the Age, Disability, Pension Income and Tuition/Education and Textbook Amounts, depending on the spouse's net income
❑ Claim for Medical Expenses, the excess of total expenses for the best 12-month period ending in the tax year, over 3% of net income, to a maximum limitation
❑ Claim for Donations and Gifts, usually based on a limit of 75% of net income; this two-tiered credit can be calculated with unclaimed donations of the prior five years. Group family claims together to exceed $200 a year to maximize tax savings.

Refundable Tax Credits

❑ The Child Tax Benefit
❑ The Goods and Services Tax Credit
❑ Provincial Child Tax Benefits
❑ Overpayments of CPP Premiums
❑ Overpayments of EI Premiums
❑ The Refundable Medical Expense Supplement
❑ Refunds of investment tax credits
❑ Employee and partner GST/HST rebates
❑ Overpaid tax instalments
❑ Provincial/Territorial tax credits

* Attach supporting documentation

Figure 9.5	**Tax Write-Offs of Investors and Seniors**

Tax Deductions from Income Lines

❑ Capital gains income is reduced by outlays and expenses like:
- brokerage fees or legal fees
- appraisal fees or surveyors fees
- finders fees or commissions
- advertising costs
- transfer taxes

❑ Revenue Property Owners may write off operating expenses like:
- mortgage interest, insurance, property tax
- maintenance and repairs
- accounting fees, advertising, office stationery costs, travelling expenses in certain cases, utility costs, condo fees
- management fees, landscaping fees
- When claiming Capital Cost Allowances on assets, you may not create or increase a loss with this deduction

Deductions from Total Income

❑ Carrying Charges. Interest and dividend income can be offset by claiming interest expenses, safety-deposit-box fees, accounting fees, investment counsel and management fees for assets held outside an RRSP/RRIF/RESP.

Tax Credits (Non-Refundable)

❑ The Age Amount is claimable by those who attain age 65 during the year, but reduced at certain net income levels.

❑ The Pension Income Amount is claimable by those who received a periodic pension from superannuation, or those aged 65 or older who receive private periodic pension income sources. Those who receive these amounts as a result of the spouse's death will also qualify.

❑ The Caregiver Amount is claimable by those who provide in-home care to parents/grandparents over the age of 65 or other relatives over the age of 18. There is an upper net income ceiling level.

❑ The Disability Amount is claimable by those who have a disability that is severe and prolonged for a continuous period of at least 12 months.

❑ The Amount for Public Transit Passes will apply to the cost of transit starting in July 2006.

❑ Amounts Transferred from Spouse allows the higher income spouse to transfer unused credits for the Age Amount, Pension Income Amount, Disability Amount, and Tuition/Education and Textbook Amounts.

❑ Medical Amount is claimable for unreimbursed medical expenses of the family in the best 12-month period ending in the tax year.

❑ Charitable Donations provide a lower tax credit on the first $200 and 29% on the balance. Donations of shares from public companies can be made on a tax-exempt basis.

Figure 9.6	Tax Deductions of the Self-Employed

Tax Deductions

❑ Accounting Fees, Legal Fees
❑ Advertising, Marketing and Promotion
❑ Asset Repairs and Maintenance
❑ Assistant's or Other Employee's Salaries
❑ Auto Expenses
❑ Bad Debts
❑ Board and Lodging while on the road
❑ Bonding and Licensing
❑ Business Meals and Entertainment (50%)
❑ Canada Pension Plan contribution payable on self-employment income (one-half)
❑ Capital Cost Allowances on Assets are subject to time limitations for adjustments. Be sure to correct errors or omissions within 90 days of receipt of a Notice of Assessment/ Reassessment.
❑ Commissions paid to Sub-contractors
❑ Convention Expenses (2 per year)
❑ Disability-Related Expenses
❑ Insurance and Interest costs
❑ Leasing costs for building or equipment
❑ Office-in-the-Home expenses
❑ Telephone and other Communications Costs
❑ Other operating expenses

Tax Credits

❑ Canada Pension Plan contributions payable on Self-Employment income (one-half)
❑ Investment Tax Credits on specified asset purchases
❑ Taxes paid during the year by installments

YOU NEED TO ASK: Your tax advisor about simple ways to make sure it's deductible for each family member by:

- Finding ways to maximize every family member's Tax-Free Zones using Personal Amounts available to your advantage
- Diversifying income sources to average down the tax you pay
- Transferring income, deductions and credits from one family member to the other
- Minimizing realized income in the year
- Deferring income to the future
- Maximizing tax-free and deferred investment vehicles
- Maximizing the tax deductions and tax credits available on your tax return every year based on your income

CHAPTER 10

How to Create Serious Wealth

"Only you can hold yourself back, only you can stand in your own way. . . . Only you can help yourself."
MIKHAIL STRABO

KEY CONCEPTS

- Recent tax changes provide excellent tax saving and deferral opportunities for small business owners.
- Every business owner should periodically discuss the evolving organizational structure of his/her business with professional advisors.
- Incorporation can offer new tax savings, income diversification and tax-deferral opportunities.
- Share ownership in a small business corporation can lead to tax-free gains on the sale of qualifying shares.
- Retirement savings and significant family wealth creation can result from such gains.

REAL LIFE: When Thomas started an electronic marketing company out of his basement office a couple of years ago, he would never have guessed what path his business venture would take him on.

Those first years were so lean. Thomas barely scratched together enough money to lease his computer. But he had an idea and a dream. He built a base of institutional buyers of his custom-designed intellectual property. His income rose steadily, from a loss of $10,000 in the first year to a profit of $60,000 in year two and $120,000 in year three. By year four, Thomas realized he was paying altogether too much income tax.

Thankfully, it was at this point that he made some strategic decisions that really paid off. You see, quite unexpectedly, Thomas would soon be approached to sell his business.

THE PROBLEM

How can there possibly be a problem? Not only did Thomas survive the start-up years, but he is bringing home more money than he ever did working for someone else! It gets even better: next year he'll bring home more, and, as time goes on, he'll see the ongoing expansion in his revenue and profits. His personal net worth is looking pretty good too.

The problem is that many start-up entrepreneurs fail to anticipate just how quickly their businesses can take off. This is particularly true of those who start an enterprise due to negative circumstances, such as the loss of a job.

What's important to understand is that besides generating profits, every business owner has the potential to build equity. The technology, product, distribution method or client base you have built and invested in represents value that another firm may someday wish to acquire. Such equity presents an opportunity with significant tax advantages, and if set up properly, the structure of the venture can greatly enhance your family's after-tax coffers.

THE SOLUTION

Every business owner should be discussing the best structure for his/her business organization with a tax advisor regularly. For many, a key question is whether the business should be incorporated or continue operating as a proprietorship.

The answer is often one of timing. For example, you may wish to earn start-up losses in a proprietorship in order to offset other income of the year, such as income from a severance package. Or, if there are excess losses in the start-up years, you may wish to carry them back and offset employment income earned in the best of the last three tax years to recover prior taxes paid.

You will also want to maximize your retirement savings opportunities, starting with your RRSP contribution room, which as you have learned is generated from actively earned sources like employment income from a full- or part-time job and self-employment income from a proprietorship.

As an unincorporated business grows and start-up losses are absorbed, personal tax rates can become an expensive way to fund needs and save for retirement wants. That's where a corporate entity can provide absolute tax relief, allowing the business owner to fund expenditures with before-tax dollars or larger after-tax dollars. In addition, a small business corporation can help the business owner diversify remuneration to earn employment income—including tax-free and taxable perks, dividends and capital gains—while taking advantage of some excellent tax deferral and income splitting opportunities.

But of equal or possibly even greater importance is the fact that upon the disposition of the shares of a small business corporation, each shareholder can take advantage of a $750,000 Capital Gains Exemption (CGE). On the tax return, 50% of the CGE will be claimed. This is known as the capital gains deduction (CGD). For a family of four adult shareholders, this can amount to $3 million in tax-free gains. Significant wealth.

Proprietors should therefore discuss the timing and potential benefits of incorporation with their tax advisors. Important questions include:

- Who will own the shares?
- What class of shares should each family member own?
- How do we determine who gets dividends and when?
- Should individuals hold the shares or should it be a holding company or perhaps a family trust?
- How do we protect the family business in case of separation/ divorce or a shareholder's bankruptcy?
- What are the costs of incorporation, tax filings and ongoing compliance or audit work?
- What differences will the new structure make to my accounting cycle and the volume of work due to new banking arrangements?
- How are shares of the company valued on sale, transition and/or shareholder's death?
- Under what circumstances can shareholders tap into the capital gains deduction?

In Thomas's case, the opportunity to sell his business came in year three. He was offered $2 million for his software company. Due to effective tax planning, Thomas's family kept much of that money for themselves.

THE PARAMETERS

Small business owners should become familiar with the key advantages of incorporation. Consider the following as starting points in your exploration of the right opportunities to leverage your productivity and investment in your business:

1. **Limited personal liability:** Corporations are set up under provincial laws, which vary from one province to another; this is true of their tax rates as well. Also, while one of the advantages of incorporation is a limitation of personal liability, be aware that practicing members and shareholders of professional corporations are **not** so protected.

Larger professional practices are more commonly organized as limited liability partnerships (LLPs), which protect individual partners by not holding them personally liable for the professional negligence of other partners. Check these variations with your lawyer and accountant and discuss how to best take advantage of a corporate structure to limit your risk exposure.

2. **Lower tax rates:** Effective January 1, 2009, the first $500,000 of active business income earned within a Canadian-Controlled Private Corporation (CCPC) that qualifies for the small business deduction is subject to a lower federal corporate tax rate. Many provinces are following suit at the time of writing. The result is that the first half-million dollars of business income earned within the corporation is usually taxed more advantageously than if it was earned by the individual directly. In addition, tax changes in recent years have significantly reduced taxes that apply to net income of business corporations.

3. **Increased purchasing power:** The federal tax rate applied to a CCPC income earning the small business deduction is 11% at the time of writing; when provincial rates are added to this, the combined rates range from 12% in Manitoba to 19% in Quebec. Contrast this to a top marginal rate for a proprietor of about 45% (exact amounts depend on your province of residence) and you can quickly see that earning your after-tax income in the corporation is much more powerful. Your larger after-tax dollars can therefore lower the costs of funding your business operations as well as expenditures that are otherwise non-deductible by you personally. Such expenditures include life insurance, 50% of meals and entertainment costs, employee loans, asset acquisitions, education and training, up to two conferences per year and group health or pension costs.

4. **Flexibility in choosing fiscal year end:** Note that a corporation can choose any taxation year it wishes, as long as the first taxation year does not exceed 53 weeks after the corporation commenced. This means that you can choose July 1 to June 30, thereby deferring taxation of personal bonuses and dividends. However, a professional corporation that is a member of a partnership must end its taxation year at the end of each calendar year.

5. **Tax deferral:** Your tax-efficient after-tax profits earned within the CCPC can be paid out as dividends to the individual. Timing plays an important role here. For example, if the corporation generates

a profit at the end of its fiscal year (December 31) of $50,000, the dividends can be declared and paid in January. This has the effect of deferring the payment of personal tax to April 30 of the next tax year. The extra money you are holding onto can be invested to earn income at lower tax rates within the corporation, to employ additional resources or to reduce borrowing costs.

6. **Optimum salary/dividend mix:** Dividends attract lower marginal tax rates than ordinary income from employment and other sources. You have learned in earlier chapters that there are two types of dividends: "eligible" and "ineligible." This terminology refers to specific tax treatment afforded to each, and you do need to know more about this if you are actively involved with your advisors in structuring your family's after-tax income and retirement savings opportunities.

   The government strives for "perfect integration" between the corporate and personal tax systems, but it's more an ideal than a reality. The theory is that an individual taxpayer should be indifferent as to whether he/she earns income personally or whether the income should be earned by a corporation, which then pays a dividend to the individual. In a perfectly integrated system, the amount of total taxes paid by the individual and corporation will be identical to the total taxes paid by the individual alone, regardless of the individual's marginal tax rate. Taxpayers and their advisors must carefully review the salary/bonus/dividend mix that generates annual taxable income for each family member and be aware of the rules described in an earlier chapter relating to changes to dividend taxation. The best time to have this conversation with your tax advisor will vary from situation to situation, but at the very least, do so in the last quarter of the calendar year when you are contemplating other year-end tax planning issues, such as tax loss selling and strategic planning for charitable donations.

7. **Bonus planning:** Any income that exceeds the small business deduction is subject to the higher "general income tax rate." This rate, fortunately, has been decreasing over the years, as described below. Dividends paid from income subject to the general income tax rate are eligible for a lower overall marginal tax rate than the ineligible dividends resulting from income qualifying for the small business deduction.

Federal Corporate Income Tax Rates, 2008–2012

	2008	2009	Rates, % 2010	2011	2012
General corporate income tax rate	19.5	19.0	18.0	16.5	15.0

For more profitable corporations, then, it might make sense to "bonus down" to the federal small business limit ($500,000 at the time of writing) to reduce the corporation's tax burden. The effect of such a move depends on the corporation's province of residence and, in the case of the individual, the tax rate at which the bonus will be taxed personally. Some time for planning is allowed: bonuses must be paid within 180 days of the corporation's fiscal year end. If a bonus is to be paid, the corporation gets the deduction now; the owner-manager or family members report the bonus later, and that's a great way to leverage your resources.

In making the decision to pay a bonus or not, ask your tax accountant to crunch some numbers to take into account the dividend taxation rules, the maximization of RRSP and TFSA room and whether the opportunity to receive "eligible" dividends in the future might result in a better income mix in retirement. (That decision will of course subject your current corporate income to the general rate, but given that it's dropping, this is a valid question and potentially a viable tradeoff.) In short, will your family unit's net position—in the corporation and personally—be better if you take the bonus, the dividends or a combination of both?

8. **Bonus on non-active business income:** The reasonableness of a bonus could be challenged by CRA where it is used to reduce otherwise non-active income of a business, as in cases where the owner-manager does not have control over the income earned. Non-active business income is income that would be taxed in the corporation as investment income. These amounts include dividends, capital gains from the sale of assets and interest income, to name a few such sources.

9. **RRSP planning:** You will want to earn sufficient salary to maximize your RRSP contribution dollar maximum for each family member. Ask your tax advisor to identify this salary figure for you when you receive your Notice of Assessment. You'll be able to do more planning that way. For example, to reduce the amount of tax that is required to be withheld from a bonus, consider paying a portion of the bonus directly into an RRSP. The amount contributed to an RRSP will be deducted from the total bonus when determining the

amount of tax to withhold. This is an excellent way to start earning tax-deferred retirement income immediately and to avoid a spike in tax rates when the bonus is paid out.

Also, always be mindful of the effect of dividends or a bonus on your requirement to make increased quarterly instalment payments regarding your personal tax liability or on social benefits repayments, for Old Age Security or Employment Insurance, for example. Taxpayers eligible for making RRSP contributions can help avoid or reduce those uninviting consequences as well.

10. **Income splitting:** Reasonable salaries paid to family members will reduce the corporation's taxable income while splitting income subject to personal taxation. We have discussed these concepts in other chapters, but remember that compensation planning, done well, partners with your retirement income and portfolio planning.

   Dividends, for example, do not qualify as earned income for CPP or RRSP purposes, so take that into account when planning your after-tax results now and your potential for future retirement income. Dividends also cannot be split with spouses, except in those cases where a transfer of dividends from the lower earner to the higher results in an increased spousal amount on the personal tax return. Dividends can also be paid to adult children who are shareholders, depending on your share structure, thereby diversifying income sources earned by each family member and averaging the overall tax burden downward (in most provinces). There are many options to choose from in planning income well throughout each family member's lifecycle. Work closely with your advisors to do so.

11. **Corporate Attribution Rules:** There are a number of ways to split family income through a corporation, but there are some obstacles to clear. These are commonly referred to as corporate attribution rules. For example, if you make a low-interest or interest-free loan to a family corporation with the main purpose of reducing your income and benefiting your spouse or minor children, you will be deemed to receive interest on the loan at CRA's prescribed interest rates, reduced by any interest you actually receive on the loan. This must be reported on your tax return.

   The second obstacle is the "kiddie tax," which prevents the transfer of income from high-earning individuals to their children under the age of 18. Kiddie tax rules provide that, rather than redirect the income to the parents' hands, the minors pay tax on the income at the highest marginal rate.

12. **Insurance planning for exit strategies/death of shareholder:** The use of a buy-sell agreement should be an important part of any shareholder's agreement. This agreement can cover everything from death of a shareholder to exit strategies for the living. Insurance planning can play an important role when considering a buy-sell agreement, especially when a shareholder dies, as the proceeds received from the insurance policy can be used to purchase the shares from the deceased shareholders' estate. Further, in the event of a living shareholder exiting the corporation, it is possible to insure someone else, usually older, and on their death use the proceeds to purchase the shares.

13. **Use of Individual Pension Plans:** Discuss this option with your tax advisors as a way to contribute more tax-deferred amounts toward your pension income planning than would normally be allowed under the RRSP rules because of the earned income limitation. It may be a good idea in particular to consider an IPP immediately before selling your company. Depending on your company's profitability, it is also possible to make past service contributions, which could be to your advantage both to increase future retirement income and to reduce corporate taxation now. However, a "Pension Adjustment" will result, which will in return reduce your RRSP contribution room for those years. Also amongst the disadvantages, spousal contributions are not allowed, funds are usually locked in and administration costs, though tax deductible, can be higher. But do discuss this opportunity with your advisors.

14. **The Capital Gains Exemption:** The Capital Gains Exemption (worth $750,000 per individual at the time of writing) is available to taxpayers who own shares in a qualifying small business corporation, a qualified farm property or—effective for dispositions after May 2, 2006—a qualified fishing property. Specific rules of eligibility must be met, however, before the claim for the deduction can be made, as explained below:

Qualified Farm Property   For those taxpayers who disposed of qualified farm property during the year, the available capital gains deduction must first be reduced by any capital gains deduction previously claimed. If you are unsure about previous claims, contact CRA for a record of previously used amounts. Then the least of the following will determine the deductible amounts:

• The annual gains limit from dispositions of qualified farm property during the current year

- The available CGD
- The cumulative gains limit

The definition of "qualified farm property" that was acquired after June 17, 1987, includes real property owned by the taxpayer, spouse or child for at least 24 months immediately before sale.

Also, a gross revenue test must be met; that is, in at least two years prior to disposition, gross income earned by the individual by active farming operations must exceed net income from all other sources.

Third, all or substantially all of the fair value of the farm assets must be used in active business operations for at least 24 months prior to disposition.

Different rules exist for farms acquired before June 17, 1987. The capital gains exemptions will be allowed, but only if the farmland and buildings were used in an active farming business in Canada in the year of sale and in at least five years prior to the disposition.

For 1988 and subsequent tax years, eligible capital property (for example, farm quotas) will constitute qualified farm property eligible for the deduction if used in the course of carrying on the business of farming in Canada.

Qualified Fishing Property   The May 2, 2006, federal budget extended to fishers each of the following benefits previously afforded farmers:

- The availability of the capital gains deduction on the disposition of qualified fishing property, which includes real property, fishing vessels, interests in a fishing licence and eligible capital property used principally in a fishing business carried on in Canada, if the individual or his/her family members were actively engaged on a regular and continuous basis in the enterprise. In addition, shares in family fishing corporations and interests in family fishing partnerships will qualify.
- Tax deferral of capital gains and recapture when qualified fishing property is transferred to the fisher's spouse or common-law partner, child or grandchild, or nephews, nieces and in-laws who may have been under the taxpayer's custody and control while under age 19, in cases where there is an active involvement on a regular and continuous basis. In these cases, it is possible to assign the value at the cost amount of the property; in the case of depreciable property, recapture can be deferred.
- Extension of the time for claiming reserves on the disposition of fishing property from five years to ten years.

The term "qualified fishing property" and the rollover and reserving rules parallel similar definitions and rules as those for qualified farm property.

Shares of Small Business Corporations   The capital gains deduction for individuals has been available on the disposition of qualified small business corporation shares after June 17, 1987.

A qualified small business corporation share is a share of the capital stock of a small business corporation owned by the individual, his/her spouse or a partnership of which he/she was a member.

A small business corporation is defined to be a Canadian-Controlled Private Corporation in which all or substantially all of the assets (90% or more) are used in an active business or carried on primarily in Canada by the corporation.

The share must not have been owned by any person or partnership other than the individual or a person or partnership related to him/her throughout the 24 months immediately preceding the disposition. During the holding period, more than 50% of the fair market value of the corporation's assets must have been used in an active business.

The allowable deduction is calculated as the least of the following four amounts:

- The capital gains deduction limit for the current year
- The individual's cumulative gains limit less any amount deducted as a capital gains deduction in respect of qualified farm and fishing property for the year
- The individual's annual gains limit less any amount deducted as a capital gains deduction in respect of qualified farm property or qualified fishing property for the year
- Net taxable capital gains for the year from dispositions of qualified small business corporation shares

Finally, you should know that if the taxpayer disposes of shares of a small business corporation, some of which do not meet the holding requirements described above, the shares are deemed to be disposed of in the order in which they were acquired.

TAX ADVISOR

When setting up a qualifying small business corporation, it is important to give thought to the ownership of the shares, asset transfer provisions (that is, possible consequences when assets are transferred in and out of operating companies, holding companies or family trusts) and compensation packages for each family member. The initiative is complicated and requires significant planning.

A small business corporation can provide great tax advantages in income planning, but a key advantage rests with the potential of selling the enterprise with a significant tax-free gain for each individual shareholder. Figures 10.1 and 10.2 serve to make an important point: the use of the $750,000 Capital Gains Exemption can help qualifying small business owners accumulate serious wealth.

In the case of Thomas's sale, had he been the sole shareholder of his corporation, his tax liability would have been calculated as shown in Figure 10.1, assuming no prior use of the Capital Gains Exemption.

Now, let's assume Thomas and his wife, Pat, were both shareholders of this small business corporation. Each could split the gain on the sale of the company and use their available capital gains deduction, resulting in much lower taxes payable (see Figure 10.2).

It pays to set up your business in anticipation of such future tax-free windfalls. Ask your advisor about multiplying the capital gains deduction with other family members or through the use of a family trust. Also ask about potential minimum tax and any net income tax implications, including quarterly tax instalment payment requirements on any unsheltered portion of the gains.

The transfer of assets from a proprietorship to a corporation, the timing of such an event and the structure of the shareholders' agreements and compensation structures all need careful consideration. These matters should therefore be discussed with your tax advisor.

Figure 10.1 Sole Shareholder Uses Capital Gains Exemption

Tax Provision	Calculation
Proceeds of Disposition	$2,000,000
Adjusted Cost Base	$ 1
Capital Gain	$1,999,999
Taxable Gain (1/2)	$ 999,999
Less Capital Gains Deduction (1/2 X $750,000)	$ 375,000
Net Taxable Gain	$ 624,999
Taxes Payable @ 46%*	$ 287,500

* Consult with advisors for accurate calculation for your province of residence.

Figure 10.2	Capital Gains Split With Two Shareholders	
Tax Provision	**Thomas**	**Pat**
Proceeds of Disposition	$1,000,000	$1,000,000
Adjusted Cost Base	$ 1	$ 1
Capital Gain	$ 999,999	$ 999,999
Taxable Gain (1/2)	$ 499,999	$ 499,999
Less Capital Gains Deduction (1/2 X $750,000)	$ 375,000	$ 375,000
Net Taxable Gain	$ 124,999	$ 124,999
Taxes Payable @ 46%*	$ 57,500	$ 57,500

* Consult with advisors for accurate calculation for your province of residence.

RECAP. YOU NEED TO KNOW:

- How to structure your business enterprise to minimize tax on business income and maximize your tax position upon sale or transfer of the business
- How to handle start-up losses in the most tax-efficient way
- The difference in tax rates applied to corporations and personal income
- How the choice of corporate fiscal year ends can facilitate tax reductions and deferral
- How to time the transfer of the business assets from a proprietorship to a corporation
- How to diversify income sources earned from the corporation
- How to determine the optimum salary, dividend and bonus mix
- What the new rules for dividend taxation are and how they affect taxpayers now and in the future
- How astute RRSP planning can help you leverage your opportunities
- How to ensure your small business qualifies for the capital gains deduction

YOU NEED TO ASK: Your tax advisor about the best way to minimize tax using a small business corporation by:

1. **Maximizing tax advantages of the proprietorship** first (i.e., excess loss carry-overs), before incorporation.
2. **Structuring your salary** within a small business corporation at least to maximize annual RRSP contribution room.

3. **Consider distributing shares** of the company to your spouse and adult family members in order to multiply the claims for the capital gains deduction.

4. **Knowing the value of your business enterprise** so you're ready if a sudden opportunity to sell comes along. Understand and determine the right valuation methods for your business and any potential tax consequences. Know how to structure your post-sale compensation as well, particularly if you are staying on in a management capacity.

5. **Anticipating the changes that rapid growth** will mean for the management of the company. Business succession can be difficult, complicated and expensive. Be ready for it from the day you open your business and you'll win. Along the way, consider what structural changes the growth of your business will require, including financing for expansion.

Remember to think big. It takes as much effort as thinking small, and it's much more fun!

CHAPTER 11

How to Turn a Tax Audit Into a Profitable Experience

"To know is to control."
SCOTT REED

KEY CONCEPTS

- The self-employed face a greater chance of tax audit under our system of self-assessment.
- CRA may question whether an expense was incurred to earn income from a commercial venture that has a potential for profit and whether the expenses bore any component of personal living expenses.
- CRA has the power not to accept your tax returns as filed and may make its own assessment of the amount of tax it believes you should pay.
- Section 152(8) of the Income Tax Act makes the assumption that CRA is correct in its assessments unless those assessments are challenged by the taxpayer.
- While the burden of proof is on you to disprove CRA's assessment or reassessment of your tax return, it is also your duty to defend your right to pay only the correct amount of tax and no more.
- The taxpayer and his/her advisor must keep up with tax law and its changes over a period of years in order to ensure the best final outcome for an audit, which can span many years and should include all tax cost averaging provisions available.

REAL LIFE: Rubin was staring down his nose at his tax auditor. "I have every receipt for every number I claimed on my tax return, including every deposit of income. There should be absolutely no problem with any of the numbers on the tax returns you are checking so thoroughly." It was hard for Rubin to hide his disdain. Three years earlier, he had been through a similar tax audit just as he was turning the corner on the popular acceptance of his passionate musical compositions.

After years of working at the symphony as an employed classical guitarist and writing music in between performances, Rubin got his first major break. A popular singer from Vancouver heard his piece *Majestic Moonlight.* Despite incurring nothing but losses for his efforts over the previous three-year audit period, that chance meeting opened doors to a recording contract. The royalties from Rubin's first CD were just starting to flow when CRA reassessed his previously filed tax returns and disallowed his business losses. Citing no reasonable expectation of profit from what they considered to be his "hobby" of songwriting, CRA presented Rubin with a tax bill of $18,000 due to the disallowed business losses that he had used to reduce his other income.

At the time, Rubin fought a hard battle with CRA. Together with his tax advisor, he successfully proved there was a reasonable expectation of profit from this commercial venture. Not long after this, Rubin got his first royalty cheque, for $85,000—more than what he earned at his day job in a year! Then the new opportunities started to roll in: an offer to become composer in residence in Tokyo as well as new concert dates and television and radio interviews. Rubin had survived his first tax audit and was on his way to international fame and fortune!

All of which brought him back to the present. Three months earlier, he was visited again by CRA. In the excitement of his burgeoning career, he had failed to file tax returns over the past several years. When he did comply (after several reminders, unfortunately) CRA decided to scrutinize his figures more closely once again. Rubin was very concerned. His auditor observed his recording studio, located in his newly renovated home. Three weeks before Christmas, Rubin learned that he had become the subject of a *net worth assessment* leading to a much higher taxable income and another potentially devastating retroactive tax bill.

THE PROBLEM

Sometimes a taxpayer can get the feeling he/she's between a rock and a hard place. While struggling to make a business run in the early years, one of the biggest threats a taxpayer faces is a CRA tax audit, the onus of proof. It is important, as we have discussed in this book, that there is commercial purpose and potential for profit. Mixing business and personal expenditures opens you up to greater scrutiny for a "reasonable expectation of profit test." That is, the taxpayer must be prepared to show that at the time the expenditures were incurred, there was a reasonable expectation of profit from a commercial activity rather than personal activities.

Then, wouldn't you know it, a few years later, having found success, the taxpayer faces a completely different (but similarly subjective) problem—the danger of being accused of under-reporting income due to a subjective assessment of living standards under the "net worth assessment" process. The onus of proof that income was not under-reported or deductions overstated? Again, it's on the taxpayer.

As a result, many taxpayers shiver with dread at the thought of a tax audit notice. The potential for a subjective dismissal of their documented claims is often enough reason to underclaim expenses. But it is not necessary that you give up your rights under the law and deliberately overpay your taxes year in and year out.

It is true that the Income Tax Act and the CRA's administrative and assessment policies can give rise to "grey areas" that create uncertainty and, in some cases, unfairness. A fair tax system is a balance between fairness and accuracy, simplicity and compliance. The taxpayer should be able to have the peace of mind and the confidence that comes with knowing the tax return was filed to his or her best benefit under the framework of the law and is audit-proof. The taxpayer should not have to guess whether a future tax auditor will disagree.

THE SOLUTION

In complying with tax law, the self-employed person automatically accepts the burden of proof that income reported is correct and that deductions are allowable, reasonable and were incurred to earn income from a commercial venture with a reasonable expectation of profit, all backed up with documentation.

That burden of proof is actually your best weapon against a subjective judgement from CRA. It presents an opportunity for you to explain your business motives and therefore to exercise your full legal rights under the Income Tax Act. Because nobody knows your business and its potential to earn profits as well as you do, you have a distinct advantage going into a tax audit.

When you combine your expert knowledge of your business with meticulous bookkeeping and the tax expertise of your financial advisors, the result should be audit-proof tax returns that reduce your overall tax costs (and the time you spend complying with the law) over the period of years in which you run your business. That allows you to focus on what you do best—build your business. It is critical, though, that the audit strategy both you and your advisors will employ is decided upon *at the time your tax returns are being filed*. This is the key to winning a tax audit.

THE PARAMETERS

In assessing your tax-filing game plan throughout the year and during tax-filing season, there are three things to analyze and discuss with your tax advisors:

Your Audit Risks

Anticipate these facts: an employed civil servant, your tax auditor, is mandated to determine whether your business is viable or whether you are operating on a "hobby" basis. He or she must make this assessment for the purposes of determining loss deductibility, without understanding the risks and challenges you may be facing in the marketplace today. The auditor will have historical and industry statistics at his/her disposal to assist in assessing whether your business is viable or not, or to test whether you are indeed reporting all of your income or overstating your deductions. Even so, you and your advisor must help the auditor understand your unique circumstances. Your auditor's interpretation of your business activities can initiate a long and costly dispute that could be left to the courts to decide. You can avoid this by providing formal budgeting and business planning documentation and making sure you do not claim any portion of expenses that contain a personal component.

Your Audit Tests

When your taxes are in dispute, you must pass five tests:

1. Will the activities of the business result in a source of income?
2. Is there a reasonable expectation of profit over time?
3. Are deductions claimed reasonable under the circumstances and supported by receipts?
4. Is all income from the venture being reported?
5. Were all personal use components of any expenditures removed?

We have discussed most of these concepts in previous chapters.

Your Tax Audit Strategy

To go into an audit battle with a winning strategy, arm your defense team with a number of powerful weapons:

- The story of the evolution of your business: yesterday, today and tomorrow
- Full use of your appeal rights
- Research of precedents set in similar cases by the courts
- A summary of the tax law of the day, current tax law and future tax proposals
- An action plan that includes your tax audit strategy

The Evolution of Your Business   We have suggested earlier that your Daily Business Journal will go a long way in helping to inform your tax auditor about the motive and intent you have in operating your business. So will the log of networking activities, business plans, budgets, cash flow projections, marketing plans and human resource plans you pull together with your bookkeeper. Don't wait for a tax audit to put these documents in place. File them with your tax return each and every year, *in anticipation of an audit*. Be prepared.

These documents will also help you make better business decisions, underscoring your commercial viability and, hopefully, leading to better results.

Rights to Appeal   There are a number of important rights you should be aware of and discuss with your tax advisor. Here are just a few of them:

- **Right to voluntary compliance:** If you have indeed overstated your business deductions or under-reported your income, you need not fear any penalties for gross negligence or tax evasion if you contact CRA first and ask that your tax return be corrected. There may be some interest charges, and CRA will expect you to either pay any resulting bill or make satisfactory arrangements to pay it over time. There may also be a late-filing penalty if you failed to file on time. However, you will avoid gross negligence and tax evasion penalties if you catch your errors before CRA does. The best (and least expensive) policy is to correct and amend those tax returns to comply with the law as soon as possible, even if you have to do this in retrospect. However, be sure to speak to your tax advisor about these matters before contacting CRA.
- **Right to Taxpayer Relief Provisions:** If you have suffered an unusual hardship beyond your control—illness, natural disaster, death of a family member and so on—and as a result of this were unable

to file a tax return, interest and penalty costs can be waived through a decision of CRA's Taxpayer Relief Provisions.
- **Right to object to the assessment or reassessment:** Discuss with your advisors the appeal routes available to you should you run into a dispute with CRA. See Figure 11.1 for a summary.

Consequences of Non-Compliance   Throughout this book we have assumed the reader is a law-abiding citizen who endeavours to file a correct tax return to his family's best tax advantage, as allowed under the law. The consequences of failure to comply with tax law are outlined in Figure 11.2.

Figure 11.1	Summary of a Taxpayer's Appeal Rights
Method of Appeal	**Basic Parameters**
1. Informal Objection	When you perceive a mistake has been made in the initial assessment of your return, have your tax advisor write to CRA to request an adjustment. If CRA refuses to make the adjustment, and you still believe they are incorrect, contact your tax professional again to discuss further options. Do this immediately.
2. Notice of Objection	This is a formal objection to the Chief of Appeals at the local Tax Services Office. It must be filed within one year after the taxpayer's filing due date or 90 days after the day of the mailing of the Notice of Assessment or Reassessment, whichever is later. You may indicate in this Notice that you wish to appeal directly to the Tax Court of Canada.
3. Appeals to the Tax Court of Canada	An appeal may be made after the Minister has confirmed the assessment or reassessment, or within 90 days after the service of a Notice of Objection to which no reply has been received. This court has an informal procedure for federal taxes in dispute of $12,000 or less, and a general procedure for amounts over this, which requires the services of a lawyer. This court may dispose of the appeal by either dismissing it or allowing it in whole or part.
4. Appeals to Federal Court of Appeal	If you have lost an appeal at the Tax Court level, informal procedures, you have 30 days from the date the decision was mailed to you or your representative to appeal to the Federal Court. A lost case under the general procedure may be appealed to the Federal Court within 30 days from the date on which the judge signs the decision. The months of July and August are omitted, so if the decision date was June 30, the taxpayer would have until September 30 to file the appeal.
5. Appeals to the Supreme Court of Canada	Appeals to the Supreme Court require the granting of permission to hear the appeal by the Supreme Court itself. The taxpayer has 60 days from the date of the judgement at the Federal Court of Appeal to file an application. The month of August is left out.

Figure 11.2	Consequences of Non-Compliance

Circumstance	Penalty
Failure to file a return on time	5% of unpaid taxes plus 1% per month up to a maximum of 12 months from filing due date, which is June 15 for unincorporated small businesses
Subsequent failure to file on time within a 3-year period	10% of unpaid taxes plus 2% per month to a maximum of 20 months from filing due date
Failure to provide information on a required form	$100 for each failure
Failure to provide Social Insurance Number	$100 for each failure unless the card is applied for within 15 days of the request
Failure to provide information with regard to foreign-held property	$500 per month for a maximum of 24 months; $1,000 a month for a maximum of 24 months if there is a failure to respond to a demand to file plus an additional penalty of 5% of the value of the property transferred or loan to a foreign trust or the cost of the foreign property where failure to file exceeds 24 months
False statements or omissions with regard to foreign properties	5% of the value of the property, minimum of $24,000
Gross negligence: false statement or omission of information in the return	50% of tax on understated income with a minimum $100 penalty
Late or insufficient instalments	50% of interest payable exceeding $1,000 or 25% of interest payable if no instalments were made, whichever is greater.
Tax Evasion	50% to 200% of tax sought to be evaded and imprisonment for up to 5 years
Failure to deduct or remit source deductions	10% of amount not withheld, or remitted
Second such failure in same year	20% of amount not withheld or remitted if this was done knowingly or through gross negligence

Penalties for Misrepresentation by a Third Party

Persons (including partnerships) who participate in planning and/or valuation activities that lead to the reduction, avoidance or deferral of taxes are subject to civil penalties under the Income Tax Act, which defines "culpable conduct," subject to penalties, as activities that are:

- Tantamount to intentional conduct

- Show an indifference as to whether the Income Tax Act is complied with, or
- Show a wilful, reckless or wanton disregard of the law

The penalties levied under this section are as shown in Figure 11.3.

Know the Tax Law of Yesterday, Today and Tomorrow

One of the interesting aspects of going through a tax audit is the fact that the auditor is usually focused only on assessing the tax years in question. This is generally the current year and/or two years back. He or she is not necessarily concerned with the concept of "tax cost averaging." This is where you and your advisor come in. Make sure the auditor prepares your reassessed return with the most advantageous tax provisions *allowed by the law of the day and how this meshes with subsequent tax law.* This is an important way to offset errors or omissions the auditor may find.

It is also important to note that, while adjustments to current year Capital Cost Allowance (CCA) claims must generally be made within 90 days after receipt of a Notice of Assessment or Reassessment, a tax auditor will generally allow retroactive adjustments to the CCA statements during a tax audit. If a tax bill results, for example, you may wish to pull

| **Figure 11.3** | **Third Party Penalties** |

Circumstance	Penalty
Misrepresentation in tax planning arrangements if made at the time of the planning or valuation activity	$1,000 or the total that the person is entitled to receive from the planning or valuation activity, whichever is more
Misrepresentation in tax planning arrangements if not made at the time of the planning activity	$1,000
Misrepresentation in tax planning arrangements if made at the time of the planning or valuation activity	$1,000 or the total that the person is entitled to receive from the planning or valuation activity, whichever is more
Misrepresentation in tax planning arrangements if not made at the time of the planning activity	$1,000
Participating in misrepresentation	Greater of $1,000 and lesser of • the penalty the taxpayer would be liable for if that person made the statement and knew it to be false or • the total of $100,000 and the amount that the person is entitled to receive from the planning or valuation activity

out all the stops and claim full CCA for the year, even if you chose not to do so in the original filings. You'll also want to claim as many carry-over provisions as possible and review reassessed tax-filing results with family members' returns, especially if there are transferable provisions available to reduce your tax outcomes even further.

You and your tax advisor must see to it that the end result of a tax audit reflects all multi-year tax-planning provisions that are available to you and your family unit as a whole. See Chapter 12 for summaries of significant provisions of recent tax years to help with this.

Also remember that while the burden of proof is on the taxpayer to disprove CRA's reassessment of taxes, it is CRA that must prove any allegations of wilful intent on the part of the taxpayer to defraud the government. The taxpayer may also challenge the appropriateness of CRA's penalties under the circumstances and request that they be removed if they are excessive or incorrect.

Be Proactive

Remember, *the Income Tax Act makes the assumption that CRA is correct in its assessments, unless those assessments are challenged by the taxpayer.* Therefore it is most important that the taxpayer make a pro-active effort to prove the tax return was correct as filed.

TAX ADVISOR

The taxpayer and his/her advisors should follow certain steps pro-actively in ensuring the taxpayer's rights under the law are upheld during a tax audit. Initiate your tax audit strategy in two parts:

I. Initial Audit Assessment Steps

1. **Act immediately:** Go see your tax advisor with all the records you can find for the tax years being audited.

2. **Determine key dates:** The deadline for filing a Notice of Objection, for example, is the first milestone. Determine whether this document should be filed and when.

3. **Have your advisor request an extension from CRA, in order to pull together the documents required:** This will take some of the pressure off and allow you to continue with your normal income-producing activities while you put together the tax audit case. But from here on in, do not miss any agreed upon dates or tasks in your dealings with CRA.

4. **Identify problem areas in your position:** These might include missing documentation, such as receipts or logbooks, or issues such as the reasonable expectation of profit or the accuracy of the auditor's net worth assessment.

5. **Identify problem areas in CRA's position:** These might include misinterpretation of facts, errors in assumptions, omissions of facts in the making of assumptions and so on.

6. **Anticipate your outcomes:** Quantify your upside and downside. Your upside is one of two outcomes:
   - No changes are made to the return
   - You uncover a tax-filing method, provision or missing receipts and use these to actually have your taxes decreased for the audit year in question

   Your downside is one of three outcomes:
   - Taxes are increased because source documents are missing
   - Taxes are increased because tax losses are disallowed
   - Taxes are increased because income reported is adjusted upward or tax deduction or credits are disallowed

   Put numbers to these circumstances to analyze your tax risk.

7. **Identify the tax provisions that were new for the tax year in question:** Do so to ensure you took advantage of them all, and understand their carry-over potential. Keep a list of these in your tax files. The top 10 questions you should ask your tax advisor follow later in this chapter.

8. **Set aside time to work with your tax advisor:** Putting together the appeal will take time.

9. **Be prepared to go back and look through old files:** You may be able to recover duplicate receipts, create auto logs from the information in your daily business journal, etc. A tax audit will require your personal resources of time and money.

10. **Determine and agree upon your Tax Audit Action Plan.**

II. Tax Audit Action Plan

1. **File the Notice of Objection:** Do this once all the documentation has been gathered.

2. **Organize your evidence:** Include documents that support your tax return as filed, any additional documents, a list of all relevant facts to support your filing position and a list of facts to address CRA's

assumptions. It would be a good idea for all of this information to be organized in such a manner that it can be referred to quickly and often. A tabular numbering system, set out at the start of the process, generally saves everyone a lot of time.

3. **Ask CRA for information:** A taxpayer is within his/her rights to ask CRA to disclose all of their findings and the exact provision(s) in the law that supports these findings.

4. **Stick to the facts at all times:** You and your tax advisor must separate emotion from fact to win the case. Remember, you have more facts than CRA does, and you know the truth: what actions were taken and why, and what your business's future potential is. Judges understand that you did not have the benefit of hindsight when you made your original business decisions.

5. **Do not express personal opinions on tax law in writing or at the audit interview:** Word your points to say, "Our position is the following:" in order to keep your presentation at a high level of professionalism.

6. **Correspond with CRA in writing throughout the audit:** For example, ask CRA to put any requests for additional information in writing.

7. **Identify your weaknesses at the outset:** If you don't have an auto log, say so. Often, the auditor will allow the taxpayer to go back and look for documentation that shows a business driving pattern. Another strategy that sometimes works is to start keeping an auto log immediately, even during the audit period. This will at least give the auditor a trend to look at.

8. **Identify any tax provisions you may have missed for the tax year in question or for prior years:** This is a good idea any time, as you always want to be in a position to recover missed provisions. In fact, it may pay to do this during your audit. For example, if you missed claiming your safety-deposit-box fees, prepare an adjustment to your prior-filed returns. Now you have 90 days from the date on the Notice of Reassessment to open up claims for CCA elsewhere on the return. This could reduce your net income, CPP liability or tax liability. It could even create or increase your spouse's claims for the spousal amount, and so on.

During the Audit Interview

Generally, once all the information is gathered, the taxpayer's advisor will meet with the auditor to have a discussion about the file. It is usually not a good idea for the taxpayer to participate in this process; let your hired advisor do the communicating at this point. Consider the following constructive ways to help your advisor represent you successfully:

1. **Meet with your advisor before his/her interview with the auditor:** Go over the materials and strategy once more. This is a good rehearsal for your advisor, who may have some last-minute questions. What you are hoping for at this point is that you have successfully communicated the story of your business, your intent for its future and your reasons the tax return should be accepted as originally filed. Because you will have all of these facts in writing, you should have peace of mind and confidence in your advisor to represent you with all the details you feel are important to express to the auditor.

2. **Overview first:** The advisor should begin the presentation with a solid overview of the taxpayer's position. It is important that supporting information be assembled so that the auditor can review it easily, as mentioned earlier.

3. **Relate to the file:** Once the facts of the position and supporting documents are identified, the advisor should proceed to explain how they relate to the way the tax return was actually filed. This is the time to identify new provisions and correct any errors on prior returns.

4. **Bring more information:** The advisor will have the opportunity to gather any additional information needed by the auditor. If the advisor doesn't know the answer to a question, or if the auditor needs additional information, the advisor should confirm this request with the auditor in writing, along with a new timeline for compliance. Make it easy for your advisor to comply.

5. **Your advisor should clearly articulate the outcome you want:** He or she should include the details of specific provisions (additions or deletions) and how they should be filed. With regard to subjective conclusions, the advisor should be prepared to stand firm on the reasons the return was filed as it was. In the case of tax losses, he/she should defend your belief in a reasonable expectation of profit from the venture. In addition to supplying the auditor with documents that support the business's future growth, the advisor may cite previous cases that address the theory of the law and present information about changes in the tax law that apply to your case.

6. **Looking to jurisprudence can help:** The case of *Johns-Manville Canada Inc.* established, for example, that where there is reasonable

doubt, the case should be resolved in favour of the taxpayer. This is especially true if the law is ambiguous or uncertain. In the end, the judge of a dispute must look to the Income Tax Act for guidance. If it can be shown that the taxpayer attempted to comply with the intent of law as it stands (without the benefit of hindsight at the time his/her actions were taken) and that the law does support the taxpayer's position, CRA's subjective interpretation of the Act is the weaker position.

Examples of Cases in Which Taxpayers Profited From the Audit Experience

While the following are based on true stories, all characters and circumstances have been changed for anonymity, and any similarities to actual circumstances are purely coincidental.

REAL LIFE: Taxpayer A succeeded in receiving a patent for an invention.

After attempting to manufacture the invention through a third party—one manufacturer was about to go bankrupt, and another repeatedly failed to deliver—the taxpayer proceeded to manufacture the invention on his own. He invested the money required to redraw plans, bought the required materials and set out to build the prototype. In the process, he claimed all the expenses on his tax return, creating an operating loss that offset the income from his day job—working as a letter carrier. CRA disallowed those losses, asserting that his business venture was actually a hobby.

In contesting this reassessment, the taxpayer was able to show, despite sketchy records, his motives and intent to find a manufacturer for the invention. He was also able to establish that the invention would already have been in the marketplace had it not been for the aborted manufacturing attempts with the first two companies. The taxpayer produced detailed cash flows and projections to show how close he was to bringing the invention to market. He was about to close a contract to sell 50 of his inventions to a national distributor on a consignment basis. In the time since he filed the tax returns in question, in fact, he'd taken a number of steps to enhance the expectation of profit.

At the end of the process, the auditor agreed that there was indeed a reasonable expectation of profit from the business, which was a viable commercial venture and not a hobby as CRA had asserted at the outset. The taxpayer's returns were reassessed, only this time more advantageously than when he first filed. That's because his sharp tax advisor caught a little-known provision about writing off the costs of a patent. After this adjustment was made, CRA actually owed the taxpayer money!

REAL LIFE: Taxpayer B had a farming enterprise.

The farmer claimed losses for years as he faced one calamity after another, from bad weather to insects to bottomed-out world market pricing. He came close to losing his asset on several occasions. While he was under this economic siege, he failed to file tax returns. A badly disorganized bookkeeper, Taxpayer B simply ignored CRA's requests to file a return until one day he was faced with a net worth assessment.

This is a little-known audit tool CRA employs from time to time under the powers of the Income Tax Act. This process begins like any other tax audit, with a request for income verification as well as receipts for expenditures. The tax auditor then sits back and takes a close look at the taxpayer's perceived surroundings and lifestyle. What they saw in Taxpayer B's circumstances included vast landholdings, Christmas vacations financed by his wife's earnings as a government worker, and a paid-off mortgage (the result, as it happens, of a family inheritance).

Taxpayer B presents a classic case for a net worth assessment. He owned tax-paid holdings but had little evidence of income to justify his apparent wealth. Further, he failed to provide an explanation when questioned about it. The auditor took a stab at assessing the value of the farmer's lifestyle, guessing at what income might have been required during the audit period to pay for it all. The auditor then computed income, deductions and credits accordingly, and presented the farmer with a bill for tens of thousands of dollars. Taxpayer B fought back tears in his advisor's office.

The good news is that at the end of a very lengthy challenge of the net worth assessment—which included combing through crates of disorganized receipts, bank records, contracts and asset transactions—CRA owed Taxpayer B more than $15,000. To his great relief, even after paying his tax deductible accounting fees, Taxpayer B's net worth actually took a jump when the audit process was finished.

Has he been a regular tax filer since? You guessed it—no. Some people are just their own worst enemies!

RECAP. YOU NEED TO KNOW:

- How to meet the burden of proof in a tax audit
- How to develop an audit strategy with your tax advisor
- How to link your business activities to revenue and profitability
- How to appeal an assessment or reassessment you think is unfair or incorrect
- What the consequences of non-compliance are
- How to hold your tax advisor accountable for misrepresentation
- How contemporary jurisprudence has ruled in grey areas
- How to profit from a tax audit with tax cost averaging

WHAT YOU NEED TO ASK:

Like it or not, the fact that you are in business for yourself increases your chance of a tax audit. One way to deal with this fact is to continually prepare yourself for a potential audit, together with your tax advisor, as you file your income tax returns annually. Remember these rules as you coach your advisor:

1. **Know your rights under the law:** The four basic provisions in the Income Tax Act that give the self-employed taxpayer guidance in self-assessment of his/her tax burden are:
   - A taxpayer's income for a taxation year from a business or property is the taxpayer's *profit* from that business or property.
   - No deduction for an outlay or expense will be allowed unless it was made for the purpose of gaining or producing income from a business or property that is a commercial activity that has *a reasonable expectation of profit.* These deductions must not include personal living expenses.
   - No deduction for an outlay or expenses will be allowed except to the extent that it was *reasonable* under the circumstances.
   - Whether you filed a return or not, CRA may reassess the taxes payable arbitrarily because they are *not bound to accept a return* as filed by the taxpayer.
2. **Never cave:** It is critical to be pro-active when you're audited. Know that under Section 152(8), CRA's assessment of your taxes will be accepted as fact unless you exercise your burden of proof and challenge CRA's assumptions.
3. **Make it a point to be a model tax-filing citizen:** File a tax return, source and sales tax remittance every year, on time, to minimize penalties and build up points for when you really need them—at tax audit time. Disorganization is absolutely no excuse. Be sure to hire help if you can't—or don't want to—keep your own records in order. Besides, for small business owners, that hired help is deductible!
4. **Make sure it's all deductible:** Defend your right to claim legitimate deductions and losses in the current year and the carry-over years by emphasizing the source of income created by your activities. By its very presence, you meet the "commercial viability" and "reasonable expectation of profit" tests.
5. **Gain confidence from the facts:** A judge must give you the benefits of reasonableness if you are making an effort to comply with the In-

come Tax Act. Your burden of proof puts you in a position of power to win a tax audit, provided you stick to the facts and remain highly professional in your approach. In many cases, CRA owes money to the tax filer at the end of the audit session.

6. **Never give CRA a reason to question your integrity:** The Income Tax Act allows you tremendous leeway to reduce gross income with legitimate tax deductions and credits that will average out your tax burden over time. Tax fraud is just not worth it. Make sure you support all income sources—cash, cheque, credit card, barter—with paper documentation and verification of deposit to separate bank accounts (that is, never co-mingle business and personal funds). Keep receipts for all personal non-taxable sources, like inheritances, so you can prove that your holdings are fully tax paid or tax exempt. When it comes to your tax compliance burden, honesty is the best—and cheapest—policy over the long term.

7. **Know why they audit taxpayers:** The answer is quite simple—to promote a level playing field for all business owners in Canada. To illustrate, we'll leave you with this story:

   Karl is in the construction business. He bases his quotes and his profit margins on the fact that he'll be paying GST/HST and income taxes every year. His competitor, Shady Sal, on the other hand, quotes "under the table." That is, he'll cut the price in half to get the job because he's paying no sales taxes and no income taxes. Can Karl compete? The answer is apparent.

   The integrity of the tax system depends on the CRA's ability to crack down on characters like Shady Sal and to protect honest taxpayers like Karl. Auditing tax returns of the self-employed is a part of this process.

CHAPTER 12

. . . .

Taxpayers and Their Advisors: The Top Check Lists

"Don't forget until too late that the business of life is not business, but living."
B.C. FORBES

KEY CONCEPTS

- Given that tax will be your largest lifetime expense, your relationship with your professional tax advisor can be the most profitable one you have.
- Choose that person carefully and begin with a review of prior filed returns to recover overpaid taxes on errors or omissions from the past decade.
- Communicate your business and financial goals for the short and long term.
- Stay current on tax changes for the future and stay in tune with tax cost averaging options.
- Make financial and investment decisions in tandem with your tax savings opportunities.
- Build on your productivity and build your business equity with smart tax planning.

REAL LIFE: Marshall, a self-employed plumber, was getting married—and he had a deep, dark secret he didn't want his bride to know. In fact, he was so worried about this that he found himself waking up in the middle of the night in a sweat. With his wedding date fast approaching, Marshall had to confess to somebody: he hadn't filed a tax return, ever.

You cannot imagine the relief on poor Marshall's face when he learned that the statute of limitations required that he file for only the last ten years. He had done the right thing the last time he woke up in a sweat: he called a local tax accountant with a very good reputation and an understanding demeanour. Marshall explained that he didn't want to go into his new marriage with this terrible burden hanging over him.

A week later, when his returns were filed, he couldn't believe CRA actually owed him money! In fact, due to the application of tax credits both federally and provincially, Marshall was going to receive enough to finance a short honeymoon.

Now that he understood how the tax system could work in his favour, Marshall wanted to know more about what he had missed. Perhaps he could have claimed more if he had known more about the rules. If only he had turned his tax files over to an advisor sooner!

THE PROBLEM

Tax is just one of those things—everyone has to deal with it, and most people have difficulty doing so enthusiastically. While many pay an advisor to help them, they often pay their fees grudgingly. They perceive the entire experience as a double negative: the only thing worse than paying taxes is paying someone to figure out how much you have to pay!

How do you choose a tax advisor, someone with whom you'll have a long-term relationship in the quest to pay only the correct amount of tax over time and not one cent more? How do you communicate with your tax advisor so that you can learn the rules to help you make tax-wise decisions all year long? How can you best leverage the professional fees you are paying to achieve peace of mind that your tax affairs are in order and that the tax system is working for you, not against you?

How do you turn the double negative around to work pro-actively with your tax advisor in building tax-efficient profits and equity in your business?

THE SOLUTION

You may be surprised at the solution to this dilemma. To find the right tax advisor, you have to decide what you want in terms of service. In short, it's your money, and it is within your control to get the most out of your professional relationships. However, as with most other relationships, this one may take a bit of research at the start. There are numerous levels of tax-preparation, tax-accounting and tax-planning services to choose from in the marketplace. Which of these will best suit your needs today and in the future?

It goes without saying that every taxpayer who pays for a professional service expects a tax return that is 100% correct. However, there can be a big difference between a return that is just mathematically correct and one that is completed to your family's best advantage over the long term.

Find an advisor who will be as protective of your financial health as your doctor is of your physical health. Your tax advisor should be someone who knows you and your goals for your family and your business very well. He or she should be someone who has earned your trust and respect by keeping up with the latest in tax law, CRA's interpretation of the law, CRA's policies and procedures, as well as your own personal, business and financial evolution. This person will also play an integral role with your other professional team members, such as your financial planner, investment advisor, insurance advisor and lawyer.

In short, your professional tax advisor can be one of the most important people in your life. For this reason, you should take some time to define this relationship carefully.

THE PARAMETERS

To find a trusted advisor, consider this action plan:

- **Seek referrals:** Ask your friends and business associates for referrals; check out the yellow pages and Chamber of Commerce or Board of Trade in your area for the names of well-respected tax advisors.
- **Expertise and services needed:** Find out what level of expertise you need. Tax advisors may offer bookkeeping and payroll services, commercial tax preparation, accounting and auditing, corporate as well as personal returns, trust returns and estate planning.
- **Reputation and experience:** Interview at least three professionals in your area. They might include independents, partners in a partnership, financial institutions and so on. It's best to include one from every group to get the best overview of potential service, quality and price. You will receive a broad sampling of services and fees and, most important, an opportunity to judge the advisors' communications skills.
- **Ask questions:** Come to the interview prepared to ask about your top taxation concerns.
- **Listen well:** When you ask your questions, take note of the way the answers are communicated to you. Can you learn from this person? Is the person willing to help you learn? Is the person interested in you and your business? Does he/she make suggestions to you?

Does he/she have a strong background in taxation? The last thing you need is to feel intimidated or unclear about the way your concerns are addressed. You are looking for peace of mind and a professional partner for the future of your business and personal affairs.

- **Find out about service:** Ask about fees, guarantee of service, billing practices, errors or omissions insurance, size of organizations and any additional services provided. What happens when errors occur?
- **Integrated services:** Ask about the professional's ability to interact with others, such as lawyers, financial planners, insurance advisors and so on, if need be.
- **Make the decision:** Choose the advisor you are most comfortable with.
- **Give a trial:** Ask the advisor to complete a small job. Evaluate the quality of the work, the ability to meet deadlines and how well he/she works with you on follow-up procedures.
- **Review the accuracy of the work:** Listen and learn as the advisor explains the results of the work to you.

TAX ADVISOR

Compile a "top 10" list of questions to ask your potential advisor, such as:

1. What are the latest tax changes that will apply to my business operations this year, and what is the tax rate I will pay on each income source earned in the coming year?

2. What tax provisions should I be carrying forward from previous filing years, and what are the latest tax changes for our family unit to take advantage of?

3. How can my family members split income and transfer deductions and credits this year?

4. What are the retirement savings strategies we should be working toward?

5. How can we plan new investments in registered and non-registered accounts to increase tax-deferred income sources?

6. How can we reduce tax withholding/tax instalment payments this year?

7. How should asset acquisitions and dispositions be timed to make the most tax sense?

8. What audit-proofing procedures should we be putting in place this year?

9. Should our business be incorporated? If so, who should own shares?

10. Who can help us value our business for a potential sale?

RECAP. Ten Skill Testing Questions to Discuss With Your Advisors

True False?

1. ❑   ❑   A small business owner can diversify income sources, de-fer the reporting of taxable income and split income with family members more easily than an employee.

True. Any investment advisor will tell you that the way to spread risk and accumulate wealth is to pay close attention to your asset mix. You want to earn income from a variety of sources: employment or self-employment, pensions, dividends, capital gains, interest and so on. When you start a small business, you'll be creating two types of income: on-going profits from the operations of the venture, and the potential for capital gains on the future sale of your business. This is a great way to diversify your taxable income sources, defer taxation of accrued wealth into the future and reduce your overall tax burden through income splitting with family members.

True False?

2. ❑   ❑   A myriad of tax deductions are available to the self-employed, but not all of them are fully deductible.

True. Unincorporated business owners are taxed only on net profits, which are added to taxable income annually and then subject to tax at the appropriate marginal tax rate. The rules governing tax deductibility of operating expenditures are not always specific. They centre around two basic concepts: your ability to explain to a tax auditor (1) why the expense you wish to deduct was reasonable under the circumstances and (2) how it was used to create income for your business, a commercial enterprise with a reasonable expectation of profit. You must also show the auditor that any personal use component of the expenditure has been removed and that you adhered to certain restrictions—like the 50% rule for meals and entertainment—when filing your return.

True   False?

3. ❑   ❑   The self-employed can't write off the value of their own labour.

That's true of unincorporated small businesses. The proprietor gets to keep the net profits (after taxes are paid). It is possible to draw from revenues throughout the year, but it is the net profit that is subject to tax. As the business grows, the proprietor may wish to incorporate, in which case he/she can become an employee of the corporation, which is a separate legal entity, and also pay himself or herself dividends, which are after-tax distributions of a corporation's profits, and/or certain perks and benefits of employment.

Under both forms of business organization, equity in the value of the business grows on a tax-deferred basis. However, when a qualifying small business corporation is sold, a capital gains deduction is available. This deduction is not available to a proprietor. Speak to your tax advisor about all of your options to stop the erosion of your income and wealth from unnecessary taxes.

True   False?

4. ❑   ❑   The self-employed must finance all the risk of building their business, without tax relief.

Not so. Here's why. What is your most precious commodity? Your time? Your money? Your health? Likely, it's all of those things. The key to preserving your resources is to use them wisely, to multiply them if possible and to have them work for you. A small business provides you with the vehicle to leverage time, money and human resources needed to build appreciating equity over time. And best of all, the costs of leveraging—hiring staff, paying interest on an operating loan, leasing computers, marketing your services—are tax deductible if you earn income from your commercial venture, which has a reasonable expectation of profit. Keeping proper records is a must.

True   False?

5. ❑   ❑   It's much better to arrange for one person in the family to earn $50,000 than for two people to earn $25,000.

False. If you understand a little about our progressive tax system, you'll know it's best to minimize realized income in the hands of one taxpayer and to "spread the wealth" into the hands of many. The taxpayer who earns $50,000 pays tax at a higher marginal rate than two who earn $25,000 each. The potential return on the process of income splitting is pretty good, and it's legal. You'll want to strive to split income with your family members now and in retirement. In fact, by starting a home-based business, you have the potential to reap double-digit returns in tax savings simply by giving family members an opportunity to work for you and build CPP and RRSP contribution room.

True   False?

6. ❑   ❑   Keeping up with tax law and its continuous change is a pointless effort.

False. Most Canadians have the educational qualifications to understand their own tax system. Motivation to understand it and use it to their advantage is often a bigger problem, which is puzzling. True, it is not possible for every taxpayer to be a tax expert. That's not your goal, nor was it the goal of this book to make you one. (I'm sure you're relieved.)

However, the essence of opportunity lies within the structure of our tax system: it is based on voluntary compliance and self-assessment. It is your legal right and duty to arrange your affairs within the framework of the law to pay the least amount of tax possible. By learning more about existing provisions within our Income Tax Act, you'll be empowered to make tax-wise decisions throughout the year. Your motivation to do so? Simple—it's *your money, your future financial freedom.*

True   False?

7. ❑   ❑   Small business owners can achieve double-digit savings—often as high as 45% or more—on each and every dollar they spend in their small business ventures, depending on their province of residence, provided the amount is tax deductible.

True. What's a tax deduction worth? It depends on your marginal tax rate. Because each qualifying business expenditure reduces business income dollar for dollar, you'll reap double-digit returns for each receipt you keep, if your income is taxable. It's important to know those income levels and sources—and how to generate them in the future—to plan to maximize the return on your tax deductible expenditures.

True   False?

8. ❏   ❏   The cost of your asset purchases can be written off in full against business revenues.

False. Many business owners fail to classify their expenditures into two main categories: operating expenses and capital expenditures. This error can be expensive in a tax audit. The former are 100% deductible against revenues of the business and can even be used to create a loss. Capital cost allowances, the partial deduction allowed for the wear and tear on depreciable assets, also can increase an operating loss, but are taken at your option. This allows you to defer the use of the deduction to a more advantageous year. So, a percentage of the asset's costs can be written off to a prescribed maximum or, if you choose, no deduction can be taken.

True   False?

9. ❏   ❏   It's difficult to justify claims for car and in-home business workspaces.

No, it's really quite easy to comply with the requirements. All you have to do is separate your personal use of the assets from your business use. In the case of the auto, this is done by keeping a representative distance log that documents your driving patterns for both business and personal purposes. At the end of the tax year, all expenses relating to the vehicle are totalled and prorated according to the business kilometres driven divided by the total kilometres driven in the year. A similar process, based on square footage of the workspace in the home over the total living area, will help you claim the properly deductible portions of home expenses. The recordkeeping process can be easily recorded in your daily business journal.

True   False?

10. ❏   ❏   Most taxpayers lose their tax audit appeals when they go to court.

Unfortunately, this is true. CRA wins appeals at the Tax Court level most of the time. However, the odds of winning are much better locally. Appealing under a Notice of Objection to the Chief of Appeals in your area reaps a successful result the majority of the time. This negotiated approach to resolving taxes in dispute can pay off for both parties, particularly when it comes to grey areas of the law. For that reason, taxpayers should never shy away from filing a Notice of Objection to a reassessment of their taxes if they believe their tax return was correct as filed.

TAX FACT SHEETS

The following information may help you and your tax advisor evaluate tax cost averaging provisions over a period of carry-over years and make adjustments for errors or omissions you may have made on the family's tax returns in the past. For more information, see www.knowledge bureau.com for a weekly electronic update of significant tax and economic news or consult *EverGreen Explanatory Notes*. Remember that adjustments to previously filed personal returns can be made for a period including the prior 10 years ending on December 31.

History of Automobile Expense Claim Limits

Automobile Capital Cost Allowance Limit   In each case, the dollar amount is increased by the amount of GST or HST plus the amount of provincial retail sales tax that is payable on the limit shown (current at the time of writing).

Period	Dollar Limit (add GST/HST/PST)
2001–2009	$30,000
2000	$27,000
1998–1999	$26,000
1997	$25,000
1995–1996	$24,000

Automobile Interest Expense Limit   The maximum monthly interest that can be deducted on a loan taken out to purchase an automobile.

Period	Dollar Limit
2001–2009	$300
1997–2000	$250
1995–1996	$300

Automobile Leasing Limit   The maximum monthly lease payment that can be deducted with respect to an automobile.

Period	Dollar Limit (add GST/HST/PST)
2001–2009	$800
2000	$700
1998–1999	$650
1997	$550
1995–1996	$650

History of Federal Personal Tax Rates

Federal Tax Brackets and Rates: Personal

Year	Bracket	Rate
2009	First $40,726	15%
	$40,727–$81,452	22%
	$81,453–$125,264	26%
	Excess	29%
2008	First $37,885	15%
	$37,886–$75,769	22%
	$75,770–$123,184	26%
	Excess	29%
2007	First $37,178	15%
	$37,179–$74,357	22%
	$74,358–$120,887	26%
	Excess	29%
2006	First $36,378	15%
	$36,379–$72,756	22%
	$72,757–$118,285	26%
	Excess	29%
2005	First $35,595	15%
	$35,596–$71,190	22%
	$71,191–$115,739	26%
	Excess	29%
2004	First $35,000	16%
	$35,001–$70,000	22%
	$70,001–$113,804	26%
	Excess	29%

Year	Bracket	Rate
2003	First $32,183	16%
	$32,184–$64,368	22%
	$64,369–$104,648	26%
	Excess	29%
2002	First $31,677	16%
	$31,678–$63,354	22%
	$63,355–$103,000	26%
	Excess	29%
2001	First $30,754	16%
	$30,755–$61,509	22%
	$61,510–$100,000	26%
	Excess	29%
2000	First $30,004	17%
	$30,005–$60,009	25%
	Excess	29%
1995–99	First $29,590	17%
	$29,591–$59,180	26%
	Excess	29%

RRSP Contribution Limits   The following table reflects the maximum RRSP contribution limits, assuming an individual is not covered by an RPP or DPSP.

2010	$22,000
2009	$21,000
2008	$20,000
2007	$19,000
2006	$18,000
2005	$16,500
2004	$15,500
1995–2003	$13,500

History of CPP and EI Contribution Room and Premiums

Employment Insurance Premiums   Employed individuals and their employers contribute to the Employment Insurance fund. The employer's contribution is calculated by applying the employer's rate factor to the employee's contribution.

Employment Insurance Premiums

Year	Maximum Insurable Earnings	Minimum Insurable Earnings	Premium Rate	Maximum Premium	Employer's Rate Factor
2009	$42,300	$2,000	1.73%	$731.79	1.4
2008	$41,100	$2,000	1.73%	$711.03	1.4
2007	$40,000	$2,000	1.80%	$720.00	1.4
2006	$39,000	$2,000	1.87%	$729.30	1.4
2005	$39,000	$2,000	1.95%	$760.50	1.4
2004	$39,000	$2,000	1.98%	$772.20	1.4
2003	$39,000	$2,000	2.10%	$819.00	1.4
2002	$39,000	$2,000	2.20%	$858.00	1.4
2001	$39,000	$2,000	2.25%	$877.50	1.4
2000	$39,000	$2,000	2.40%	$936.00	1.4
1999	$39,000	$2,000	2.55%	$994.50	1.4

*Beginning in 2006, rates for Quebec employees will vary.

Canada Pension Plan Contributions   Both employed and self-employed individuals contribute to the Canada Pension Plan. Where an individual is employed, the employer matches the employee's contribution. Where an individual is self-employed, the individual funds both parts of the contribution.

Year	Maximum Pensionable Earnings	Basic Exemption	Contribution Rate	Maximum Employee Contribution	Maximum Self-Employed Contribution
2009	$46,300	$3,500	4.95%	$2,118.60	$4,237.20
2008	$44,900	$3,500	4.95%	$2,049.30	$4,098.60
2007	$43,700	$3,500	4.95%	$1,989.90	$3,831.20
2006	$42,100	$3,500	4.95%	$1,910.70	$3,821.40
2005	$41,100	$3,500	4.95%	$1,861.20	$3,722.40
2004	$40,500	$3,500	4.95%	$1,831.50	$3,663.00
2003	$39,900	$3,500	4.95%	$1,801.80	$3,603.60
2002	$39,100	$3,500	4.70%	$1,673.20	$3,346.40
2001	$38,300	$3,500	4.30%	$1,496.40	$2,992.80
2000	$37,600	$3,500	3.90%	$1,329.90	$2,659.80
1999	$37,400	$3,500	3.60%	$1,186.50	$2,373.00

History of Corporate Tax Rates

	Years	Rate
General corporate rate	2012–1995	38%
General rate reduction	2012	13%
	2011	11.5%
	2010	10%
	2009	9%
	2008	8%
	2007	7%
Abatement for income earned in a province	2012–1995	10%
Surtax (Note 1)	2007–1995	4%
Manufacturing and processing credit	2009	9%
	2008	8.5%
	2007–1995	7%
Small business deduction (Note 2)	2009–2008	17%
	2007–1995	16%
Tax on small business income up to $500,000	2009	11%
	2008	11.5%
	2007–2006	12%
Small business tax rate reduction	2009	1%
	2008	0.5%
Refundable surtax on investment income (Note 3)	2009–1996	6 2/3%

Note 1—Corporate surtax was eliminated January 1, 2008.
Note 2—The federal annual business limit for the small business deduction was $200,000 from 1995 to 2002, $225,000 for 2003, $250,000 for 2004, $300,000 for 2005 and 2006 and $400,000 for 2007 and 2008. Effective January 1, 2009, the annual business limit was increased to $500,000.
Note 3—The refundable surtax on the investment income if a CCPC applies only from July 1, 1995.

History of Prescribed Interest Rates

	2007				2008				2009			
Quarter:	1	2	3	4	1	2	3	4	1	2	3	4
Overdue taxes	9%	9%	9%	9%	8%	8%	7%	7%	6%	5%	5%	5%
CPP/EI premiums	9%	9%	9%	9%	8%	8%	7%	7%	6%	5%	5%	5%
Tax over-payments	7%	7%	7%	7%	6%	6%	5%	5%	4%	3%	3%	3%
Taxable benefits, or no low interest loans	5%	5%	5%	5%	4%	4%	3%	3%	2%	1%	1%	1%

Foreign Exchange Rates   The Income Tax Act does not prescribe a method for translating into Canadian dollars transactions that are denominated in foreign currencies. CRA accepts that a taxpayer may use the rate in effect at the date a transaction takes place or an average rate for the period in which the transaction occurs. The following are average annual exchange rates for U.S. dollars as computed by the Bank of Canada.

2008	1.0660	2003	1.4015	1998	1.4831
2007	1.0748	2002	1.5704	1997	1.3844
2006	1.1162	2001	1.5484	1996	1.3636
2005	1.2116	2000	1.4852		
2004	1.3015	1999	1.4858		

WHAT YOU NEED TO ASK:

1. **Is your tax advisor qualified and experienced enough to represent you?** Look for a recent in-depth tax course and infrastructure that includes a double-checking service for your current tax filing needs, accuracy guarantees and multiple years of experience in the industry so that your tax returns can be planned, adjusted for prior errors and omissions and properly represented over a period of years in a tax audit.

2. **Am I informed enough?** CRA also has a wonderful, free Web site, which is easy to navigate and contains a wealth of information for business owners. Visit www.cra-arc.ca/tx/bsnss/menu-eng.html. It pays to be informed and ask the right questions. This site can really help you. Make a commitment to learning more, and on an ongoing basis, about the tax deductions, credits and benefits available to you as an individual, a family and a company.

3. **Is your tax advisor a team player?** No one person can know it all. It is important that you work with a professional team on an ongoing basis to get the results you want. Is your tax advisor a leader of a professional team and well connected to insurance, legal, accounting and investment advisors who can build your family's wealth with you and keep you out of trouble with a tax auditor? That's important. Again, look for ongoing certification from the most recent professional education on the subject, including courses on providing in-depth tax and compliance services, such as the DFA, *Tax Services Specialist*™. Also important are the tax efficient elements of Real Wealth Management™ taught under the *MFA, Retirement Services or Investment Services Specialist*™ programs, both available to professionals from www.knowledgebureau.com.

Conclusion

Entrepreneurs are, by nature, an optimistic breed. They take on risk to-day for the potential of realizing a vision tomorrow. They happily retire several years later than others, they think they are rather invincible and they like to be in control. These very same traits, which are necessary to build an empire from the germ of an idea, can play havoc with the planning that is required to build financially sound family legacies.

Within the next decade, more than half of Canada's small business owners are expected to retire, with approximately $1.2 trillion in business assets expected to change hands. In a 2005 report by CIBC World Markets, only two in five small business owners had scouted out a clear succession plan for their businesses, with 60% of entrepreneurs aged 55 to 64 yet to have a discussion about their existing plans with family members or business partners. Only 15% of those have definite plans to transfer or sell the business to a family member. The Canadian Federation of Independent Businesses has produced similar findings in more recent surveys of its members too.*

This trend is disturbing in the context of an aging demographic and an economy in need of repair in the aftermath of the most significant financial crisis (Fall 2008) since the Great Depression. While tough times often give birth to new entrepreneurial ventures, they can also bring with them other changes—illness of employees or founders, for example, or even bankruptcy.

Canada, in fact, finds itself home to the world's highest percentage of baby boomers in its total population, with 9.8 million individuals, representing almost 30% of the population. (The United States, due to its sheer size, has the largest overall baby boom population. The U.S. population aged 65 and over is projected to grow from 40.2 million in 2010 to 71.4 million in 2030 to a staggering 86.7 million by 2050.†)

Canadians depend on their small business community for economic output, employment, philanthropy and taxes. Given that there are only

---

* Canadian Federation of Independent Businesses (CFIB), A Survey of SMEs on Productivity, April 2007.
† U.S. Census Bureau, 2004.

23 million tax filers in Canada, the danger of an aging and disappearing tax base is a real one, causing shifts in tax-filing patterns as well as the source of tax dollars themselves. Recently more provinces in Canada have moved to a Harmonized Sales Tax (HST), for example, to complement the personal and corporate income tax system and advance Canada's competitive position in the global economy. This shifts an increasing burden of responsibility for tax collection and remittance to the small business community—a role that is important, if not always welcome.

The small business community, in short, is a vital player that creates tax revenues for governments from its own economic outputs and the employment of taxpayers. However, it is also an increasingly significant partner in its role as income and sales tax collector and remitter. The continued success of those twin roles depends on the business community's ability to tap into future economic growth, even in the most challenging of times. It is therefore in everyone's interest that a strong and healthy business community work in harmony with both employees and governments within a fair and efficient tax system.

This will require some extra "TLC"—tender, loving care—over the next several years. That's because the incubation of successful businesses that thrive over the longer term is not always achievable. For example, according to Statistics Canada, of all firms that were created in Canada during the end of the last decade, roughly one-quarter ceased to operate within the first two years, just over one-third survived five years or more, and only one-fifth were still in operation after 10 years. *Being in business is tough; staying in business even tougher.*

Today this staying power is critical for boomers and their families to thrive well into the twenty-first century. Their business legacies are important to our economy now and in the future. At a time when business founders contemplate retirement, business start-ups may take a completely different path in the near future—the adoption, continuity and transition of successful businesses to a next generation of owners. *How prepared will the new guard of today's small business enterprises be to take over and steward their inheritance—a living legacy?*

The challenge for new owner-managers will be to understand at what stage of the existing firm's lifecycle the change occurs and what the vision for the firm's future is once the founder moves on in his or her lifecycle. *If the transition is well planned, then financial coffers will not be depleted by taxes at the very same time they are depleted by the driving force behind the business and his or her expertise.*

Taxes are the biggest eroder of income during the lifecycle of an individual and potentially the biggest eroder of wealth upon the transition of assets on his or her death. Fortunately, there is much we can do, working together with financial advisors, to arrange affairs within the framework of the law to pay the least income tax possible—personally and on behalf of the business—while contributing to the well-being of society with healthy economic output.

That's important in this time of change, and the new guard must understand that overpaying taxes—now or in the future—brings with it an unwanted element of risk that no one can afford and is wasteful at a time when every intact dollar counts in rebuilding a strong economic future.

For these reasons, it's important that you take the time to ***Make Sure It's Deductible***, paying only the correct amount of tax and not one cent more within your small business and family unit. By protecting your precious energy and the wealth you create from tax erosion, you will be in a better position to secure not only your own future but also that of your employees, your suppliers and your community.

I sincerely hope that this book has helped you to do that.

Evelyn Jacks

Index

Accounting fees, 73–74, 85
Accrual method of reporting income, 41
Adjusted gross sales, 68
Adjustments to net income, 73
Adoption expenses, 176
Advisor (*see* Tax advisor)
Age amount, 176, 207
Aging demographic, 253
AgriInvest/AgriStability, 135
Appeal, 89, 228, 246
Artists, 130–133
Asset(s):
   depreciation, 93
   disposition, 8,12
   half-year rule, 95
   interest costs, 78–79, 85, 96
   write-offs, 91–105
Asset tracking system, 97
Attribution Rules, 129n, 186–194, 215
Audit (*see* Tax audit)
Audit proof, 5, 31
Auto log, 110, 111
Automobile Capital Cost Allowance limit, 247
Automobile distance log, 48
Automobile expenses, 45–46, 83, 84, 107–120, 246
   auto log, 110, 111
   CCA, 114–115
   CRA worksheet, 112
   dispositions, 115
   maximum deductible costs, 113
   more than one vehicle, 115
   operating/fixed expenses, 113
   worksheet, 116
Automobile interest expense limit, 247
Automobile leasing limit, 247–248
Automobile log, 54–55
Automobiles, 99–100, 114
Average tax rate, 12

Baby boomers, 253
Basic parameters:
   audit-proof, 5
   business start-up, 4
   family first, 3–4
   source of income from business, 4–5
Basic payroll equation, 157
Basic Personal Amount (BPA), 175, 176
Beverages en route, 77
Bonus, 56, 213–214
Bookkeeping practices, 88
Buildings, 100
Burden of proof, 231

Business, 36
Business bank account, 38
Business expenses:
   business/personal use classification, 82, 83–85
   general rule, 66, 237
   Statement of Business or Professional Activities (Form T2125), 68–73
   types, 67–68
Business inputs, 43
Business organization structure, 59
   (*See also* Corporation; Partnership; Self-employment)
Business/personal use classification, 82, 83–85
Business profile overview, 148
Business relationship, 154
Business start plan, 51, 52
Business start-up (*see* Starting up a business)
Buy-sell agreement, 216
Buy vs. lease, 101–102

Canada Child Tax Benefit (CCTB), 193
Canada Disability Savings Bond (CDSB), 192
Canada Disability Savings Grant (CDSG), 192
Canada Education Savings Grant (CESG), 190–191
Canada employment amount, 176
Canada Employment Credit, 198
Canada Pension Plan (CPP), 28–29, 158–159
Canadian-Controlled Private Corporation (CCPC), 212
Capital accumulation, 174
Capital Cost Allowance (CCA), 91–105
   adjustments, 230
   automobiles, 99–100, 114
   buildings, 100
   calculating the CCA, 96–98
   cost of additions, 95
   dispositions, 98
   farmers, 143
   half-year rules, 95
   how it works, 43–44, 246
   interest costs, 96
   land, 100
   patent/licence, 99
   recapture, 99
   short fiscal years, 96
   tax advisor, 101
   tax audit, 230–231
   taxpayer's option, 29, 93
   terminal loss, 99
   UCC, 98–99
Capital expenses, 67, 85

Capital gain, 8, 183, 184–185, 196
Capital gains deduction, 216, 219, 220
Capital gains income, 207
Capitalizing expenditures, 94
Capitalizing interest, 79
Car payments, 83
Caregiver amount, 176, 207
Carry-over provisions, 26–27
Carry over years, 4
Cash method of reporting income, 41
Charitable donations, 207
Charities, 76–77
Child care expenses, 134
Child care provider, 133–135
Child Tax Benefit, 193
Children's Fitness Tax Credit, 176, 198
Children's wages, 138
Child's RRSP, 190
Clawback zone, 199
Clothing, 83, 84
Common-law partner, 187
Common-law partner amount, 176
Communication costs, 137
Computer equipment, 92
Computers, 85
Construction industry, 146
Consultant's billings, 77
Contract for service, 154
Contract of service, 154
Convention expenses, 74
Corporate Attribution Rules, 215
Corporate tax rates, 214
Corporation:
    buy-sell agreement, 216
    compensation planning, 56
    fiscal year end, 41, 212
    insurance planning, 216
    limited liability, 211
    reducing personal taxable income, 56–57
    tax filing deadline, 54
    what is it, 14
Cost of goods sold, 72
Credibility, 65
Credit card balances, 199
Current expenses, 67
Current year tax review, 9

Daily Business Journal, 51, 53, 227
Damages and settlements paid, 74
Death:
    of shareholder, 216
    of spouse, 193–194
    of taxpayer, 203–204
Deductions (*see* Business expenses; Tax
    deductions)
Deemed disposition, 8, 95, 98, 184–185
Defer tax, 27–28, 212–213
Dependants, 176
Disability amount, 176, 207
Diversify income sources, 29–30, 182–185, 243
Dividend, 30, 57, 183, 184, 215
Dividend Tax Credit, 30

Earned income, 200
eBay sellers, 150

Education amounts, 176
Education credit, 198
Eligible capital property, 74, 99, 143
Eligible dependants, 176
Employee vs. sub-contractor, 154–156
Employer-employee relationship, 154
Employer-operated cafeteria, 77
Employer-sponsored events, 77
*Employers' Guide—Payroll Deductions and
    Remittances*, 158, 159
Employment contract, 165–166
Employment income, 6, 196
Employment Insurance (EI):
    employer's obligations, 159–161
    premiums, 249–250
    overpayments, 160–161
Entertainment expenses, 76, 83
EverGreen Explanatory Notes, 81, 95, 247
Exit strategies, 216
Expense restrictions, 88

Failure to file, 82, 229
Fair market value (FMV), deemed disposition
    or transfers, 95
False statements or omissions, 82, 229
Family business, 151–169
    CPP, 158–159
    EI, 159–161
    employee vs. sub-contractor, 154–156
    employment contract, 165–166
    formalizing hiring practices, 153
    payroll procedures, 157–158, 166–167
    tax-free perks, 163–165
    tax return, 167
    tax withholding, 161–163
    time cards, 166
Family farm rollover, 144–146
Family income splitting, 185–186
Family members:
    Attribution Rules, 175, 186–187, 188, 215
    Capital Gains Exemption, 219–220
    CPP contributions, 154
    formalize hiring practices, 153
    income splitting, 16, 28, 153, 170, 175,
        185–189, 215
    non-arm's-length transactions, 153
    tax review, 13
Family tax planning, 171–208
    Attribution Rules, 186–194
    diversify income sources, 182–185
    invest with tax efficiency, 180–182
    maximize deductions and credits, 194–198
    maximize Tax-Free Zones, 175–177
    minimize income realized, 177–180
    overview, 174–175
    split income earned by family, 185–186
Farmer, 135–146
    accounts receivable, 142
    AgriInvest/AgriStability, 135
    Capital Gains Exemption, 143–144
    CCA, 143
    eligible capital properties, 143
    family farm rollover, 144–146
    filing methods, 135–136
    forms, 135

Farmer *(continued)*
  GST/HST, 142
  ineligible expenses, 139
  instalment payments, 136
  inventory valuations, 139
  land improvement costs, 140
  livestock income tax-deferral program,
    140–141
  loss deductibility, 141–142
  Mandatory Inventory Adjustment,
    139–140
  Optional Inventory Adjustment, 140
  prepayments, 140
  reporting expenses, 136–137
  restricted farm loss, 142
  vehicle costs, 138–139
  wages, 137–138
Federal budget summary, 32
Federal Court of Appeal, 228
Federal refundable tax credits, 197, 206
Federal tax brackets/rates, 178
First Nations Goods and Services Tax
  (FNGST), 42
Fiscal year end, 41, 212
Fishing property, 217–218
Food and beverage business, 76
Footwear, 83
Forbes, B. C., 239
Form CPT1, 138n
Form of business organization, 14
  (See also Corporation; Partnership; Self-
    employment)
Frequent flyer points, 179

General Anti-Avoidance Rules (GAAR), 86
Generally Accepted Accounting Principles
  (GAAP), 7
Gifts, 84
Goods and Services Tax (GST), 41–43, 100, 101
Grandparents gifts, 188, 193
Grey areas, 59
Groceries, 83
Gross negligence, 229
Gross profit, 72

Half-rate rule, 92
Half-year rules, 95
Harmonized sales tax (HST), 41–43, 100, 101, 254
Health care premiums, 75
Historical overview:
  automobile expense claim limits, 247–248
  corporate tax rates, 251
  CPP contributions, 250
  EI premiums, 249–250
  federal personal tax rates, 248–249
  foreign exchange rates, 252
  prescribed interest rates, 251
  RRSP contribution limits, 249
Hobby vs. business, 39–41
Home-based business:
  auto expenses, 45–46
  deductible debt, 200
  personal use allocation, 44–45
Home office, 46, 116–120, 137, 246

Hospitality, meals and entertainment, 76
Hospitality business, 76

Imputed interest, 57
Income assessment procedure:
  current year tax review, 9
  form of business organization, 14
  previous errors and omissions, 13–14
  RRSP contribution room, 9–11
  tax cost averaging, 14–15
  tax rate, 12
  tax review for each family member, 13
  TFSA, 12
Income splitting, 16, 185–186, 215
Income Tax Act (ITA):
  capital appreciation, 8
  personal use allocation, 45
  reasonable expectation of profit, 36
Income tax preparation fees, 85
Incorporated company *(see* Corporation)
Individual Pension Plan (IPP), 216
Infirm dependants, 176
Informal objection, 228
Input tax credit, 100
Insurance payments, 83
Insurance planning, 216
Integration, 213
Interest-bearing loans to family members,
  192
Interest costs, 78–79, 85, 96
Invest lower earner's money, 189
Investment counsel fees, 85
Investors, 207

Johns-Manville Canada Inc., 234
Joint accounts, 188–189

Kiddie tax, 215
Know about tax changes, 31–32
Knowing the law, 245, 247
Knowledge Bureau, 169, 192

Land, 100
Legal fees, 73–74, 85
Legitimizing your claims, 87–88
Letter of Authority, 161, 163
Leveraged buy-out, 79
Licence, 99
Licences and bonding, 84
Life insurance policies, 26, 34, 45, 136, 189,
  193, 203
Limited liability partnership (LLP), 212
Livestock income tax-deferral program,
  140–141
Long-distance calls, 84, 137
Lottery tickets, 194
Low-hanging fruit, 88
Loyalty programs, 179
Lunches, 84

Management fees, 85
Mandatory Inventory Adjustment (MIA), 139
Manufacturing and processing equipment, 93
Margin analysis, 72

Marginal tax rate, 12
Maximize Tax-Free Zones, 175–177
Meals and entertainment, 76, 83
Meals at conferences, 77
Medical amount, 207
Medical expenses, 176
Medical/pharmacy expenses, 84
Methods of reporting income, 41
Minimize income realized, 177–180
Minors, 201
Model Citizen Factor, 65
Mortgage, 83

Net research grants, 196
Net worth assessment process, 225
Non-active business income, 214
Non-allowable expenses, 68
Non-competition agreement, 75
Non-compliance, 228, 229
Non-deductible debt, 199
Non-refundable federal credits, 206
Non-refundable tax credits, 197
Non-registered accounts, 182
Notice of Objection, 228, 246–247

Office rent, 85
Office supplies, 84
Onus of proof, 46, 59
Operating expenses, 43, 85, 246
Optional Inventory Adjustment (OIA), 140
Other income, 196
Overtime meals/allowances, 179

Parking, 84
Partnership, 127–130
    assets, 127
    compensation planning, 56
    individual expenses, 128
    special rules, 127
    between spouses, 129
Passenger vehicles:
    half-year rule, 115
    tax write-offs for fixed costs, 113
    terminal loss, 115
Patent, 99
Penalties:
    misrepresentation by third party, 229–230
    non-compliance, 229
    other missteps, 82, 86
    tax evasion, 82, 86
Pension Adjustment, 216
Pension income amount, 176, 207
Pension Income Credit, 198
Perfect integration, 213
Perk, 57
Personal amounts, 176
Personal tax brackets/rates, 25–26, 29
Personal use allocation, 44–45
Prepaid costs, 67
Previous errors and omissions, 13–14
Prior-filing review, 15
Prior years (*see* Historical overview)
Private pension income, 202–203
Professional practice, 211, 212

Proprietorship, 14, 124–126
Public Transit Passes, 198

Qualified farm property, 216–217
Qualified fishing property, 217–218
Quarterly tax instalments, 24–25
Questions, 204

Reasonable expectation of profit, 63–64, 89
Recaptured CCA, 99
Receipts, 51, 54
Record keeping, 46–48
Record retention, 47–48
Redundant income, 181
Refundable medical expense credit, 176
Refundable tax credits, 197, 206
Register the business, 49
Registered accounts, 181–182
Registered charities, 76–77
Registered Disability Savings Plan (RDSP),
    191–192
Registered Education Savings Plan (RESP),
    190–191
Registered Retirement Savings Plan (RRSP),
    15–16, 189–190, 200–201, 214–215
Rental income, 196
Repairs/maintenance, 83
Restricted expenses, 67
Restricted farm loss, 65, 142
Restrictive covenant, 75
Retirement compensation arrangement
    (RCA), 161
Retroactive tax adjustments, 32
Revenue property owners, 207
Rights under the law, 227–228, 237
RRSP contribution room, 9–11, 176

Safety deposit box, 85
Salary/dividend mix, 213
Salary to assistant, 85
Self-employment, 3–5, 6–8, 49, 55, 56, 74,
    121–150, 154–156, 208
Seminar, 81
Seniors, 207
$750,000 Capital Gains Exemption, 8, 143–144,
    216, 219, 220
Shares of small business corporation, 216, 217
Skill testing questions, 243–247
Small business corporation, 143, 216, 217
Small tools, 92
Sole proprietorship, 124–126
    (*See also* Self-employment)
Source deductions, 161–163
Source documents, 48n
Special clothing, 84
Split income earned by family, 185–186
Split income with family members, 16
Spousal RRSP, 190
Spouse:
    amounts transferred to, 203
    death of, 193–194
    defined, 187
    partnership, 129
    RRSP, 190

Spouse *(continued)*
transfer dividends to, 192–193
wages, 137–138
(*See also* Family business)
Spouse amount, 176
Spread the wealth, 244–245
Starting up a business, 35–59
automobile log, 54–55
business bank account, 38
business start criteria, 39
business start plan, 51, 52
CRA's considerations, 40
Daily Business Journal, 51, 53
fiscal year end, 41
formalize books/keep receipts, 51, 54
hobby vs. business, 39–41
record keeping, 46–48
register the business, 49
required reports, 54
tax compliance discussion points, 49, 50
tax-efficient profits, 55
tax filing deadlines, 54
tax-filing framework, 41–46
tax losses, 48–49
Statement of Business or Professional
Activities (Form T2125), 68–73
Stewart v. Queen, 63
Sub-contractor, 154–156
Support payments, 196
Supreme Court of Canada, 228

Tax advisor, 239–247
finding an advisor, 241–242
questions to ask, 242–243
skill testing questions, 243–247
Tax audit, 37, 223–238
action plan, 232–233
audit interview, 233–235
audit risks, 226
audit tests, 226
CCA, 230–231
changing laws, 230–231
initial audit assessment steps, 231–232
proactive, 231
profiting from the audit experience, 235–236
strategy, 226–227
Tax brackets/rates, 29, 178, 183
Tax compliance action planner, 147
Tax cost averaging:
audit-proof, 31
build equity that will be tax free, 30–31
carry-over provisions, 26–27
CPP, 28–29
defer tax, 27–28
defined, 21
diversify your income sources, 29–30
know about tax changes, 31–32
personal tax brackets/rates, 25–26, 29
retroactive tax adjustments, 32
tax audit, 230
tax-exempt income, 26
Tax Court of Canada, 228
Tax credits, 197–199, 206–208
Tax deductions, 194–197, 206–208

Tax deferral, 27–28, 212–213
Tax efficiency, 3
Tax evasion, 86, 229
Tax-exempt income, 26
Tax filing deadlines, 54
Tax-filing framework, 41–46
Tax-filing profile, 15
Tax-free perks, 163–165
Tax-Free Savings Account (TFSA), 11, 12, 181,
187–188
Tax-Free Zone, 12
Tax losses, 48–49
Tax planning:
importance, 254–255
income over $126,000, 202
income under $126,000, 201–202
minors, 201
taxpayer's death, 203–204
Tax planning R & D, 16
Tax refund, 2
Tax return:
failure to file, 82, 229
family business, 167
farmers, 135–136
who files, 5
Tax saver, 20
Tax Savings Blueprint, 23, 33, 34, 178
Tax withholding, 161–163
Taxable capital gain, 184, 196
Taxable income, 6
Taxpayer Relief Provisions, 86, 227–228
Terminal loss, 99
Textbook tax credit, 176, 198
TFSA contribution room, 11, 177
Third-party misrepresentation, 86
Third-party penalties, 229–230
Time cards, 166
Tools and equipment, 84
Training expenses, 79–81
Transfer dividends to spouse, 192–193
Transit passes, 198
Travel within municipality/metropolitan
area, 179–180
Tuition fees, 84, 176, 198

Undepreciated capital cost (UCC), 98, 99
Universal Child Care Benefit (UCCB), 193
Unused TFSA contribution room, 177
Utilities, 83

Voluntary compliance, 227
Voluntary Disclosures Program (VDP),
86–87

Wage loss replacement benefits, 196
Wages:
to children, 138
to spouse, 137–138
Walker, Harold Blake, 171
Walls v. Canada, 64
What-if scenarios, 34
Withholding taxes at source, 161–163
Writers, 130–133
www.knowledgebureau.com, 32, 81, 95, 247